DUMFRIES AND

D1448234

AN ILLUSTRATED ARCHI1

I remembered from the map that if I went north I would come into a region of coal pits and industrial towns. Presently I was down from the moorlands and traversing the broad haugh of a river. For miles I ran alongside a park wall, and in a break of the trees I saw a great castle. I swung through little old thatched villages, and over peaceful lowland streams, and past gardens blazing with hawthorn and yellow laburnum. The land was so deep in peace that I could scarcely believe that somewhere behind me were those who sought my life.
John Buchan, *The Thirty-Nine Steps*, 1915

John Buchan's sketch encapsulates the essence of the beauty and mystery pervading the Galloway hills and the flatlands of Solway, the southernmost region in Scotland. Only on a closer inspection are its secrets revealed – this excellent guide is essential in that discovery.

During the Scottish Enlightenment of the 18th century, Dumfries was second only to Edinburgh as a centre of artistic endeavour, with Burns in residence and William Adam working on several mansions in the area. A prosperous, self-confident region, which was important in the development of modern Scotland, it has a strong affinity with Glasgow, as the quarries at Locharbriggs provided sandstone for most of the great 19th-century expansion of the city.

This well-researched publication records the history of the architecture which contributes to the sense of place of Dumfries and Galloway, and, in doing so, reveals its true character, whilst providing a fleeting glimpse of some of its mysteries. I hope readers will investigate further.

Gordon C Murray
President
Glasgow Institute of Architects

© *Author: John R Hume*
Series editor: Charles McKean
Series consultant: David Walker
Editorial consultant: Duncan McAra
Cover design: Dorothy Steedman
Index: Oula Jones

The Rutland Press
ISBN 1 873190 34 4
1st published 2000

Cover illustrations
Front *Caerlaverock Castle from the south-west (Crown Copyright: reproduced by permission of Historic Scotland)*
Insert *Bridge of Cree, Newton Stewart (Hume)*
Back top *A Galloway landscape by George Henry (Glasgow Museums)*. Bottom *The Tolbooth, Kirkcudbright by William H Clarke (Glasgow Museums)*.

Typesetting and picture scans by
The Almond Consultancy, Edinburgh
Printed by Pillans & Wilson Greenaway, Edinburgh

Dumfries and Galloway, that region of Scotland bounded by the Solway Firth, the Irish Sea and the massif of the Southern Uplands, is today cut off from the rest of the country, or seen by many travellers as landscape to be driven through as quickly as permissible on the way to places further north or south. A great pity, for it is an area to be explored and savoured, as it yields its secrets.

Romantically associated with smugglers and gypsies, celebrated by John Buchan, Dorothy L Sayers and S R Crockett, and depicted by artists' colonies in Moniaive and Kirkcudbright, the area covered by this volume consists essentially of a series of river valleys – Esk, Annan, Nith, Urr, Cree and Luce – which break up the land mass into fingers reaching into the Solway Firth. Until the coming of the railways to the area in the 1840s-60s, Dumfries and Galloway relied heavily on the sea for transport. Most significant towns were on the coast or on navigable rivers, and were linked to the Irish Sea economy, depending more on trade with the English coast down as far as Liverpool, with the Isle of Man and with Ireland itself, than with other parts of Scotland.

Top *Broughton House, Kirkcudbright.* Above *High Street, Kirkcudbright.* Left *Dalbeattie Station.* Below *Near Moffat.* Opposite *Tongland Dam.*

Beyond the coast, with the exception of the fertile lower valleys and tributaries of the Nith and Annan, the area was sparsely populated until the late 18th century, when many new planned towns and villages were laid out, and the enclosure and improvement of land became common. Better roads followed, with the construction of the strategic Carlisle/Portpatrick road giving an effective east/west land link across the three counties for the first time, also significant to the infrastructure of the United Kingdom by virtue of the short sea link to Ireland.

Right *Birtwhistle's cotton mills, Gatehouse of Fleet*. Below *East Cluden Mill*.

During the early Industrial Revolution, the water power of the area had attractions for entrepreneurs, and both cotton and woollen mills were established, together with hand-loom weaving settlements. Their ability to compete with major urban centres of textile manufacture was, however, limited. After the coming of the railways, Annan, Langholm and Dumfries all became industrial towns, as did, to a lesser extent, Sanquhar and Kirkconnel, on the area's more successful coalfield; the Canonbie collieries were comparatively short-lived. Red sandstone quarries at Locharbriggs and Corncockle, and granite quarries at Dalbeattie and Creetown developed extensive markets. The mining of lead ore, particularly associated with Wanlockhead, was also practised in the hills west of Carsphairn, and in the west of Kirkcudbrightshire.

The enduring influences on the area, however, have been agriculture and forestry, and, more recently, tourism. All the major settlements had – and still have – a market-town function, and Dumfries, Castle Douglas, Newton Stewart, Stranraer and Thornhill still have livestock marts. Dumfries and Galloway have long been renowned for both dairy and beef cattle, with the *Belted Galloway* a badge of the latter. The processing of raw milk into a range of dairy products, carried out on farms until the late 19th century, moved into centralised creameries and is now concentrated on a few large plants.

Tourism, like dairy farming, was initially linked with the opening-up of the area by the railways. Though a few attempts were made to develop seaside resorts on the English and Irish models, the area has consistently attracted people seeking quiet family and sporting holidays, and the charm of the area means that many people return year after year.

The west coast of the Rhins.

This book has been written to intrigue those people who are not aware of the delights of Dumfries and Galloway, to provide a guide for visitors, and to encourage residents to appreciate the variety, fineness and distinctiveness of the towns and parishes of this most delightful part of Scotland.

Organisation of the Guide
The guide is based on the river valleys that break up the land-mass of the eastern part of the area, and on the peninsulas that constitute most of Wigtownshire. It begins with Dumfries – 'Queen of the South' – the capital of the area, followed by the parishes of Nithsdale. Annandale comes next, centring on the river-mouth port of Annan, and then Eskdale, at the eastern edge of Dumfriesshire, with the town of Langholm as its focus.

West of Dumfries is the valley of the Urr, with two major communities, Castle Douglas and Dalbeattie; next, the Dee valley, with Kirkcudbright at its mouth, then the Fleet organised round Gatehouse of Fleet.

The Cree is the boundary between the Stewartry of Kirkcudbright and the Shire of Wigtown, with Newton Stewart at the head of the estuary and Creetown on the eastern shore. West of the Cree is the broad peninsula known as the Machars, with its principal burghs Wigtown and Whithorn, with Port William on its western coast. Luce Bay separates the

Top *A planned estate village.* Above *Drumlanrig Castle.* Left *Hills Tower, Lochrutton.*

INTRODUCTION

The Southern Upland Way is Britain's first official coast-to-coast, long-distance footpath running 212 miles south-west to north-east. From Portpatrick in the west, the route heads along the coastal cliffs before turning inland, passing through farmland, parkland, broadleaved and coniferous woodland, as well as open moorland. It skirts ponds and lochs, weaves along small upland burns, follows forest tracks and ancient drove roads, passes ruined castles and crosses over exposed summits before reaching the east coast at Cockburnspath.

Below *Sinclair Memorial, Dumfries Museum.* Middle *Rhino-topped bus shelter in Priory Avenue, Lincluden, a stage point on the Southern Upland Way.* Bottom *Threave Visitor Centre, Kelton.*

Machars from the Rhins, the T-shaped peninsula west of Stranraer, the town itself being on the narrow isthmus between Luce Bay and Loch Ryan, and now the westmost administrative centre in Dumfries and Galloway. The parishes of the Rhins end, significantly, with Kirkmaiden, whose southernmost point, the Mull of Galloway, is also the furthest south-west point of Scotland.

Text Arrangement

Entries for principal buildings follow the sequence of name (or number), address, date and architect (if known). Lesser buildings are contained within paragraphs. Both demolished buildings and unrealised projects are included if appropriate. In general, the dates given are those of the design (if known) or of the beginning of construction (if not). Marginal text offers anecdotal and less technical aspects of the story of Dumfries and Galloway.

Map References

Guideline maps are included for the main urban centres with a larger map covering the region. Numbers refer not to pages but to numbers beside the particular text entry. Where buildings are concentrated, space has allowed only a few numbers sufficient for visitors to take bearings. Numbers in the index refer to pages.

Access to Properties

Many of the buildings described in this guide are open to the public, or are visible from a public road or footpath. Some are private, and readers are requested to respect the occupiers' privacy.

Sponsors

The generous support is gratefully acknowledged of the Landmark Trust, Groundbase, Historic Scotland, Solway Heritage, Portrack Charitable Trust, Robert Potter & Partners, Dumfries & Galloway Council, Crichton Trust, Architectural Heritage Society of Scotland, DuPont, Galloway Preservation Society, British Nuclear Fuels Ltd, Dumfries & Galloway Council Educational Trust.

Dedication

To all my former colleagues in Historic Scotland and its predecessor bodies, with gratitude.

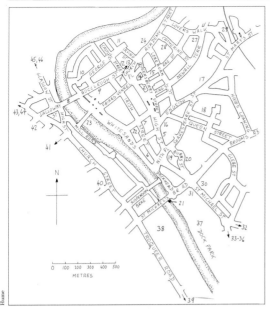

Mid Steeple.

DUMFRIES

Dumfries owes its importance to its situation as the lowest crossing point on the River Nith, and its rich agricultural hinterland. It was a place of significance by the 12th century, with a royal castle, and received its first charter from David I. It had a chequered history in later medieval times, being sacked by English invaders more than once, but after the Union of the Crowns in 1603 it became a town of some significance. After the Union of the Parliaments in 1707, its merchants seized the opportunity offered of free trade with the colonies to establish a trade in tobacco. This trade later moved to the Clyde, but with agricultural improvement during the later 18th century and early 19th the town's role as a market improved significantly. Since the mid 19th century it has also been a manufacturing centre, though its once-important woollen textile trade has long gone; as have its engineering industries, leaving rubber and chemicals as the largest employers.

The Nith was formerly the border between the burgh and the separate Maxwelltown on its west bank, but the two were united in 1928. **Maxwelltown**, too, had textile mills of importance, the largest of which now forms an industrial estate.

The burgh has an irregular town plan dating from medieval origins. High Street was the

RCAHMS

Dumfries, from the New Bridge, by A S Masson.

The New Bridge from south-east.

Hume

original market place, with Friars Vennel leading down to a ford on the River Nith. At one end of High Street was the castle, on a mound, and at the other the parish church. To mark the mid-point of this street the Mid Steeple (see p.10) was built in 1705-7. As the burgh grew, streets were added to form a very rough grid. To the west was Irish Street and to the east Loreburn Street, while English Street and Bank Street formed transverse links. By the early 19th century the medieval bridge which had replaced the ford had become a serious constraint on east/west traffic, as wheeled vehicles became more numerous. The New or Buccleuch Bridge was built in 1791-4 by Thomas Boyd, and to provide it with a level approach Buccleuch Street was constructed on an embankment which cut across both Irish Street and Brewery Street. In the years following, Dumfries's *New Town* was laid out to the north. This comprised Castle Street, George Street, and Irving Street and was, at first, like Edinburgh's New Town, residential.

Victorian developments took place along a series of routes radiating out of the town, except to the north, where the meanders of the Nith constituted a barrier, and the spaces between them were laid out for development, mainly for housing. To the south there were roads to the outports of Dumfries, **Kingholm Quay** and **Glencaple**, and to the east roads to

Annan and Carlisle, and to Moffat, for
Edinburgh.

As befitted a county town, however, these
areas also accommodated schools, hospitals
and administrative buildings, and a limited
amount of industry. Railway links with
Glasgow and Carlisle came to Dumfries in
1850; subsequently a cross-country competing
route to Lockerbie was opened, and lines to
Stranraer and Portpatrick, and to Moniaive.

The advent of motor transport in the early
20th century created a bottleneck at the New
Bridge, and consequently **St Michael's Bridge**
was built (see p.18). This increased the degree
of integration with Dumfries and its neighbour
Maxwelltown, whose development had been to
some degree independent, and inter-war
building was funnelled into the flat land to the
west. Maxwelltown was in Kirkcudbrightshire,
but housed the Dumfries town mills. In the
19th century it provided sites for large woollen
mills, for churches, schools, a prison and court
house, and for extensive working- and middle-
class housing, but the settlement relied heavily
on Dumfries for shopping and commercial
services. During the 20th century council
housing estates were built to the north at
Lincluden and **Lochside**.

Other satellites developed at **Heathhall** and
Locharbriggs to the north-east, **Lochfield**
and **Georgetown** to the west. Heathhall is
best known for its motor-car – now rubber –
works; Locharbriggs for its large and still-
working sandstone quarries; and Georgetown
for the ICI factory.

1 **Greyfriars Church**, Church Place, 1865-8,
John Starforth
Built to replace the New Church of 1724 and to
complement St Michael's, it crowds onto a tiny
site a soaring mass of pinnacles and a gigantic
spire, giving a dramatic termination to views
along High Street. **Robert Burns' statue**,
1882, Mrs D O Hill, sculpted in Italy, is the
formal focus of Church Place (colour page 49),
but its impact has been reduced by rather
heavy-handed floorscape improvement. It was
moved to this position in 1938 to form the
centrepiece of a roundabout. The earlier 19th-
century **Nos 9-15 Castle Street** has a unique,
though inelegant, concentration of Venetian
windows at first-floor level, and its contemporary
No 17 had a notable Greek revival shopfront
added later in the 19th century.

Below *Greyfriars Church before
recent townscape improvements*
Bottom *Robert Burns' statue,
Church Place.*

Above Mid Steeple, leaded cap.
Right No 120-4 High Street.

7 Church Place, 1895, Frank Carruthers
The town centre's most striking commercial building, a three-storey-and-attic red sandstone wedding-cake in a style which would be more at home in Glasgow. From there to the Mid Steeple, High Street is lined with mainly three-storey buildings, mostly of late 18th and early 19th century, typical burgh architecture of the period. Behind these frontages, buildings extend along the old burgage plots creating a dense urban form. Once these backlands incorporated the many inns serving the bustling market town: a few survive including the lion-flanked **Hole in the Wa'** at **152-8 High Street**, early 19th century, though it claims to have been founded in 1620.

Mid Steeple, 1705-8,
probably Tobias Bachup or Bauchop
One of the largest early town-houses in Scotland, and the symbol of Dumfries. Six-storey square tower, with three-storey flat-roofed wing to the south and a later block of one- and two-storey shops to the north. The three-storey block and the tip of the tower have Netherlandish strapwork balustrades, and the tower is capped by an ogee-headed leaded steeple of a type fashionable in the 17th century, and used, for example, in the Old College of Glasgow, the Tolbooth in Stirling and

Tobias Bauchop (or Bachup), died *c*.1710, was one of a family of master masons working in the Alloa area (see *Clackmannan & The Ochils* in this series). At first he built in the vernacular style, but became involved with Sir William Bruce, and worked on several of Bruce's late 17th-century projects. He built the Dumfries Town Steeple on a model supplied by John Moffat of Liverpool, the steeple itself being based on that of the College at Glasgow.

The Mechanics' Institute movement began in the early 19th century as a means of improving the education and training of working 'mechanics' – that is artisans/craftsmen – at a time when technical knowledge was increasing rapidly. The Dumfries Institute was housed in a two-storey-and-basement, five-bay former town house of the Stewarts of Shambellie (see p.78). Demolished 1970s.

the Manse of Leith (see *Central Glasgow, Stirling & The Trossachs* and *Edinburgh* in this series). The south front of the building has a forestair running diagonally across its face, and bears a series of plaques, including one showing the royal arms of Scotland, and another indicating the distances from Dumfries of major towns. Reclad in polished ashlar, 1909, by James Barbour (colour page 49).

High Street
Beyond the Mid Steeple, High Street widens to form what was once a market-place, and the buildings become grander (colour page 49). **No 120-4**, 1809, is a splendid early 19th-century nepus-gabled building, with beyond it the massive bulk of **Burton's**, 1934. The junction with **English Street** is marked by an
4 elaborate cast-iron **fountain**, 1882, George Smith's Sun Foundry, now a focal point in a pedestrianised and *enhanced* floorscape. Facing the fountain is a pleasing group of Italianate buildings which once formed the **County Hotel** and, on the east, an apparently contemporary colour-washed block part of which is a façade retention, the remainder being new-build of the 1980s. **No 79** was built as a town-house for Richard Lowthian of Stafford and was heightened, 1860; the body of the building was demolished in 1984-5, and a new steel structure inserted. Other new buildings here are the **Bank of Scotland**, replacing Binns' department store, an inter-war building and **Marks & Spencer**. Both are deferential, incorporating stone façades and semi-traditional treatment and, as a consequence, though well-mannered, are rather disappointing. Beyond Marks & Spencer High Street narrows; with the mid 18th-century
5 **Globe Inn**, a Robert Burns' howff, and a 1980s **supermarket**, sandstone-faced, with a curious glazed pediment, built partly on the site of the delightful Georgian **Mechanics' Institute**, originally the 18th-century town-house of the Stewarts of Shambellie (see p.78).

Irish Street
Roughly parallel to High Street, Irish Street was formed probably in the early 18th century, as the burgh expanded, and cut across the old High Street rig pattern. The buildings here form the richest architectural group in Dumfries. **No 18** is a modest, late 18th-century villa.

Top High Street fountain by George Smith, Glasgow. *Above* Close leading to the Globe Inn.

29 Irish Street.

Brick was rarely used in Scotland before the 19th century. Apart from the two houses in Irish Street, another early example is Kirkconnell House (see pp.77-8). The influence in all these cases was probably from England.

Clydesdale Bank.

6 **29 Irish Street**, early 18th century
Two-storey, attic-and-basement, baroque town-house, said to have been for the Gilchrists of Spedloch and, most unusually for Scotland at that date, constructed in brick. It has some good interior details, including fielded panelling, a timber stair and plaster cornices. Beyond this gem is a distinguished, plain Greek revival red sandstone **villa** of 1828, now the **Albert Club**. The east side of the street here is made up of the back premises of rebuilt High Street stores, with the charm they so often possess, but the former **British Linen Bank**, remodelled 1872, John Starforth, latterly part of Binns' store, has been converted to **housing** as part of the Bank of Scotland's redevelopment of the Binns' site. A sad loss opposite is the former **British Legion Club**, once a grand early 18th-century brick mansion.

7 **The Old Bank** (formerly Commercial Bank), 92-94 Irish Street, *c*.1830
Attractive Georgian block facing the single-storey Edwardian baroque **Clydesdale Bank**, *c*.1914. Between Bank Street and Friars Vennel the west side of Irish Street is a marvellous mixture of buildings. **Greyfriars Hall**, *c*.1840, is Tudor-Gothic and at **No 135**, now a **Job Centre**, the main body of the pedimented house is set back, with little single-storey pavilions.

Buccleuch Street, from 1794

If Irish Street is Dumfries's richest street architecturally, Buccleuch Street is its most pretentious, laid out as an elevated approach to 8 the **New** or **Buccleuch Bridge**, 1791-4. **Nos 75, 77 & 79** are original terraced houses with distinctive round-headed recessed doorways, with similar at either end of the street. The replacement buildings, in red sandstone, are much larger in scale, and generally grander, than their predecessors: **Bethany Hall**, a rather plain Gothic revival church, built as Buccleuch St UP Church, 1861-3, Alexander Crombie; a very grand **Clydesdale Bank**, 1892, James Thomson; the multi-turreted 9 **Sheriff Court**, 1863-6, David Rhind; and the plain but decent **Nos 24-36**, a family store, 1878-9, James Barbour. The north side is less spectacular, starting with the shell of the neoclassical former **Methodist Church**, built as an Episcopal chapel in 1817, F J Hunt, awaiting restoration; **Nithsdale District Council Offices**, a late example of Edwardian baroque, built as the Municipal Chambers, 1931-2, James Carruthers; and the terraced **Nos 75-9**, now a veterinary surgery, more elaborate than most of its neighbours.

Top *Sheriff Court.* Above *Terraced house, north side of Buccleuch Street. Beautifully crisp sandstone ashlar masonry.* Left *Methodist Church.*

George Street

Buccleuch Street is the southern edge of Dumfries's *New Town*, planned by Robert Burn in 1806. Its heart is George Street, distinctively eclectic, with the elaborate free-style former 10 **Freemasons' Hall**, 1889-90, A B Crombie, and the Netherlandish **Dumfries Workshop**, built as a primary school, 1897-9, A B Crombie. Good Georgian terraces at **Nos 34-40**, with the

Robert Burn, 1752-1815, was an important Georgian architect-mason, father of the famous architect William Burn. He worked mainly in the east of Scotland, his most conspicuous surviving building being the Nelson Monument, 1807, on the Calton Hill in Edinburgh (see *Edinburgh* in this series).

Walter Newall, 1780-1863, the son of a New Abbey farmer, was the leading Dumfries architect in the mid-19th century. He designed several churches and minor country houses and villas, and many farm buildings especially on the Buccleuch estates in Dumfriesshire.

curious classical **St George's Church**, built as a Free Church in 1843-4, remodelled 1892-3, James Halliday, an appropriate place of worship for this polite area. At the east end are 11 **Moat Brae**, a very handsome detached villa with an Ionic portico, *c*.1832, Walter Newall, and the **Assembly Rooms**, 1825, a rather clumsy building at the corner of **Irving Street**, breaking a line of Georgian terraced houses in both streets.

St George's Church.

Inscription on Queensberry Monument:
This column, Sacred to the memory of Charles Duke of Queensberry and Dover, was erected by the County of Dumfries as a monument of their veneration for the character of that illustrious nobleman, whose exalted virtues Render him the ornament of Society and whose numerous acts of public beneficence and private charity endeared him to his country.
Ob 22ᵈ Octʳ 1778 Etat 80

Castle Street
Castle Street and Irving Street form the rest of the *New Town* grid. The former is Dumfries's finest Georgian street, with four terraces 12 surviving: **Nos 25-37**, **41-47**, **26-30** & **14-24**. **No 27** is said to have been occupied by a Dr Scott, who performed the first operation in Europe under general anaesthetic. Irving Street has its terraces broken by **Dumfries Congregational Church**, 1835, with its flat, idiosyncratic façade with tall round-headed windows and mock machicolations, and the former **Reformed Presbyterian Church**, 1831-2, altered 1866, a simple Gothic box. Irving Street leads to **Church Crescent**, a short street with some vernacular character, broken by the classical **Dumfries Savings** 13 **Bank**, 1847, John Gregan (colour page 50), complete with marble bust of **Henry Duncan** (by John Currie), who founded the savings

bank movement in Ruthwell (see p.31). Duncan stands in the arched opening of a Venetian 'window' set between pairs of Ionic columns over a strongly rusticated ground floor. The best features of **St Andrew Street** are some unaltered shopfronts.

Queensberry Street

A narrow, twisting thoroughfare, very obviously a secondary street, but with some buildings of real character and even distinction. The early 20th-century art nouveau 14 **warehouse** at **No 128**, with its three little bowed windows at eaves level, is probably the best, but the four-storey Renaissance red sandstone blocks at **No 109** are also impressive. Amid these comparative giants one could overlook a fine, simple public house, the **Tam o' Shanter Inn**, at **No 117**.

Queensberry Square was 18th-century Dumfries's attempt to modernise the town centre. It diverts attention from the Mid Steeple, as do some less than appropriate shopfronts.

15 **Queensberry Monument**, Queensberry Square, 1780, Robert Adam Topped by a flaming urn and set on a plinth with rams' heads at the corners, it was designed for the Square, but moved to the front of the County Buildings in English Street, returning to the Square in 1990. The most eye-catching feature of the Square is, however, the pedimented **Trades Hall**, 1804-6, Thomas Boyd, refronted, but retaining most of its distinction. On the north side is the fussily post-modern **Lloyds TSB Scotland**, 1993, Sutherland Dickie & Copland.

English Street

Curving away from High Street and preserving, to a considerable degree, the character of an old county-town street (as does Queen Street, which leads to Shakespeare Street), English Street has a real mixture of buildings, both in style and date, most listed. Many retain Victorian shopfronts – **Nos 36 & 41** are particularly fine – and highlights are **No 8**, good Renaissance former **Union Bank**, 1875-7, William Railton, well detailed, and the 16 extraordinary frontage of the **Queensberry Hotel**, 1869, James Barbour, with rich low-relief carving. **No 48** has a pedimented wallhead chimney, a good example of the type.

Top *Statue of Henry Duncan, founder of the savings bank movement.*
Middle *128 Queensberry Street.*
Above *Queensberry Monument.*

15

Hume

Hume

Hume

Beyond **Loreburn Street** the character begins
to change. **Jubilee Buildings**, 1887, sports a
bust of Queen Victoria, but the most striking
features are the exuberant baronial towers of
the former **County Police Barracks**, 1876,
James Barbour, and a similarly inspired
tenement, **Nos 102-4**, at the gushet. Beyond
that the street opens out with a neat Victorian
17 terrace and the massive U-plan **County
Buildings**, 1912-14, J M Dick Peddie & Forbes
Smith, its plainness relieved by giant three-light
windows with heads based on windows in the
Baths of Diocletian, Rome. **St Mary's Church**,
St Mary's Street, 1837-9, John Henderson, next
to the County Buildings and on a medieval
chapel site, is a tall Perpendicular building with
a gabled front. The chancel was added in 1896.
Interior mainly of 1878 and 1896.

High Street ends at **Shakespeare Street**, a
victim of *road improvement* for most of the
buildings which once lined the street have
gone. The steeple of the former **St Andrew's
RC Cathedral**, tower 1843, John H Bell, with
a spire of 1858, Alexander Fraser, and the
tower of the former **school**, 1831, loom up
rather forlornly, while on the site of the rest is
18 the chunky modern **RC Church of St
Andrew**, 1963-4, Sutherland & Dickie, in
Brooke Street.

Theatre Royal, Shakespeare Street/
Brooke Street, 1790-2, Thomas Boyd
Its plain classical exterior belies its
significance, for this is the oldest surviving

theatre in Scotland. Robert Burns attended it, though the building was substantially remodelled in 1876, C J Phipps, and again, 1959-60, Colin Morton. Boyd's building had a portico, replaced by a narrow solid range by Phipps, whose cast-iron gallery front has been retained.

19 24 Nith Place, 1753

An unexpected joy. Charming but rather compressed pedimented town-house built for Archibald Maxwell, Town Clerk of the burgh at the time of Bonnie Prince Charlie's stay in Dumfries. Its lugged and keystoned window surrounds, and Corinthian-columned, pedimented and swagged doorway give it a welcome exuberance.

20 Burns' House, 24 Burns Street

Very plain two-storey red sandstone building, memorable only for its poetic association: the poet lived there between 1793 and his death in 1796. **St Michael Street** has a pleasing jumble of minor vernacular buildings, with one unusual shopfront at **Valentine**'s bar, basket-arched windows separated by pilasters.

Below *Burns' House*. Bottom *24 Nith Place.*

Devorguilla's Bridge from The Antiquities of Scotland *by Francis Grose.*

James Abernethy & Co, of the Ferryhill Foundry, Aberdeen, were the leading producers of structural cast-iron, wrought-iron, and steel-work in north-east Scotland. They specialised in making suspension bridges, of which a number survive in Aberdeenshire and Moray (see *Gordon* and *The District of Moray* respectively in this series).

Below *Nith Suspension Bridge, ornamental arch with burgh arms.* Bottom *Royal Bank of Scotland.*

Whitesands

This riverside route, notorious for flooding, provides a grandstand view of the Nith and its bridges, and of Maxwelltown. The lowest crossing is the stone-faced reinforced-concrete
21 **St Michael's Bridge**, 1925, J Boyd Brodie. Between it and the **Nith Suspension Bridge** the only building of note is a former aerated-water **factory**, now a garage. The suspension bridge was designed by the Aberdeen engineer John Willet, and built by James Abernethy & Co in 1874-5, for the convenience of millworkers in the large tweed mills on both banks of the Nith. Little is left of the original structure, for it was almost completely renewed in 1985, W A Fairhurst & Partners.

North of the bridge Whitesands widens out to become a market place, though cars now take
22 the place of cows. The **Royal Bank of Scotland**, 1982, Rowand Anderson Partnership, is the grandest structure, with massive red sandstone-clad battered base, bronze glass strip-glazing and oversailing slated roof, but there are several market-related buildings including public houses and a market building. **Bank Street**, which links to High Street, is conveniently to hand, with a pair of dignified red sandstone banking establishments complementing those already identified in Irish Street: the Italianate, heavily corniced **No 17**, **Royal Bank of Scotland**, 1856, Peddie & Kinnear, and the more elaborate former **National Bank of Scotland**, 1862, Alexander Fraser, richly detailed, with segmental panels over the first-floor windows, carved by William Flint, and vermiculated rustication round the ground-floor windows.

23 Devorguilla's Bridge, *c.*1430-2
Rebuilt in 1620 and repaired afterwards, it still retains the character of a medieval structure with massive triangular cutwaters and small round arches. It lost three spans at the Whitesands end in the early 19th century and is now a footbridge. A motley group of two- and three-storey buildings, mostly much altered, runs up to Buccleuch Street, and the character of this group, with pubs, cafés and small shops jostling each other, carries on up Friars Vennel and its cross-street **Brewery Street**. By virtue of the narrowness, the vennel has a medieval character, but its buildings are generally disappointing. The three-storey **71-75** is of some antiquity, and **Nos 80-82** has some quality, but only at **Church Place** does one encounter any building of real character: **No 114-116** is distinctive and rather fine late 19th-century, red sandstone with cast-iron elements in its façade.

Whitesands.

Devorguilla was the mother of John Balliol, King of Scots (*Toom Tabard*). She founded Sweetheart Abbey (see pp.80-2) in memory of her husband, and also added to his endowment of Balliol College, Oxford (see also Buittle Place, pp.135-6).

24 Dumfries Academy, Academy Street, 1895-7, F J C Carruthers
Originally elaborate baroque with much sculptural detail. Large red sandstone addition, 1936, in the rather heavy style of the then County Architect, John R Hill, and more recently further extensions to the north and east. Short row of two-storey buildings with notable shopfronts, at the corner of **Loreburn Street**.

Nunholm Road
Two terraces, the first late Georgian, lead to Dumfries's two railway viaducts; low structures over the Nith, with skew-spans. The earlier, on the Glasgow Dumfries & Carlisle Railway, was

Left *Dumfries Academy.* Below *Nith Viaduct.*

John Miller, of the Edinburgh civil engineering firm of Grainger & Miller, was the most accomplished designer of masonry viaducts in Scotland in the 1830s/1840s. His finest work was Ballochmyle Viaduct, near Mauchline (see *Ayrshire & Arran* in this series) which still has one of the longest masonry spans in the world. His son succeeded him as a viaduct designer.

opened in 1850, designed by John Miller, perhaps the finest designer of masonry
25 viaducts of all time. The other, **Nith Viaduct**, from 1859, John Miller jun, on the Castle Douglas railway line, has five segmental arches, unusually sharply skewed.

Edinburgh Road
No 28, Gracefield Arts Centre, a mid-Victorian red sandstone villa with open eaves and carved bargeboards, has a good collection of pictures and a not-undistinguished, mid 20th-century, single-storey range at the rear incorporating **studios**, **gallery** and **restaurant**. **Church of Christ Jesus of the**
26 **Latter Day Saints**, 1963-6, Paul Oliver, very typical, decent, clean, in rendered brick with a slender spire, but bland. **No 105**, **Mile Ash**, English Arts & Crafts house of considerable charm with large canted bay window, timber-framed veranda and prominent eaves. This is the inner edge of villadom, with a wide range of house sizes, and two churches of which the finer
27 is **St John the Evangelist Episcopal Church**, Lover's Walk, 1867-8, Slater & Carpenter, successor to the little chapel in Buccleuch Street, its broach-spire a landmark. North aisle added 1888, Alexander Ross. **War Memorial** with bronze infantryman on white granite plinth, 1921-2, J S Stewart. Mainly terraced houses in **Newall Terrace**, but on the corner with **Catherine Street** is the rather stuffy classical **Dumfries Baptist Church**, 1880-1, Francis Armstrong, and further west **Loreburn Halls**, with a pleasing glazed veranda and door guarded by two listed lions. Across the road is the Gothicky former **Loreburn Street Primary School**, 1876, R K Kinnear, an early Board School. Dignified
28 **Ewart Library**, Catherine Street, 1900-4, Alan B Crombie, with high relief carvings of symbolic figures. **Rae Street**, a gloomy thoroughfare of red sandstone terraces, punctuated by the simple Gothic **St John's School**, 1885.

Loreburn Street
Police Headquarters, 1938, Dumfriesshire County Council
Vast and in the rather heavy neoclassical style of Dumfries public buildings of the inter-war period, recently extended in post-modern style. Cliff-like **Telephone Exchange**, 1958-63, H M Office of Works. These monumental structures contrast with the three-storey, four-bay

Below *St John the Evangelist Episcopal Church*. Bottom *Ewart Library*.

Threshers Arms at No 46, a survivor of the days when nearby Buccleuch Square was a market.

Station Hotel, Lover's Walk, 1896-7, W J Milwain
Built for the Glasgow & South Western Railway, a wooden cupola offsets the bulk of this red sandstone edifice. Facing it is

29 **Dumfries Station**, 1858-9, with only one platform originally; late Victorian single-storey building on the southbound side, rare *moderne* signal box and an unusually large warehouse, built for the Caledonian Railway's branch from Lockerbie.

Above *Station Hotel*. Left *St Michael's Church.*

30 **St Michael's Church**, St Michael's Street, 1742-9, Alexander Affleck & Thomas Twaddell, masons, and James Harley, wright
Built to replace a medieval building, this fine dark red burgh church, with a steepled tower, is approached through a pair of monumental red sandstone gatepiers. Tower by William Hanna, mason, and Henry Williamson, wright. Interior refurnished, 1869, rather gloomy, though sumptuous, in the manner of the time.

St Michael's Church is on the site of the medieval parish church of Dumfries. The gatepiers are hollow, providing shelter for elders collecting alms for the poor.

Churchyard remarkable for style and richness of its monuments – the easily worked red freestone of the area lends itself to monumental sculpture – the most famous being the dignified domed classical **Burns Mausoleum**, 1815-16, T F Hunt.

31 **Moorheads Hospital**, 1751-3, Alexander Crombie, mason, and James Harley, wright
Built as a pauper hospital, two-storey simple but charming H-plan, with piended roofs – *Built at the expence of James and William Moorheads Merchants MDCCLIII.*
To the south is a mixed range of houses and shops, terminating in a recent housing development, built on the site of the **Nithsdale Tweed Mills**, founded 1857, Robert & Walter Scott. Demolished *c.*1990, this complex comprised a distinguished polychrome brick spinning mill and an extensive area of single-storey weaving sheds, with an octagonal chimney.

Top *Burns Mausoleum, St Michael's Churchyard.* Middle *Moorheads Hospital, St Michael's Street.* Above *Nithsdale Tweed Mills, 1974.*

32 **St Joseph's College**, founded 1907
Main centre of Roman Catholic education in south-west Scotland. Originally a boys' school, it became co-educational with the closure of St Benedict's Convent School (see p.26). Main building is North European Renaissance, 1907, Charles Hay. Behind is the Roman baroque **chapel**, with tall tower, 1923, Charles J Menart, which replaced a *tin church* brought from Greenock. On the edge of the school grounds is **Aldermanhill House**, 19th century, perhaps by Walter Newall, pedimented and urned. College extended, 1957-60, John Sutherland, and in 1981, Dumfries and Galloway Regional Council.

33 **Dumfries and Galloway Health Board offices** (former Royal Infirmary), North Bank, 1869-72, John Starforth
Front block two-storey, Italianate, with pyramid-roofed end bays and three-bay central section with ornamental gable. Entrance flanked by statues of **Aesculapius**, god of medicine, and **Hygeia**, goddess of health, his daughter, both by John Currie.

John Starforth, 1823-98, a noted designer of churches, was responsible for Greyfriars Church, Dumfries (see p.9). There are other notable examples of his work in Kelso (see *Borders & Berwick* in this series), Moffat (see p.108) and Nairn.

34 **Dumfries and Galloway Royal Infirmary**, Bankend Road, 1970-4, Boswell Mitchell & Johnston
Large and uncompromising flat-roofed Modern Movement building in brown brick with shuttered-concrete details. At the entrance are

two female herms, perhaps 17th century, which probably came from the town's Christy's Well, via the former Royal Infirmary.

Crichton Royal Hospital

For many years Scotland's premier mental hospital, housing patients from all over the country whose families could afford the substantial fees for the private accommodation.

Crichton Royal Infirmary was founded with money left to his widow by Dr James Crichton, a doctor with the East India Company. Frustrated in her first wish to found a university she decided, in 1833, to establish a *lunatic asylum*. William Burn, who had designed asylum buildings in Perth and Dundee, was commissioned to produce a design, which was too expensive. The cut-down version, now known as **Crichton Hall**, opened in 1839, providing accommodation for all classes of patients.

The late Victorian ward blocks provided were separate from each other, on a continental model and, as was characteristic of the period, a large farm steading was constructed to provide therapeutic employment and to produce food for the institution. Electric power was also introduced.

New approaches to mental health care in recent years have meant that many of the patients have been released into the community, and in 1996 most of the buildings were sold to a Trust which has been adapting them to new uses, including an outstation of the University of Glasgow, thus realising in part Mrs Crichton's original intention.

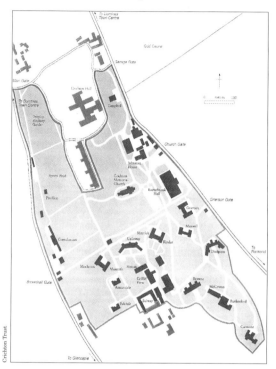

Crichton Trust

35 **Crichton Hall**, 1839, William Burn

A cut-down version of the original Burn scheme designed on a double-cross plan as a three-storey palace; only one cross was completed, with the central link. T-plan extension, 1867-71. New entrance inserted, 1910. Further additions to the rear, 1852 and 1926. Very little remains of Burn's interior, most of it is 1870-1, William Lambie Moffat. A second building was added in 1848-9, William McGowan, to house pauper patients from Dumfries and Galloway. Major extensions were made in the 1890s, when mental health provision throughout the country was revised.

The grounds, which slope down to Glencaple Road, were very handsomely laid out, for the recreation of patients, with a cricket pitch, bowling greens, and a fine garden.

Left *Crichton site plan.* Below *Crichton Hall.*

Hume

Crichton Memorial Church.

Arthur George Sydney Mitchell, 1856-1930, was an Edinburgh architect notable in the late Victorian and Edwardian periods. His early works included the model housing at Well Court in the Dean Village, Edinburgh, and the reconstruction of the Edinburgh Mercat Cross in the High Street (see *Edinburgh* in this series). In 1887, he went into partnership with George Wilson and, between then and 1911, designed a wide range of buildings, including more than a dozen churches and both country and town houses. His hospital buildings included, apart from those at Crichton Royal, the Roxburgh District Asylum, the Opthalmological Pavilion in the Edinburgh Royal Infirmary and the Royal Victoria Hospital. He worked in a range of styles, but his work is always relaxed, intelligent and expansive.

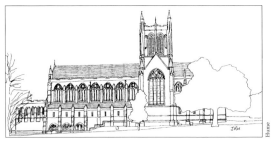

Crichton Memorial Church, 1890-7, Sydney Mitchell
Unquestionably the finest building on the site; decorated cruciform of considerable size with a splendid interior (colour page 49). Stained glass, by the Glass Stainers Co, is exceptional, with black and pale colours against a clear background. Of the same period is the **Farm & Solway House**, 1890-2, John Davidson with Colonel F R Dudgeon, a two-storey north range with central clock tower and single-storey ranges to the rear, providing steading accommodation, dormitories for male patients and staff quarters. Now workshops.

36 **Easterbrook Hall**, 1934-8, James Flett
Long one- and two-storey building in plain art deco style. Remarkable for its pioneering community functions rather than for its architecture, it was built to provide recreational facilities, including a swimming pool and gymnasium.

The **ward blocks**, built between 1890 and 1912, were designed by Sydney Mitchell mostly in Scots Jacobean. Inter-war blocks were by James Flett, in a plainer style. Remarkable for its early date is the **electricity generating station**, 1894-5, with crowstepped gables and a sandstone ashlar chimneystack.

Easterbrook Hall.

Dock Park

37 Site of the original harbour of Dumfries, the quay walls of which are still visible. Typical Victorian park, with small but graceful **bandstand**, 1906, and **monument** to two local men who died on the *Titanic*, 1912-13, Kirkpatrick Brothers; a white granite obelisk bearing a low-relief sculpture of the doomed vessel.

Troqueer

38 On the west bank of the Nith and dominated by the great Victorian **Rosefield & Troqueer** tweed mills, 1885-9, Alan B Crombie. Though now much reduced by demolitions, the remains are still impressive. The Venetian Gothic **weaving sheds**, 1886, facing the river are the most elaborate, obviously designed as a showpiece. The remaining buildings are generally plainer, though the offices in **Troqueer Road**, vaguely French Renaissance, have some intriguing detail. Behind these, in **Ryedale Road**, is a smaller, later knitwear factory. Also of 39 note are the fantastic Gothic **Parish Church**, originally built 1770-1, Andrew Crombie, subsequently remodelled in a heavy manner, 1886-8, James Barbour, and its former **manse**.

Maxwelltown

Between Devorguilla's Bridge and the Suspension Bridge is what is left of **Dumfries Mill**, now the **Burns Heritage Centre**, clearly a very ancient mill site. Present building, *c.*1781, Andrew Meikle, originally five-storey, cut down to three storeys in 1911, when converted to a hydro-electric power station. The weir or *caul*, *c.*1705, Matthew Frew, is constructed of massive stone blocks with a fish ladder at each end.

Church Street, lined by uniform terraced early/mid 19th-century housing, leads to 40 **Dumfries Museum**, 1862, extended 1981, dominated by a converted windmill. This mill was built in 1798, but had a short life as such and was converted to an **observatory** and **camera obscura**, 1836, Walter Newall, to coincide with an appearance of Halley's Comet. Beside the windmill is the **Sinclair Memorial**, 1841, John Gregan, a tempieto housing sculptures of Sir Walter Scott's *Old Mortality* and his pony by John Currie. The sculptures were won in a lottery by Dr John Sinclair, an assistant surgeon with the Royal Navy, who died the day after his win (see p.6).

IN MEMORY OF
JOHN LAW HUME, A MEMBER OF THE BAND
AND THOMAS MULLIN, STEWARD,
NATIVES OF THESE TOWNS
WHO LOST THEIR LIVES IN THE WRECK OF
THE WHITE STAR LINER "TITANIC"
WHICH SANK IN MID-ATLANTIC
ON THE 14TH DAY OF APRIL 1912.
THEY DIED AT THE POST OF DUTY

Top *Monument to* Titanic *victims, Dock Park.* Middle *Rosefield Tweed Mill.* Above *Dumfries Museum, camera obscura.*

The converted windmill houses a wooden gear wheel, probably part of the sack hoist mechanism, which is a rare survivor of 18th-century mill technology.

James Barbour, 1834-1912, was the leading Dumfries architect of the later 19th century, and worked throughout Dumfries and Galloway. His work was generally heavily Victorian, often to the point of clumsiness.

On the summit of Maxwelltown is the former 41 **Dominican Convent of St Benedict**, Maxwell Street, 1880-4, Pugin & Pugin, with a wing added, c.1890, James Barbour. Closed as a religious house c.1990, and since used as a temporary **Sheriff Court**. At **No 1 Hill Street** there is an unexpected well-composed Modern Movement **villa**, 1966, John A Copland, Sutherland Dickie & Partners.

Laurieknowe and **Cassalands** contain a number of large villas including **No 16**, **Chapelmount House**, c.1840, much extended in the 1850s, a rambling picturesque house with a tower. **No 30**, **Laurieknowe**, is an early 19th-century villa with a remarkable cast-iron veranda round 42 two sides. **Maxwelltown West Church**, 1865-6, James Barbour, clumsy but imposing decorated Gothic, sits above the street, while nearly opposite, in **School Lane** is the Gothic former **Laurieknowe Church**, 1843, John Thomson; now a **leisure club**. **Laurieknowe Primary School**, c.1900, an extensive complex with a family resemblance to the Dumfries primary schools. On the corner of Laurieknowe and **Galloway Street** is a handsome early 19th-century two-storey **terrace** with some good doorpieces and railings. **Palmerston House**, 42 Terregles Street, is a pleasing two-storey villa with an attractive doorpiece; beyond is the former 43 **Maxwelltown Court House**, 1892-3, Alan B Crombie, a Jacobean building with some good features, recently converted to houses after a long period of disuse, and **Queen of the** 44 **South**'s football ground. **Dumfries Prison**, 1883, Major General T B Collison, is a castellated structure of relatively modest scale but considerable presence, with additions of 1988.

Right *1 Hill Street*. Below *Maxwelltown Court House before conversion to flats.*

Left *St Teresa's RC Church.* Below *Footbridge over the Dumfries bypass.*

Galloway Street is a short thoroughfare, lined on both sides with modest two-storey buildings of a vernacular character. Though many suffer from unfortunate alterations, the general effect is very pleasing. On the east side of **Glasgow Street** is the striking **St Teresa's RC**
45 **Church**, 1956-8, John Sutherland of M Purdon Smith & Partners, with steeple slating extending almost to ground level. Further north, the route intersects with the Dumfries bypass on the A75, 1988-90, marked by a monumental cable-stayed **footbridge**, designed by Hugh Murray of Dumfries and Galloway Regional Council.

46 **Lincluden College**, Abbey Lane, from 1160 Richly detailed and sophisticated collegiate church of the 14th century, with significant remains of the domestic range which housed the priests who served the church; the only substantial surviving component of priestly accommodation at a Scottish collegiate church. Community founded as a Benedictine priory and converted to a collegiate church at the request of Archibald the Grim, Lord of Galloway, in 1389. Extended, 1429, by Princess Margaret, daughter of Robert III, and by others in the mid 15th century, when the church was remodelled with a new choir, featuring the

Lincluden College is one of the more modest ecclesiastical establishments that were founded by Scots noble families after the endowment of abbeys became too expensive. Collegiate churches had a number of priests who were paid to say masses and to pray for the souls of the patron and his or her family. The survival of substantial remains of the priests' accommodation is unique in Scotland.

Lincluden priests' quarters from The Antiquities of Scotland *by Francis Grose.*

tomb of St Margaret. South nave aisle rebuilt, and transept added all in flamboyant French Gothic, probably by John Morow, who also worked at Melrose and Paisley.

The layout of a formal garden of some distinction can be discerned, with a former motte remodelled as a knot, probably in the early 17th century.

Historic Scotland; open to the public

Before the houses were built, Lincluden was a small estate, and the Tudor stable range survives, a two-storey, U-plan building with a three-storey tower, c.1824, Walter Newall.

Below *St Margaret's tomb*. Right *Lincluden collegiate Church, early 20th century.*

LOCHARBRIGGS

A long straggling village with little of distinction.
It merits inclusion because of its sandstone
47 **quarries**, now the last operating in
Dumfriesshire, which supply stone for buildings
all over Scotland. A memento of former methods
of stoneworking is a hand-crane now mounted at
the quarry entrance. Between Locharbriggs and
48 Heathhall lies Dumfries **Aerodrome**, built
during the Second World War as a reception
centre for aircraft delivered from manufacturers.
Some of the hangars are still standing, used for
storage or as workshops, and the control tower is
the centre of an **aviation museum**.

Top *Locharbriggs Quarry.*
Above *Cluden Bridge.*

NEWBRIDGE

49 A hamlet clustered round the elegant **Cluden
Bridge**, a three-arched structure, 1758-9,
Thomas Twaddell & Thomas Porteous. The
smiddy has a round-headed doorway
surrounded by a roll-moulding.

Ladyfield West (formerly Hannayfield), 1830,
Walter Newall
Smart and ingeniously planned small classical
villa; single-storey painted ashlar over
rusticated basement, concealed by front
elevation fully exposed to garden. Three-bay
entrance front with pedimented Ionic porch,
shallow piend and platform-roof behind
blocking course. Door with semicircular
fanlight enters vaulted vestibule giving on to
pilastered hall lit by cupola.

Arrol-Johnston Ltd was one of the
leading firms of motor-car
manufacturers in Scotland in the
early 20th century. It was founded by
George Johnston, with financial
support from Sir William Arrol, the
celebrated civil-engineering
contractor, but by the time the
Heathhall works were built most of
the shares were owned by Sir William
Beardmore, Glasgow forgemaster and
armaments' manufacturer.

Netherwood, early 19th century,
Walter Newall
Svelte two-storey classically inspired villa set
on raised platform and approached from
gardens up flight of stone steps. Symmetrical
five-bay front with shallow bays flanking
recessed doorpiece with inset Doric columns.
Pair of single-storey wings flank main block, all
painted ashlar. Detached 1930s garage block.

Rubber Works, Heathhall.

50 **Rubber Works**, Heathhall, 1913, Albert Kahn
and Arrol-Johnston Co Ltd
Large group of three-storey reinforced-
concrete-framed flat-roofed buildings, very
advanced in technique when built as a motor-
car factory resembling, in construction, Kahn's
factories in the United States, and at the
forefront of British factory design. Some of the
much-altered houses in the vicinity are
contemporary, built to house workers.

Top *Craigs House*. Middle *Ellangowan House*. Above *Netherwood Bank*.

51 Craigs House
Very pleasing late Georgian or early Victorian single-storey-and-attic villa, with sunk storey at the rear, handsome tetrastyle Doric portico and broad triangular dormers.

Ellangowan House, *c*.1869
Elaborate, eclectic two-storey red sandstone building in the style of James Barbour, with octagonal stair-tower as its central feature, with Gothic doorway flanked by open roundels at first-floor level.

The mid-19th-century, two-storey, L-plan stable range at **Kelton**, with its projecting three-bay pedimented centrepiece, is, very unusually, of red and white brick.

Ladyfield East House, earlier/mid-19th century
Uncompromising piend-roofed two-storey-and-basement block with rather ungainly porch and Venetian window with gablet above.

52 Marchmount, Marchmount Avenue, earlier 19th century
Heavily handsome, two-storey and basement house, with massive pedimented Doric porch, piend roof and chimneystacks ranged along the inner spine walls.

Netherwood Bank has, at its core, an earlier 19th-century, three-bay, symmetrical two-storey-and-basement laird's house, with inset Tuscan porch with columns *in antis*. Extended at each end, later 19th century, by a canted bay, with a balustraded stone-framed conservatory at one end.

Comlongon Castle.

53 Comlongon Castle, 15th century
Vast rectangular rubble tower of the Murrays of Cockpool connected, since *c*.1890, to a large baronial mansion house, now a **hotel** (colour page 50). The tower rises through five storeys to a heavy machicolated embattled parapet; the south elevation appears symmetrical with regularly placed paired windows to each floor. Paired crowstepped caphouses at the parapet added 1620, the westmost housing a small long gallery running the width of the castle. Entry at ground floor to vaulted basement and a full-height spiral stair in the south-east angle. Thick walls honeycombed with mural chambers, and pit-prison. Well-preserved

CAMLONGAN CASTLE.
DUMFRIESSHIRE.

PLAN OF MEZZANINE FLOOR

SECOND FLOOR PLAN

GROUND FLOOR PLAN

FIRST FLOOR PLAN

One of Ruthwell's cottages was Scotland's first savings bank, founded in 1810 by Dr Henry Duncan, the local minister, now a Savings Bank Museum. The savings bank movement, now surviving in Scotland only in North Lanarkshire with the Airdrie Savings Bank, became an important vehicle for working-class investors.

carved hall fireplace and elaborate cusped aumbry. Adjoining mansion (replacing smaller early 18th-century house), c.1890, James Barbour & Bowie, tacked on the east side, suitably rubbly and crowstepped three-storey block with square machicolated entrance tower, a smaller version of the original. Overpoweringly baronial interior, 1900, today furnished, in keeping, with suits of armour.

54 CLARENCEFIELD

Estate village for Comlongon Castle, with some limewashed vernacular buildings complemented by modern bungalows. Crowstepped former **police station**, 1911, James Barbour & Bowie, and pre-Education Act **school**, 1869, A B Crombie.

RUTHWELL

A small agricultural village dating from the 18th/19th century in its present form but probably a much older settlement judging by the existence of the Ruthwell Cross.

55 Ruthwell Parish Church

Originally a medieval building to which a 17th-century burial aisle was added. The main body was shortened and broadened, 1801-3, and the north apse added, 1886-7, by Campbell Douglas & Sellars, to house the Ruthwell Cross. James Barbour & Bowie further recast the building in 1906. The plaster ceiling and belfry are 1801, pews 1863.

Left *Comlongon Castle, plan by William Bell.* Below *Ruthwell Parish Church.*

Ruthwell Cross.

Ruthwell Cross, probably early eighth century Of Anglo-Saxon origin and of the Jarrow/Monkwearmouth school. At the time of its erection the Anglians controlled a strip of southern Scotland extending across to Whithorn. Sculpture on the south face depicts incidents in the life of Christ and the Christian life, and on the north face the presence of Our Lord. The sides depict birds and beasts in stylised foliage. It was in the church in 1642, but was smashed in 1842. The pieces were used as seating in the church until 1771 when they were placed in the **graveyard**. Re-erected by Dr Henry Duncan in the manse garden in 1802, and further restored in 1823. Finally placed in the apse formed for it in 1887.

Good monuments in the churchyard, including a vigorous headstone to Gilbert Couper, *d*.1709. **Hearse house**, 1875, beside the churchyard.

The Caerlaverock area has a long history of fortification: from the Iron Age fort on Ward Law and its successor Roman camp to the 'first' Caerlaverock built south-east of the present castle in the early 13th century. The remains of this first Maxwell castle are marked by a grassy mound and it was abandoned shortly after construction began, perhaps owing to weak foundations.

Caerlaverock Castle, entrance front.

56 **Caerlaverock Castle**, from late 12th century Built on a rocky outcrop, the present castle was described following a siege by Edward I of 1300 *in shape it was like a shield, for it had only three sides round it, with a tower at each angle; but one of them was a double one, so high, so long and so large, that under it was a gate with a drawbridge, well made and strong ... It had good walls and good ditches filled to the edge with water ... .* Triangular castle, now roofless shell, rises tranquil from its moat. Twin-towered north front entered by satisfactorily knightly (though modern) bridge. The Maxwell family retained the keepership, from *c*.1200 onwards, by dint of political wit untrammelled by moral scruple or emotional attachment, alternately forming and breaking alliance with the Scottish or English crown, successive Maxwell generations defending, dismantling or re-building the castle as demanded by the prevailing powers. In all, five major sieges and three dismantlings occurred followed by successive campaigns of building evidenced by the different types of masonry in the walls.

The first phase of building began in the late 12th century under Aymer Maxwell laying out the distinctive shield-shaped plan with round towers at each angle. From this period dates the fine ashlar lower portions of the west and south-east towers which survived a

Caerlaverock Castle, Nithsdale Apartments in courtyard.

dismantling, 1312 (by Aymer's great grandson, Sir Eustace, who defected to join The Bruce). The upper courses, built of chunkier ashlar with wide mortar joints, indicate post-1312 work. The walls linking the towers were rebuilt, mostly in the early 15th century, with adjustments for artillery in the form of gunloops, from the 16th century.

The Sleeping Beauty within the walls is the outstanding **Nithsdale Apartments**, as fine a Renaissance palace front as any in Scotland. Begun 1621 for Robert Maxwell, recently elevated as Lord Nithsdale, most of the east range survives. Strictly symmetrical design outweighs all considerations of internal layout. Each opening crowned by a steeply pitched pediment, either triangular with heraldic motifs or segmental showing scenes from classical myth: iconography balancing courtly ideals of lordship with humanist and academic concerns. Alas, it was a brief flowering and the final denouement came in 1634 when a party of Covenanters laid siege to Catholic Caerlaverock and, after 13 weeks' bombardment, both the castle and the *delicate fabric of the new lodging* lay in ruins. Caerlaverock remained a Maxwell possession but was never again inhabited and was given over to state care in 1946. *Historic Scotland: open to the public; guidebook*

Detail, Nithsdale Apartments.

33

Caerlaverock House, 1837, Walter Newall
Extensive former manse in stugged red ashlar; two-storey, three-bay west front with advanced gabled centre bay. Typical Newall pedimented canopy over door and chunky diagonally set-square chimneys flourish at all gable heads. Double-pile full-height wing to rear links to steading range.

57 **Kirkconnel Lea**, 1870
Station-style Gothic villa for Great Eastern Railway magnate, Captain Anderson. Originally bedecked with gables, turrets, bargeboards and lead-canopied veranda, set in gardens stocked with architectural and botanical exotica. Recently turrets sadly decapitated and impoverished of ornament.

Right Kirkconnel Lea. *Below* Conheath.

58 **Conheath**, late 18th century
Two-storey three-bay Georgian country house; garden elevation preserves original flavour with balustraded fish-tail steps, full-height curved bow. Entrance elevation altered, 1909, James Morris of Ayr; semicircular Doric portico with three-light window above. Single-storey north wing added by Morris, harled with balustraded parapet. Rubble-walled garden with round **summerhouse**. Nineteenth-century hood-moulded lodge.
Chapel, 1909, James Morris; simple T-plan burial vault for R Y Pickering of Conheath. Completed, 1928, R S Lorimer, with interiors in simple Arts & Crafts style.

R Y Pickering was a notable builder of railway rolling stock with works at Wishaw.

Conheath Farmhouse, 1912, Robert Lorimer
Two-storey, three-bay, with deep-hipped roof pulled down to eaves; canted bay windows,

slate-hung between floors. Difficult not to dismiss as a commonplace semi out of kilter with its setting, so now familiar are its legion of suburban cousins. Earlier 19th-century steading, with **doocot** tower.

Isle Tower, near Bankend
Ruins of a three-storey-and-attic T-plan tower, probably rebuilt 1622 from an earlier structure, by Edward Maxwell.

59 **Glencaple pier**, 1836-40
With its corrugated-iron sheds, an obvious reminder of bygone commerce; mooring posts in the grass testify to the numbers of vessels that once berthed here (colour page 50). The village itself consists of a row of cottages, some scattered individual houses, an inn, now much altered, a **church**, built as a Free Church in 1856, William McGowan, the **Barbour Memorial Hall**, 1938, and both an old (late 19th century) and a new **school** in **Church Street**; the latter, **Caerlaverock School**, 1978-99, Dumfries and Galloway Regional Council Architects.

Netherwood Bank, early 20th century
Two-storey, classically inspired, symmetrical, shallow, bow-fronted house with central Doric recessed portico. 1930s garage.

BANKEND
Small 19th-century settlement on a hillside overlooking the Solway Firth, with a single-span **bridge** over the Lochar Water, 1812-13, John Robieson. Focal point is the former
60 Jacobean **Hutton Hall Academy**, 1892, James Barbour, replacing a school founded in 1712 by Dr John Hutton. On the east side of the village stands **Caerlaverock Parish Church**, 1781, a T-plan building recast and re-roofed, 1794, by James Barbour. Interesting **graveyard** containing late 18th-century burial enclosure and **hearse-house**. The **manse** is a handsome two-storey, three-bay ashlar building in Tudor style.

TORTHORWALD
Probably a medieval settlement. A few 18th/19th-century houses of which the best are **Crossway House**, early 19th century, and the former manse, **Torr House**. Set among 20th-
61 century buildings is **Cruck Cottage**, later 18th century, restored, 1993, as a monument; a

Glencaple is one of the places from which haaf-net fishing for salmon is practised. This involves a party of fishermen standing side by side across the Nith holding rectangular nets.

Top *Haaf-net fishing on the Nith at Glencaple.* Below *Hutton Hall Academy.* Bottom *Caerlaverock Parish Church manse.*

35

rare survival of the pre-improvement rural vernacular in Dumfriesshire with, as the name implies, cruck frames set in low rubble walls, with a thatched roof.

The **school**, vaguely Tudor in character, was built in 1911, and the hall, built as the **Nicolson Bequest Female Industrial School**, in 1868. In front is the **schoolhouse** and, behind, the simple school, extended, c.1935.

The T-plan **parish church**, 1782, incorporates earlier work; enlarged, 1791 and 1809, and plainly refurnished. Good monuments in the graveyard (colour page 52).

62 **Torthorwald Castle**, 14th and 15th century
Substantial remains of a large tower-house on a small hill, with ditch and rampart, and formerly curtain-wall defence, built for the Kirkpatricks and Carlyles of Torthorwald.

63 **Amisfield Tower**, 16th and early 17th centuries
Unquestionably the finest late tower-house in southern Scotland. A quart in a pint pot; simple rectangular base developing above second floor into a sophisticated interplay of

Top *Cruck Cottage, Torthorwald.*
Above *Torthorwald Castle.* Right *Amisfield Tower.*

Amisfield Tower is unique in southern Scotland for the elaboration of the treatment of the upper section. The nearest parallels are castles in north-east Scotland such as Craigievar (see *Gordon* in this series) and Crathes, but Amisfield is dependent for its aesthetic effect more on its solid geometry than the Aberdeenshire examples.

flat and curved-surfaced turrets. A Charteris family stronghold since 1200; the lower floors are early 16th century, extensively enlarged and remodelled, 1600, by Sir John Charteris. Generously proportioned windows, nail-head decoration enriching roll-moulded jambs. Once-harled rubble walls contrast with ashlar for the turrets; dormer corbelled on fake machicolations over door in jest at *murder-hole* tradition. Stair in north-east angle, vaulted basements, halls to first and second floors, one public, one private, linked by a laird's lug to eavesdrop on *public hall* conversation. Paired bedchambers to third, and attic rooms aplenty in the upperworks. Both halls have handsome shafted fireplaces with saltbox and aumbries; fragments of painted decoration survive.

Amisfield Tower, corner turret.

Amisfield House, 1631 and 1837
Commodious horizontally planned house built to south of tower by 11th Lord Charteris. Considerably remodelled, now presents 18th-century appearance with windows enlarged. This block now forms rear wing of an 1837 classical house. All red ashlar, two storeys, five bays, with pediment over centre canted-bay window. Pretty gabled and bargeboarded **gatelodge**, mid 19th century. The **walled garden** was probably an original feature though the present fabric dates from early 19th century.
Open to the public; guidebook

Glenae
William Hyslop, the mason, was paid *for polished ashlar 4d per foot, for droved work 3d and 7s 6d for each of the steps.*

Below *Glenae*. Bottom *Tinwald House*.

64 **Glenae**, 1789, Thomas Boyd of Dumfries
Genteel classical house in droved ashlar with polished margins. Two storeys with lower wings, raised basement oversailed by steps to Ionic doorpiece. Good interior, pilastered hall screen, cantilevered stair, elaborate chimneypieces.

65 **Tinwald House**, 1740, William Adam
Palladian mansion built for Charles Erskine, sometime Lord Advocate. Two-storey, seven-bay front with canted bays to side elevations (see also **Knockhill** (p.121) and **Greenlaw** (p.144)). Balustraded perron stair to pedimented keystoned doorway; windows in lugged architraves. As at **Craigdarroch** (p.64), Adam planned pavilions which were never executed. Interior fire-damaged, 1946; restored by Simpson & Brown. Re-roofed and stacks raised from existing to match Adam drawing; ground plan altered (colour page 51).

Above *Tinwald Parish Church*. Right *Dalswinton Mission Church, interior*.

Tinwald Shaws Farm, late 18th century
Incorporates a large piend-roofed farmhouse.

TINWALD

The village consists of a small group of houses
66 close to the **parish church**, 1763-5; porches
added, windows and roof replaced, 1898-9, by
James Barbour, interior recast at the same
time (colour page 52). Interesting **graveyard**.
The views over Nithsdale are striking.

AMISFIELD TOWN

Just a row of cottages, a school and schoolhouse.

DALSWINTON

The ultimate in simple planning: two terraces
of cottages, *c.*1790, facing each other across a
wide street; that on the north has had a storey
added. Nearly hidden in trees to the south is a
real gem – a '**tin church**' with original pitch-
pine pews, pulpit and panelling, built, 1881, as
a Mission Church.

Dalswinton Village.

'Tin Churches' – churches made of
corrugated-iron – were popular in late
19th- and early 20th-century Scotland,
and were also exported by Glasgow
and Edinburgh makers, in kit form, to
countries overseas. The Dalswinton
church is one of the few surviving in
ecclesiastical use and is probably the
best of its kind in Scotland.

67 **Dalswinton House**, 1785,
?Alexander Nasmyth; additions 1919
Modest classical mansion, for Patrick Miller,
perched on high ground above a crossing of the
River Nith and on the site of a 13th-century
castle. Plain in the extreme; ashlar fronted,
three storeys, five bays with central porch to
the east elevation, it was re-orientated and
recast, 1919-20, by Barbour & Bowie, the
original porch replaced by a wide single-storey
bow window. The north elevation promoted to
entrance front with full-height addition and
stodgy entrance bay with giant thermal
window over simplified broken pedimented
Doric porch – more municipal chambers than

Dalswinton House.

country house. In the grounds, simple timber **boathouse** oversees artificial lake; pair of 18th-century classical **lodges**. Ruins of 16th-century predecessor, Dalswinton Old House, consisting of buried vaulted ground floor, with remains of round stair tower. **Stable block** now converted to housing. Large, formal stable court, central entrance pend under pediment surmounted by tall square clock tower, its roof a (now) truncated spire.

In the grounds of Dalswinton House, an 18th-century, roofless, square-plan **doocot** on the edge of Dalswinton Loch. **Dalswinton Mill**, early 19th century, a water-powered oatmeal mill with a low-breast paddle wheel, sympathetically converted to a dwelling house, early 1990s.

Dalswinton is a name to conjure with in Scotland's industrial history. It was in 1788 on little Dalswinton Loch that, under the patronage of Patrick Miller, a banker who, by his own admission, had made and spent three fortunes, William Symington tried out Scotland's – and one of the world's – first steamboats. A full-scale version was tried out the following year on the Forth & Clyde Canal. Robert Burns is said to have been a passenger on one of its inconclusive trials.

Kirkmahoe Parish Church.

KIRKTON

A settlement to one side of the rather plain red
68 sandstone **Kirkmahoe Parish Church**, 1822-3, Walter Newall, a large *Heritors' Gothic* building with pinnacled tower.

Manse, 1798-9, probably John McCracken Two-storey, three-bay house, with engaged-pillared porch, flanked on the ground floor by tripartite windows, later single-storey service wing.

The cottages round a green are neat but unpretentious, giving a settled feel to the place,

CARNSALLOCH HOUSE

Some very fine 18th- and 19th-century monuments in Kirkton graveyard include one to Mary Lindsay, a motherly spinster, who died in 1832, whose epitaph reads:

Stranger! one fleeting moment save,
For this is MARY LINDSAY'S GRAVE
Who practised, in her low estate,
Virtues that well become the great:
Who, self-denying, chaste and kind,
An honour was to womankind,
Near yon rude cot she first drew breath,
And there she closed her eyes in death
– Pattern to all who wish to thrive –
At the ripe age of eighty-five,
No husband Mary ever had,
Nor offspring age's ills to glad;
Yet all the children round and round
In her a foster-parent found
Their eggs she boiled, their Josephs dried
And soothed and coaxed them when
they cried
And when the burn was wide and wild
She ferried over every child
Proficient in each nurturing art,
The fremit [spinster] had a mother's
heart
A janitress from love not hire
How blest was Mary's winter fire!
Disturb not but respect this stone
Raised to her memory by one
Who even in death would Mary shield.
Hannah of Bayhall, Huddersfield.

Below *Castle Hill Windmill.*
Bottom *Duncow House.*

the warm red sandstone sitting well with the green. Pair of Tudor cottages (**Lukeview**), perhaps by Walter Newall, spoiled by the removal of the mullions from the windows.

Newlands House, 1911
Large two- and three-storey-and-attic, red sandstone, heavily baronial, with castellated and turreted lookout tower incorporating mid-19th-century house. Norwegian servicemen billeted here, 1940-5.

69 **Castle Hill Windmill**, probably 18th century Squat tapering rubble tower of wind-powered corn-mill (colour page 51).

70 **West Galloberry Steading** contains a circular horse-engine house, still with its wooden engine, the only complete survivor of the hundreds that once worked in Scotland.

Milnhead House, *c.*1760
Delightful small laird's house, two storeys and basement, three bays, with piended roof and spine-wall chimneys. Central bay advanced and pedimented, with rusticated quoins. Later 18th-century, square-plan **doocot**, two-storey, with brick upper section, in the grounds.

Duncow House, 1860, Alexander Crombie
Demolished, but some estate buildings survive, including the former **stables**, 1878, a mildly Tudor quadrangle, with towered carriage entrance and advanced end bays, all in rock-faced red sandstone masonry. **South lodge**, *c.*1878, is crowstepped, on an L-plan, with gabled porch. Adjacent entrance retains a full set of very fine cast-iron gates and railings.

71 **Clonfeckle Tower**, 1810, circular rubble tower built by Patrick Miller of Dalswinton as a monument to the Revd Dr William Richardson of Clonfeckle in Ireland, pioneer of the cultivation of fiorin grass.

72 **Carnsalloch House**, 1757, Isaac Ware
Built for Alexander Johnstone, a London chemist, by a fashionable London architect; tall, narrow, three-storey, three-bay, Palladian villa, only one room deep looking, from the side, like a slice of a house of normal proportions. London swank in the details though: three tall Burlington windows, enriched by Ionic columns with full entablature, light the first floor; exquisite iron anthemion-pattern stair

40

RCAHMS

balustrade. Early 19th-century work includes the pedimented pilastered porch and some internal refitting. Single-storey corridors link to two-storey, piended, seven-bay pavilions. The north pavilion encloses an earlier five-bay laird's house with much early 18th-century panelling *in situ*. Now a Leonard Cheshire Home; miscellaneous modern flat-roofed extensions to rear. Solemn Doric-columned Newallesque **lodge**.

Carnsalloch House.

Carnsalloch Stables, ?Isaac Ware, 1755, Palladian inspiration; square on plan with single-storey outer range encircling vast central two-storey block. All four elevations roughly identical; tall-arched pedimented doorway with Diocletian window above. Swept pyramid roof ends abruptly; a cupola was probably intended to finish the composition; spectacular interior.

Tiny, decorated Gothic **chapel**, 1850, E B Lamb, for the Campbell-Johnstons of Carnsalloch; bristling buttresses now wreathed in ivy and gently decaying. Elaborate curvilinear tear-drop tracery, five-sided apse.

Carnsalloch Chapel.

73 **Riddingwood House**, 1830, Walter Newall Four-square Newall gravitas: two-storey, three-bay front, heavy pedimented Doric porch, chunky chimneystacks; polished ashlar dressed

Anderson

Quarrelwood Church and manse.

Quarrelwood
The church and manse were built by *Cameronians*, followers of the Covenanter Richard Cameron, a member of the Reformed Presbyterian Church, which refused to join the Presbyterian Church of Scotland as restored under William and Mary in 1690.

work contrasts with stugged walling. **Garden house** is a tiny castellated folly with bartizans and gun-ports.

74 **Quarrelwood**, 1798
Former Cameronian manse, two storeys, three bays, central arched doorway flanked by plain Venetian windows, low pitched roof; adjoining octagonal **former church** restored from ruins, 1969, A C Wolffe & Partners.

AULDGIRTH
Small village with superb three-span classical old **bridge**, 1781, David Henderson, built of red sandstone, unusually with half-domed refuges above cutwaters. New **bridge**, 1979, Dumfries and Galloway Council, is a composite 75 concrete/steel construction. Gothick **Auldgirth Inn**, *c.*1804.

AE
Village created, from 1947, by Forestry Commission to service large area of new planting. Housing plan, John A W Grant, reminiscent of pre-war *garden suburb* public 76 housing. Forestry Commission **offices** and workshops on floodplain below, some of timber construction.

77 **Ross Mains**, 1728, attr James Smith
Fully fledged classicism for the smaller mansion, here executed for the Queensberry Estate. Two-storey, five-bay, symmetrical front dominated by deep piend and platform roof, heavy axial stacks, gracefully swept eaves. Boldly rusticated corners flank five regular bays, central open-pediment doorway bears Queensberry arms. Internally some 19th-century alterations, but original doors, panelling and bolection-moulded fireplaces survive.

78 **Barony Agricultural College**, 1834, William Burn
Modern block and brute baronial, rambling, asymmetric, Jacobean house in purply-red Locharbriggs sandstone; two storeys with bay windows, mullioned and transomed, gloomy gables, pedimented dormers. Over the door, strapwork pediment with ball finials. Interior alterations and refit by James Barbour & Bowie of Dumfries suits well its present institutional use. Infinitely more cheerful modern courtyard block for Barony Agricultural College, 1984-91, by Peter Nelson

Below Auldgirth Bridge. Middle *Auldgirth Inn.* Bottom *Ae village.*

of Dumfries and Galloway Regional Council.
Red brick incorporating echoes of Burn's detail
given post-modernist expression.

Dalfibble.

79 **Dalfibble**, early 19th century, Walter Newall
Two-storey, three-bay, piend-roofed farmhouse
crowned with heavy pair of ashlar
chimneystacks and six cans apiece. Pilastered
corniced doorpiece. Newall variations on this
theme also at **Kirkland**, with stacks placed
transversely, and at **Burrance**, with good
margin-glazed fanlight.

Kirkmichael Parish, because of its
relative flatness and dryness, is one of
the best grain-growing parishes in
south-west Scotland. This is reflected
in the scale of its farm steadings and
in the number of cottage rows
provided for farm servants. Cumrue
appears to have been the largest on
both counts.

80 **Kirkmichael Parish Church**, 1813-15,
John McCracken
T-plan church, recast late 19th century.
Belfry, in typical Dumfriesshire fashion, is on
the downstroke of the T. Good monuments in
the **churchyard** (colour pages 51&52).

Cumrue Steading, early 19th century, has
an unusually large granary and cart shed of
1827, with eight cart bays. Large two-storey,
three-bay, symmetrical **farmhouse** with
later porch. Nearby village consists of a long
row of farmworkers' **cottages**, one of the
longest in Scotland.

Cumrue village.

81 **Courance House**, *c.*1840, style of
Walter Newall
Symmetrical, two-storey, three-bay, red-
sandstone ashlar house, with advanced central
bay and machicolated porch; flanking window
bays also slightly advanced. Lying-pane glazing
at first floor.

82 PARKGATE

Hamlet dominated by large and now decaying **farm steading**. **Village hall** rebuilt from Kirkmichael Free Church.

83 CLOSEBURN

Nineteenth-century planned village, probably founded by Revd James Stuart-Menteth of Closeburn Hall and laid out on an L-plan; the single-storey cottages are early 19th century, originally roofed probably with stone slabs quarried locally. Early 20th-century corrugated iron **village hall**, and former **railway station**, 1850, a simple sandstone ashlar structure.

The front of the **primary school**, 1909, by James Barbour & Bowie, is a rather heavy design in red sandstone; the back is more open, with extensive glazing. Next to it is the former **Wallace Hall Academy**, founded by a native of Closeburn, John Wallace, who had become a successful Glasgow merchant. The first school was built, 1724-9, by William Lukup, reworked, 1842, by Walter Newall, and recast into Scots Jacobean in 1882. Between it and the primary school is the three-storey **boarding house**, 1795.

84 Closeburn Parish Church, 1878, James Barbour

Dominated by tower with tall crocketed finials. Hammerbeam roof and many original furnishings inside. The **churchyard** contains the remains of the old parish church, 1741, heightened, 1779, by Archibald Cleland, and the belfry houses a bell of 1606. Some fine gravestones and the classical **Thomas Kirkpatrick Mausoleum**, 1742. The ball-finialled **gatepiers** have adjoining offertory shelters.

Top *Closeburn Parish Church*. Middle *Closeburn Parish churchyard*. Above *Closeburn Castle*.

85 Closeburn Castle, late 14th century

Kirkpatrick family stronghold, set on a plateau and formerly moated. Simple rectangular tower on three storeys with vaulted basement and attics; entry direct to first-floor hall via external steps. Defence against attack and arson was ensured by massively thick walls and stone vaults over basement, ground and attic level; all crowned with a stone-flagged roof and wallhead battlements. Ironically the Kirkpatricks moved out to a smart new 17th-century house, which burned out in 1748 thereby forcing their return to the old tower and occasioning the re-fit which enlarged all windows to their present size and subdivided rooms internally. Further 19th-century alterations titivated the battlements with mock crenellations and added a new single-storey wing and a castellated porch to the old tower (colour page 51). Single-storey **South Lodge**, early 19th century, classical with Doric-columned porch.

Park smithy.

Dalgarnock Graveyard
A forest of 18th- and 19th-century stones all with fluted pilasters and draped urns, nicely euphemistic in their iconography. Scattered between these, a number of earlier Covenanters' memorials, simpler and more direct: skulls, crossed bones, winged souls and skeletons facing the hereafter head on.

Closeburn Mains steading, *c*.1780
Massive two-storey range with central pedimented cart entrance, formerly the stable block for Closeburn Hall.

86 **Park Village & Limeworks**
One of the most advanced limeworks in the west of Scotland, with a waterwheel-operated inclined plane to hoist limestone to the block of three single-draw kilns. The village has several single-storey buildings (including a **smithy**) roofed with sandstone tiles from nearby **Gatelawbridge quarries**.

87 **Cample Mill & Viaduct**
Large, early 19th-century, two-storey-and-attic, six-bay, possible early woollen mill, now gutted and used as a store. Viaduct opened, 1850, by

The limeworks of Upper Nithsdale, at Barjarg, Porterstown (see p.68) and Park were the largest in Dumfries and Galloway, and were intensively worked during the agricultural improvements of the late 18th and early 19th centuries. The Park works was probably the most technically advanced.

Park Limeworks.

Cample Viaduct.

the Glasgow, Dumfries & Carlisle Railway, John Miller, engineer.

88 **Barburgh Mill**, early 19th century
Two-storey woollen mill of seven by nine bays on an L-plan, spinning and weaving local wool for local use; closed since 1950. A complete and unaltered example of a once-common building type in south-west Scotland.

Rosebank, early 19th century
Single-storey cottage, with flattened Venetian bay windows flanking an arched doorway. Later extensions to both ends.

Below Barburgh Mill. Bottom 57 Drumlanrig Street.

Auchencairn steading, *c.*1830
Retains its all-iron overshot waterwheel, fed by fireclay-pipe siphon, which drove a threshing machine inside the adjacent barn.

THORNHILL
Generously planned settlement with tree-lined streets on a cross-plan, this estate village for Drumlanrig, founded by the Earl of Queensberry as a burgh of barony in 1664, developed in the late 18th century, largely as a consequence of road and agricultural
89 improvement. **Drumlanrig Street** has a pleasing mix of 18th- and 19th-century buildings, with a good arched shopfront at **Nos 57/58**, more elaborate towards the south end, where a simple Gothic former **Congregational Church**, 1873-4, Charles Howitt, sits comfortably among the houses. At the crossing of **East** and **West Morton Street**, marked by the **Cross**, 1714, on an octagonal base, are the **George Hotel**, and the **Buccleuch & Queensberry Hotel**, the latter of 1855,

Charles Howitt. The former **Virginhall Church**, simple red sandstone Gothic built for the United Presbyterians, 1897-8, John B Wilson, is a visual stop to West Morton Street.

East Morton Street is the civic centre, with the remarkable abstract mosaic front of the **Drumlanrig Restaurant**, and the **parish hall**, 1893-4, James Barbour, dignified by a bronze bust. At the end of the street is a **monument** to Joseph Thomson, African explorer, with low-relief panels of African scenes round the base, 1896-7, Charles McBride. Behind are the Jacobean **primary school**, 1909, Edward J Dakers; the **Wallace Hall Academy** and **schoolmaster's house**, 1864-5, Charles Howitt; and the present **Academy**, 1959-78, Dumfriesshire County Council; with the towered Romanesque

90 **Morton Parish Church**, 1839-41, William Burn, on a road leading to the former **railway station**, opened 1850, by the Glasgow, Dumfries & Carlisle Railway, and **Thornhill Auction Mart**, with an octagonal wooden auction room with slated pyramidal roof.

Unusual and striking, relaxed and spacious layout, the light red sandstone giving a lightness absent from southern Dumfriesshire settlements.

Nithbank House, c.1800
Mildly Tudor, two-storey-and-attic house, with slightly advanced gables and finialled end bays. Broader wing added mid-19th century, with two-storey canted bay window.

91 **Carronhill Viaduct**, 1850, John Miller, engineer
Six-span masonry structure, with semicircular arches for Glasgow, Dumfries & Carlisle Railway.

92 **CARRONBRIDGE**
This ducal village has a wonderful setting, its main street twisting down and up again, with picturesque houses and an old smiddy, now a shop. Apart from a few vernacular buildings, and a handful of modern ones, the houses reflect the design characteristics of Walter Newall, who designed many of the Buccleuch Estate buildings in Dumfriesshire. The former **school** and **schoolhouse** date from 1844.

Carronbridge Mill steading, earlier/mid 19th century, contains a magnificent long two-storey sandstone range with 12 arched cart

Drumlanrig Restaurant.

Joseph Thomson, 1858-95, African explorer, was born in Penpont. His monument has on the front a low-relief plaque featuring a depiction of Mount Kilimanjaro, reflecting his explorations in what are now Tanzania and Uganda in the 1870s and 1880s. Though he did not discover Kilimanjaro, he visited it on his third expedition in 1883.

Below *Morton Parish Church.*
Bottom *Carronbridge.*

bays, certainly the largest of its kind in south-west Scotland.

Morton Castle.

93 **Morton Castle**, 14th century
Perched on a promontory amid the rolling Nithsdale hills, Morton is more manorial Douglas hunting-seat than fortified castle. Round towers flank a long hall block plentifully lit by fine arched mullioned windows, and warmed by hooded fireplaces with carved capitals. Twin gatehouse towers (*à la* Caerlaverock) secured a drawbridge and portcullis entrance, though the cubed ashlar walls are devoid of arrowslits or other defences. *Historic Scotland; open to the public*

Rowantree House.

94 **Rowantree House**, 1855, W L Moffat
Former poorhouse; long symmetrical range, its 11 bays articulated by bold painted quoins and tall coped stacks. Entrance through tiny gatehouse pend flanked by tall stacks.

Holmhill, 1827
Whitewashed rubble two-storey house, three wide bays flanked by pedimented wings; that to right heightened. Projecting rear bow holds stair.

Top *Dumfries High Street looking north from the Mid Steeple.* Middle *Statue of Robert Burns, Church Place.* Above *Royal Arms of Scotland on the Mid Steeple.* Above left *The Mid Steeple.* Left *Crichton Memorial Church.*

Top *Comlongon House and Tower, Clarencefield.* Top right *Dumfries Savings Bank, Church Crescent.* Above *Detail, Tourist Information Office, Whitesands.* Right *Tourist Information Office, Whitesands.* Far right *Portico, Dumfries Academy.* Below *The Nith from Glencaple.*

50

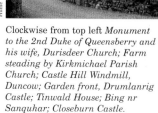

Clockwise from top left *Monument to the 2nd Duke of Queensberry and his wife, Durisdeer Church; Farm steading by Kirkmichael Parish Church; Castle Hill Windmill, Duncow; Garden front, Drumlanrig Castle; Tinwald House; Bing nr Sanquhar; Closeburn Castle.*

51

Stirling Smith Art Gallery and Museum

Hume

Hume

Hume

Left from top *Tinwald Parish Church; St Mark's Church, Kelloholm; Torthorwald Parish Church; 'From Bedrock to Sunlight' by Sybille von Halem, sculpture in front of Sanquhar Tolbooth; Tombstones, Durisdeer Churchyard.*
Top *Dunglaston by James Paterson.* Middle *Monument to the Sanquhar Declarations.* Above *Kirkmichael Parish Church.*

95 **Nith Bridge**, 1778
Two-arch rubble bridge consisting of narrow carriageway with pedestrian refuges and V-shaped cutwaters. £680 was collected by the presbytery to begin work in 1774; a collapse two years later resulted in an appeal to the Commissioners of Supply in 1778 to fund the present structure.

Burn Farm, 1834, William Burn
Drumlanrig Estate two-storey baronial farmhouse with crowsteps and turret. Steading, to plans by Walter Newall, grouped around central roofed midden, later rebuilt as cattle court. Hierarchy of materials: pink sandstone for the house; whin rubble for the steading with sandstone for the dressed work only.

96 **Dabton House**, 1820, William Atkinson
Classically detailed two-storey house by a fashionable London architect in pink ashlar for the chamberlain of the Drumlanrig Estate. Three-bay front with recessed centre bay. Functional **stable block** around courtyard; T-plan **lodge** with pilastered doorpiece.

DURISDEER
Parish kirkton for Drumlanrig; the Dukes of Queensberry, as heritors, had the patronage of the church, and responsibility for it, hence a very remarkable church in this apparently remote spot.

The farm steadings on the Drumlanrig Estate, many of which were designed by Walter Newall (see p.14), are the most elaborate and most varied in south-west Scotland, reflecting the ducal status of their owner.

Top *Nith Bridge*. Above *Burn Farm*. Left *Durisdeer Parish Church, postcard view c.1960*.

About 1.5km north-east of **Durisdeer Church**, in the valley of the Kirk Burn is the best-preserved Roman fortlet in the area. It dates from the Antonine period, and consists of two banks and a ditch, enclosing a rounded rectangular area.

97 **Durisdeer Parish Church**, 1716-20, probably James Smith
T-plan church in harled sandstone rubble with tall round-headed windows, rusticated ashlar quoins and dressings replacing its medieval predecessor. Two-storey session house and retiring rooms for the Duke, and central tower

finished 1729, originally crowned by a leaded spire, removed, 1825. Original platform roof on the church and leaded ogee roof on the south aisle replaced by simple piended roofs, 1784.

The oldest and most glorious part is the sandstone ashlar **Queensberry Aisle**, 1695-1708, designed by James Smith and built for the burial of the 1st Duke of Queensberry: a tall square pavilion with ogee-domed lead roof – appropriately, for the Duke's lead mines were at nearby Wanlockhead. Roof profile lowered, 1881, and curvilinear Gothic window in north wall removed when baroque **monument** to the 2nd Duke and his wife Mary inserted, c.1713, John van Nost. Aisle linked to church by low segmental arch, with wrought-iron screen. Over entrance to burial vault is a twisted-columned *baldacchino*, designed by James Smith in the style of that over the high altar in St Peter's, Rome (colour page 51).

Late 18th- and early 19th-century galleries within, and pulpit of earlier 19th century placed in its present position, c.1870. Box pews at the back of the south aisle with pews in front converting for communion.

Churchyard contains exceptionally fine tombstones and monuments of 18th and early 19th century (colour page 52). **Cottages** round the churchyard mainly mid-19th century; **manse**, 1763, altered 19th century.

Durisdeer Parish Church, Queensberry monument.

Durisdeer Parish Church
The whole is an extraordinary thing and especially in this remote upland place. It may seem rather grandiose, but the Duke was the most influential nobleman of his day, representative of the monarchy in Scotland, and much involved in the Union of the Parliaments. The architect was probably James Smith who studied for the Roman Catholic priesthood in St Luke's Rome in 1671-5, so would have known St Peter's.

Drumlanrig Castle, plan, from Vitruvius Britannicus.

98 **Drumlanrig Castle**, mainly 1675-90, James Smith
Ducal palace of the Queensberrys *rises from the Dumfriesshire hills like a pink marble palace in the steaming heat of the Indian Subcontinent* (Macaulay). Until its remodelling, Drumlanrig was substantially as reconstructed in the mid-16th century, with a tower in the north-west corner of an irregular courtyard. First scheme for rationalising the house devised in 1618, and involved a south range with towers at both ends, probably inspired by Culross Abbey House, 1608, for Lord Bruce of Kinloss, then the acme of advanced taste in Scotland.

Nothing done with these plans, and it was not until 1673 that the 3rd Earl of Queensberry (later the 1st Duke) sought advice from Robert Mylne, and from Sir William Bruce about a new scheme of rebuilding, implemented between 1675-90, under the general superintendence of James Smith, who had worked at Holyroodhouse with

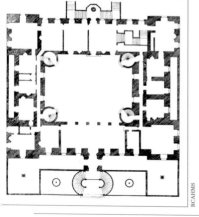

Bruce. Plan resembles that of George Heriot's Hospital, Edinburgh (see *Edinburgh* in this series), but with the north front reduced in height by a storey and given an arcaded advanced base, to approximate more closely to the arrangement of the Palace of Holyroodhouse, itself influenced by the design of Christian IV's Frederiksborg Castle, at Hillerød in Denmark, both of which had U-plan main blocks with lower entrance fronts. Drumlanrig also resembles the Palace of Holyroodhouse (and other high-status houses of the period) in having the central entrance flanked by blocks of reducing height to give a theatricality to the entrance itself.

The design as constructed seems to have been substantially altered during building, and

Douglas is the family name of the Earls, Marquesses and Dukes of Queensberry. They trace their lineage back to the Sir James Douglas, supporter both of William Wallace and of Robert the Bruce, who took the embalmed heart of Bruce to Spain, where he was killed in 1330. Drumlanrig is liberally embellished with the winged heart – emblem of the Douglas family.

Left *Drumlanrig Castle, entrance front.* Below *Drumlanrig Castle, garden front.* Bottom *Drumlanrig Castle, entrance porch.*

embodied part of the old east range, but most of the rest was new. **South-east** and **west ranges** form a relatively uniform U-plan, with four-storey blocks and five-storey corner towers, all with balustraded flat lead roofs, an indication of taste and wealth. Double-angled **stair** to first floor on the garden front with elaborate, 1684, wrought-iron railing (colour page 51). Display reserved for the **entrance front**, elaborate confection with twin curved staircases (a perron) rising to advanced entrance bay, elaborately swagged, with semicircular open pediment enclosing the Queensberry Arms, and topped by octagonal **clock tower** with ducal coronet round its domed roof. Frontage has giant-order Corinthian pilasters, and lugged windows have richly moulded pediments, with sculpture in the tympani, the whole giving a feeling of, at times slightly awkward, richness. Overall effect is stunning.

Internally, the ground-floor entrance between the arms of the perron leads into an open loggia (glazed over to form a hall, 1875), thence into central open courtyard. A choice of four round

55

Drumlanrig landscape
Extensive grounds laid out by the 1st
and 2nd Dukes; formal terraces and
parterres around the house opening to
wider formal vistas. Reactions varied:
Defoe, nervous of nature in the raw,
declared Drumlanrig *a fine picture in
a dirty grotto ... environed with
mountains, the most hideous aspect in
all South Scotland.* Gilpin criticised
the terracing, *a contrivance to deform
beauty*, finding the environs
delightful. The profligate 4th Duke,
Old Q, was no gardener, felling trees
wholesale and necessitating careful
restoration and replanting throughout
the 19th and 20th centuries.

Right *Drawing room, Drumlanrig.*
Above *Limewood carving of fish,
fruit and birds.*

stair-towers or, from the south range, the scale-
and-platt main stair to the *piano nobile*
apartments. **Dining room**, 17th century apart
from heavy Jacobean ceiling with fine wood
carving in the style of Grinling Gibbons added
19th century, **drawing room**, **bedchamber**
and **closet**, all with 17th-century panelling
framing tapestries, luxuriantly carved flora and
fauna in over-door panels. The first floor of the
north range originally given over to a *very* long
gallery, subdivided into bedchambers in 1813.

Numerous estate buildings include **stables**, now
craft shops; 19th-century timber rustic
98 **summerhouses**; **Creel Bridge footbridge**
suspended from slender iron columns; **East
Bridge**, two-arch, red ashlar, springs high over
the Nith – late medieval in origin and put in good
order, 1710, by William Lukup; roadway widened
on corbel table, 1810. **Bridge Cottage**, 1840,
William Burn, picturesque single-storey lodge with
hood-moulded mullioned windows. **Laundry
Cottages**, remodelled, 1871, by Charles Howitt.
Low Garden Cottage, 1831, William Burn, is
picturesque gabled *cottage orné* with veranda.

Ashlar-walled **kitchen garden** formerly
with heated glasshouses producing pineapples
for Edinburgh dinner tables. To avoid smoke
and smuts from the boilers, flues ran
underground discharging from a tall, masonry
chimney on a distant hilltop. Nearby **Heather
House**, mid-19th-century summerhouse, with
rustic timber walls.
*House open to the public in summer; grounds
all year*

Low Garden Cottage.

99 **Sweetbit Steading**, 1829-31, probably
Walter Newall
Two-storey barn and fine three-bay cart shed,
with single-storey **farmhouse**; all limewashed.

Carronbank Cottage, *c.*1830, William Burn
Single-storey Italianate composition, with
prominent open eaves and semi-octagonal bay
with iron-columned veranda.

Sanquhar Post Office was founded
in 1712 when a *Change Post* was set
up at Sanquhar where postal runners
would change horses and pick up post.

SANQUHAR

Market town, originally a burgh of barony
linked to the castle whose gaunt and
enigmatic remains lie at the south end, then a
royal burgh from 1698. General scale of
buildings is modest, and the two-storey shops,
houses, commercial and administrative
buildings which line High Street give it a
strongly uniform character.

100 **Sanquhar Castle**
The logic of the building is difficult to decipher
but it seems to have been built from around
1400, and extended in the 15th, 16th and
possibly 17th centuries. The site is bounded on
three sides by natural and artificial defences,
the masonry structures consisting of a curtain-
wall enclosing an outer and an inner
courtyard, the latter with ranges on two
sides. Significant restoration work undertaken,
1895-1901, Robert Weir Schultz, for the 3rd
Marquess of Bute.

*Below Sanquhar Castle. Middle St
Ninian's Baptist Church. Bottom
Post office.*

101 Worthy of note in the village are **St Ninian's
Baptist Church**, 1841-2, built as a United
Session church in pinnacled Gothic *college chapel*
style, with **manse**, 1849, next door; granite
obelisk **monument** to the Sanquhar
Declarations, 1864, D H & J Newall – an oath of
allegiance sworn by Richard Cameron, the
Covenanting leader, to Charles II and James VII
(colour page 52); and **Council Offices**, 1814, a
well-detailed town-house with a plaque to Robert
Nivison, 1st Baron Glendyne of Sanquhar.
Lawrie's Wynd leads to the former **Crichton
School**, 1823, founded under the provisions of
the will of Dr James Crichton (see p.23),
consisting of two classical blocks, with recent
additions, now a **nursing home**. **Post office**,
mid-18th century, is reputed to be the oldest in
Britain; **Crown Hotel**, early 19th century,
displays late 19th-century cast-iron lettering;
and **Royal Bank of Scotland**, and **Bank of
Scotland**, both two-storey, five-bay, are set back
from the street frontage. High Street narrows to
102 squeeze past the **Tolbooth**, 1735-7, William
Adam, paid for by the 3rd Duke of Queensberry
and built by Thomas and George Lawrie and
James McCall, the burgh's finest building,

Sanquhar Tolbooth.

Sanquhar has a tradition of hand-knitting, with a distinctive black-and-white pattern of squares and diamonds, usually applied to scarves and gloves.

Hume

To the north of the railway the **Buccleuch Terracotta Works** operated from the late 19th century until the 1960s, with a row of circular downdraught kilns with conical hoods (*below*), to give the high temperature necessary to make terracotta bricks.

Hume

probably marking the medieval core. Two-storey, five-bay, piend-roofed with pediment over central three bays, and **clock tower** with octagonal belfry and leaded flat ogee cap. Double forestair rebuilt, 1856-7. In front, a small square, now a car park, has a recently commissioned sculpture inspired by the local geology (colour page 52).

Beyond the tolbooth the urban grain becomes more open. Note the ruined **office** of the Sanquhar & Kirkconnel Coal Co, built of the firm's own terracotta bricks, and the red sandstone **Town Hall**, 1882, J Robert Pearson, mildly baronial, with a Diamond Jubilee **fountain** in front of it.

Former **Sanquhar Academy**, Queensberry Square, is part 1870s Tudor and part 1890 Jacobean; sadly derelict. The T-plan **Parish Church of St Bride**, 1822-4, James Thomson, *Heritors' Gothic*, has pinnacled tower; chancel added, 1930-1, J Jeffrey Waddell & Young; interior completely remodelled on ecclesiological lines at the same time. The present **Sanquhar Academy**, Church Road, 1970, Dumfriesshire County Council, is plain Modern Movement and **Sanquhar Station**, Station Road, 1850, Tudor cottage-style, recently reopened. A skew **bridge**, 1850, leads to **Blowearie Road**, a row of Victorian villas with some

103

good cast-iron detailing. In **St Mary's Street**, **EU Congregational Church**, 1844-5, built as Sanquhar Free Church, a very plain structure, and Gothic former **North United (Presbyterian) Church**, 1849, with very pretty ogee-headed gable window, now a hall, with unfortunate extension, 1954.

Wanlockhead is not obviously a place for the architectural pilgrim, but it is well worth visiting for its frontier-town atmosphere, its feeling of having defied the elements for centuries, and for that slightly haunted air that old metal mines exude.

Left *Wanlockhead*. Below *Water-powered beam pump*. Bottom *Miners' library*.

WANLOCKHEAD

Wanlockhead and the neighbouring community of **Leadhills** (in South Lanarkshire) are Scotland's highest villages, brought into being to house the miners who worked the country's richest seams of lead ore. Beneath the hillsides marked with old waste heaps, with tracks and water courses, lie many miles of underground workings, most now flooded. Here and there are the much-reduced surface remains of lead-mining, most notably the **water-powered** 104 **beam pump** on the Straitsteps vein. The houses are mostly tiny and rather ramshackle, with a few later terraces. The **miners' library**, 1850, Charles Howitt, is second only to the Leadhills one as a subscribing library, now owned by the Wanlockhead Museum Trust, which also owns the former **church**, designed by John Douglas, clerk of works at Drumlanrig Castle. The trust also looks after the consolidated ruins of the **Pates Knowes lead smelter**, and a row of **cottages** sitting above Straitsteps engine. The museum proper was established in the mine workshops; much extended mid-1990s. The scale of the Tudor 105 former **school**, 1846, John Douglas, is a graphic reminder of the number of families then in the village.

Eliock House.

James Crichton, 1560-83, 'the Admirable Crichton' born at Eliock, *flashed like a meteor across the literary firmament of Europe.* A brief but brilliant career as linguist, orator, intellectual and swordsman, he was appointed tutor to the son of the Duke of Mantua, but inspiring only jealousy perished at his recalcitrant pupil's hand.

Fauldhead Colliery, before closure in 1968.

Kirkconnel Parish Church.

106 **Eliock House**, late 16th century
H-plan house of three storeys, part harled, part ashlar, which developed in several stages, though at first glance it appears homogeneous. North wing (burned out 1940 and still derelict) is earliest, containing tower-house nucleus and preserving wide-mouth gunloops, probably built by Robert Crichton, Lord Advocate of Scotland (father of 'the Admirable Crichton'), in the reigns of Mary, Queen of Scots and James VI. Long three-storey centre range in two builds with a circular stair-tower midway. To left of the stair, 1658, and right of tower together with the south wing, is a 1770 addition, built to complete H-plan. Most windows regularised at this date giving a symmetrical appearance to the west front. Further additions to the east side, c.1910.

Brandedleys, early 19th century
Characteristic L-plan farmhouse with single-storey dormered cottage wing. Overlapping skews, tall corniced stacks and lying-pane glazing throughout.

KIRKCONNEL

Large village which grew in the late 19th century to serve the coalmines of the Sanquhar & Kirkconnel Coal Co, and at the south end of the village there are terraces of housing dating from that period. Originally centred on the
107 **parish church**, 1728-30, which replaced an earlier medieval church situated to the north. Present T-plan **church**, 1805-6, Adam Laidlaw, commissioned by the 1st Earl of Glasgow and built by John Weir. Radically recast, 1896, by MacGibbon & Ross, who extended the jamb and added a vestry and apse incorporating, in the apse, architectural fragments from St Conal's churchyard.

    Main Street is composed of 18th- and 19th-century one- and two-storey cottages and at the end are the simple **RC Church of St Conal**, 1921, and the **Salvation Army Hall**, formerly the Kirkconnel UF Church, 1911.
Queensberry Arms Hotel, early 19th century, is one of the oldest buildings, and there is a red sandstone **Bank of Scotland**, 1922. Perhaps the most attractive is what is now **Mac's Bar**, built as a hall, 1922, in mildly Jacobean style. **Miners' Memorial**, 1983-4, erected after the closure of the last pit in the area, features a bronze bust of a miner. The **police station**, 1897, is by James Barbour,

108 and the **railway station**, opened 1850 by the Glasgow, Dumfries & Carlisle Railway, is still remarkably intact.

The coal produced in **Fauldhead Colliery** had an unusually high content of sulphur, which made it unsuitable for use as house coal, or in power stations. It could, however, be burned in steam locomotives, which spread the pollution round the country. When steam locomotive operation in Scotland ended, Fauldhead closed.

Kirkconnel Railway Station.

KELLOHOLM
Model suburb, begun 1921, to house miners in better conditions, expanded after the First World War with a large number of **prefabs**, and later by more orthodox public housing. Large **school**, 1925, massively extended, 1952-6, George Bartholomew, Dumfries County Architect, and
109 **St Mark's Church**, a typical post-war hall church (colour page 52). North of the village is **Guildhall Bridge**, John Smeaton, widened late 19th century, and again, in concrete, *c.*1990, Dumfries and Galloway Regional Council.

Left *Guildhall Bridge before widening in 1990.* Below *Miners' Memorial.*

Kirkland Farmhouse, *c.*1840, ?Walter Newall
Three-bay, two-storey symmetrical *Tudorbethan* with gabled porch. Windows all have hood-moulds, lying-pane glazing and dormer heads at first floor.

The Relief Church was the second important secession from the Church of Scotland in the 18th century over the issue of the right of landowners to appoint ministers to parish churches. It was predominately an urban church, and joined with the United Secession Church in 1847 to form the United Presbyterian Church.

The Holm

Converted steading range, with central pedimented two-bay range flanked by single-storey piend-roof wings, formerly with pairs of cart arches.

BURNHEAD

110 Attractive hillside village with **Relief Church**, 1839, with round-arched windows, and larger **Penpont Free Church**, founded 1843-4, remodelled 1886, with attractive cast-iron classical belfry. **Free Church manse**, 1847, is large L-plan Tudor. Houses a mixture of local vernacular and red sandstone Tudor estate cottages.

Hume

Grovehill House, *c*.1800

Begun as two-storey farmhouse, with later bow windows; extended to the north, *c*.1830, with pedimented centre, flanking round-arched windows and bowed end.

Right *Grovehill House.* Below *Parish Church and War Memorial.* Bottom *Penpont crossroads.*

Anderson

PENPONT

Early 19th-century planned village, round four earlier hamlets, built to accommodate people displaced by improved farming. **Main Street** has two rows of mid-19th-century cottages with front gardens; the **War Memorial**, 1920, a life-sized bronze sculpture of a soldier; the steepled 111 Gothic **Parish Church**, 1867, Charles Howitt; and the Tudor **school** and **schoolhouse**, 1844-5 (extended 1864 & 1869). Further along are the Tudor **Moor House**, 1888, and the **Volunteer Arms Hotel**, early 19th century. Four two-storey buildings at the cross have doors on the chamfered corners, one with an elegant wallhead chimney, and several with porches of monolithic slabs of the local sandstone. **Marrburn Road** ascends into *villadom*, with **Albury** (formerly two cottages),

Hume

1831, and the **Smithy** (now a house), the earliest. **Burnbrae House**, earlier/mid 19th century, is the finest, with Greek-Doric porch set in rusticated arched frame.

Up **Carse Brae** is a former granary, c.1850, now a most unusual house; former **Reformed**
112 **Presbyterian Church**, 1791, now much altered, and its manse, c.1840, Walter Newall, now **Scaurbridge House**, two-storey, three-bay, with steep-pitched roof and tall quadruple stacks, lying-pane glazing in hood-moulded windows, pilastered doorpiece. **Keir Road**, the southern arm of the cross, opens out to a village green.

Arkland Cottage, 1830, William Blore
Small gabled rubble cottage; tall stacks, overlapping skews.

113 **Eccles House**, late 16th century
May incorporate part of a tower-house barmkin. Tower itself remodelled as an asymmetric house, c.1830, with curved bay and Venetian windows to the left of a plain door. Complex remodelled, 1965, Gordon J Kinghorn. **Eccles Lodge**, attractive single-storey, piend-roofed, Gothic, with central chimneystack, now roofed with corrugated asbestos.

Former Reformed Prebyterian Church.

The Reformed Presbyterian Church, also known as the Cameronian Church, came into being in 1690, when Covenanters who did not support the Church of Scotland, revived as a Presbyterian Church by William and Mary, decided to stay independent. There are still a few Reformed Presbyterian congregations in existence, including one in Stranraer (see p.205).

Left *Tynron school and schoolhouse.*
Below *Tynron Parish Church.*

TYNRON

One of the unexpected delights of Dumfriesshire. Set in a wooded hollow, it is a classic *kirkton* – a single row of early 19th-century cottages, curving round a knoll on
114 which sit the **church**, **manse**, former **school** and schoolhouse. The simple Gothic church, now being converted to a house, is by William Burn, with Tudor vestry chimneys. Some 18th-century tombstones testify to an earlier building on the site.

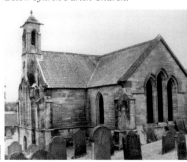

Though **Tynron Doon**, on a spur of Auchengibbert Hill, is fundamentally an Iron Age hill fort, with a series of ramparts and ditches protecting the round-houses in the summit enclosure, its excellent defensive position led to its use as late as the 16th century, when an L-plan tower house was built on the site. There are finds from the excavation of the site in the Dumfries Museum (see p.25).

Auchenhessnane, *c*.1830
Two-storey, three-bay, piend-roofed farmhouse with Roman-Doric doorpiece.

115 **Lann Hall**, later 18th century
Two-storey, attic and basement, three-bay main range, with piended roof and bellcast platform; lower piend-roofed wings. Dormer windows added, *c*.1900, James Barbour & Bowie. Roman-Doric doorpiece approached by a perron.

Right *Lann Hall.* Below *Glencairn Parish Church.* Bottom *Craigdarroch as planned by William Adam and illustrated in his* Vitruvius Scoticus.

KIRKLAND
Dominated by simple Gothic **Glencairn**
116 **Parish Church**, 1836-7, William McCandlish, in whinstone rubble with red sandstone dressings and slender tower. Original pews survive in the galleries, but those at ground floor date from 1902, when the church was recast in ecclesiological form. Fine **churchyard** with gables of the medieval church, adapted in the 17th century, which preceded the present building, and elegant early 19th-century **mausoleum** of the Gillespies of Parton. Fine mid-19th-century range of Tudor cottages, with Tudor former **manse** beyond, 1840-1, Walter Newall. The 1776-7 **manse** is on the south side of the road.

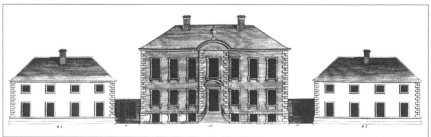

117 **Craigdarroch**, 1726-9, William Adam
Compact classical mansion, two storeys over
basement; not as extensive as Adam intended
– his client Alexander Fergusson wished a
simple humble house for his bride Bonnie
Annie Laurie. Therefore no quadrants and no
pavilions, segmental pediment replaced by
more conservative, almost equilateral,
triangle with urns; on plan, main public
rooms on first floor. Extended 1840, to double
size; fire 1984, since repaired. Estate
buildings include **Sawmill Cottage**,
Italianate *cottage orné* with unusual
casement glazing on its garden front.

Crawfordton, 1865, Peddie & Kinnear
Multi-faceted baronial; turrets, towers and
tourelles at every angle; an extended version
of the architects' plans for Cargen House (see
p.76). A **school** since 1940; flat-roofed
gymnasium to left and large classroom block.
Shingle-roofed clapboard **chapel** in grounds.
East Lodge, 1882, gabled with veranda.

118 **Maxwelton House**, 17th century; restored
1969-73, Michael Laird & Partners
Roughly U-plan three-storey mansion around
courtyard extended from earlier core evident in
the vaulted east range. Successive layers of
addition removed in restoration to *bring the
house back to its former appearance of
simplicity* – chiefly expressed by a unifying
coat of harl with (often newly indented)
exposed dressed stone margins, roll mouldings
and Stenhouse heraldic panels. Interiors
include beautifully rib-vaulted **Annie Laurie's**
boudoir. Grounds with **stable block**, gazebo on
turntable and rustic bowers.
Open to the public; tearoom

Maxwelton Episcopal Chapel, 1868
Small stocky Gothic chapel, built as a memorial
to John Minet Laurie, with cusped traceried
windows and endearing lead-work. Well-
preserved interior with leaded lights and
stencilled east wall. Oak-gabled lych-gate, 1884.
Open to the public; guidebook

119 **Glenluiart**, 1900, W West Neve, London
Rubbly Arts & Crafts vernacular country house
with *Jacobethan* details, designed for the
widow of a minister of Glencairn parish, a
relative of the architect. Asymmetric
elevations; slab canopy porch 'hung' from

The Fergussons of Craigdarroch
were prominent anti-Jacobites;
during the '45 Rising the house was
occupied by the Prince with a
demand for victuals. Fergusson took
to the hills, returning to find
Craigdarroch in a state *worse than I
could possibly imagine*.

Top *Craigdarroch*. Middle
Crawfordton. Above *Maxwelton
House*.

Stephen Laurie bought Glencairn
Castle in 1611 and changed the name
to Maxwelton.

Glenluiart.

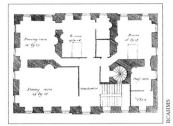

insubstantial wrought-iron brackets; large mullioned and transomed windows with leaded glazing. Swept roofs and deep eaves; English rosemary tiles proved no match for Scots' weather, soon replaced by slate. Inside, regulation Arts & Crafts **living hall** with ingle-nook. **Lodge** and **stables** by the same hand. Initials EMM for Elizabeth Mary Menteith, client and benefactress for almshouse row in Moniaive.

120 **Caitloch House**, 18th century; remodelled *c*.1860
Not high architecture, but a singularly pleasing small baronialised mansion with an attractive swept-roof Victorian conservatory.

Top *Craigdarroch, first-floor plan, from* Vitruvius Scoticus. Middle *Caitloch House.* Right *Moniaive.* Above *Market Place.*

MONIAIVE
A 17th-century burgh of barony, picturesquely sited in the wooded Cairn Valley, established by the Earl of Dumfries in 1636. Originally confined to the west side of the Dalwhat Water, but enlarged to the east on a more regular plan in the 18th century, it never developed commercially, functioning mainly as an agricultural service community until the mid-19th century, when it became something of a resort. The opening of the Cairn Valley Railway in 1905 made it attractive to commuters from Dumfries.

Best approached via the A702 from Dumfries, along a straight 18th-century street with a mixture of one- and two-storey detached houses and terraces, some Arts & Crafts, testifying to the late 19th-century appreciation of Moniaive as an 'artistic' village, frequented by the Glasgow Boys. A hump-backed **bridge** over the Dalwhat Water, 1796-1800, William Stewart, leads to the short, narrow **High**

Moniaive
The scale and arrangement of the small-scale buildings give the village extraordinary charm, and it is not surprising that turn-of-the-century artists, such as James Paterson, found it so congenial. (See Roger Billcliffe, *The Glasgow Boys*, 1985, pp.163-8)

Street, and to the **Market Place**. **George Hotel**, early 18th century, is a historic two-storey inn with lugged doorway, and **Craigdarroch Arms Hotel** is later 19th-century Scots Arts & Crafts. The **Mercat Cross** comprises shaft dated 1638 on 19th-century drum base.

Chapel Street contains **Bank of Scotland** (former Union Bank & Bank House), *c.*1850, an attractive building with round-headed openings, and **primary school**, 1883-4, James Barbour, a mildly Gothic range. **Memorial Institute**, built as United Secession church, 1834, and remodelled as a hall, 1919, J M Bowie. Further along are the remains of the **railway station**, 1905, a little timber Arts & Crafts building.

Tower House, Market Place, late 19th century, is a villa with large clock tower.

121 **St Ninian's Church**, built as chapel of ease of Glencairn, 1887-9, W West Neve, a curious building with continuous clerestory glazing above lean-to aisle roofs, and early 19th-century single-storey terraces.

Ayr Street is also lined with terraced houses, the westernmost group of which is **Cottage Row**, an unspoiled single-storey range.

122 **Kilneiss House**, 1884, J J Burnet, an English Arts & Crafts reworking of an older cottage (Burnet's only essay in this style) for the painter James Paterson, brother of architect A N Paterson. The dramatic timbering of the attic floor was harled over for many years, but has recently been recovered. Two early 19th-century houses, **Broomfield House**, two-storey and basement, three-bay mansion, with flat-curved bays flanking arched central doorway with columned porch, and **Broomfield Bank**, a smaller house also two-storey and basement, three-bay, with cavetto-moulded doorway.

Top *Primary School*. Middle *Tower House*. Above *Kilneiss House*.

KEIR MILL
Small village, founded late 18th century, with
123 **church**, 1813-15, William Barr, altered 1880, by James Barbour, when chancel and vestry were added; (former) **school**, later 19th-century Tudor-Gothic; and **mill**, 1771, much altered during domestic conversion. **Old Manse**, early 19th-century, seven-storey, three-bay, with piend-roof.

James Paterson, 1854-1932, was born in Glasgow and studied there and in Paris. He was one of the *Glasgow Boys*, and was particularly noted for his landscape and flower paintings (colour page 52).

In 1974, though almost all of the machinery had been removed from Keir Mill, it still contained a wooden pit wheel, one of the main drive wheels for the grindstones, and a very rare survivor from pre-cast-iron mill technology.

There were important **limeworks** at Barjarg and Porterstown, and remains of kilns can be seen at both sites, now much overgrown. An underground waterwheel (*below*), used for pumping, was recovered from the limestone mines of Barjarg, and is now in the Museum of Scotland in Edinburgh.

Hume

Barjarg House.

124 **Barjarg House**, 16th–early 20th centuries
Extensive country house sprouting from L-plan home of Thomas Grierson, *c.*1587, growing by a block a century since then. Original building at north-east angle with turrets elongated, parapet crenellated and mullioned bay window added, 1914, J M Bowie. Spreading west from the short jamb of the L, late 17th-century range with advanced canted centrepiece, 1806, links to balancing late 17th-century L-plan with angle turrets to match Grierson's tower. Interior mainly J M Bowie refit in baronial manner; oak panelling, minstrel's gallery to **ballroom**. Estate buildings include the **Drybridge**, 1810, carrying drive over public road, and **Front Lodge**, 1810, a crowstepped cottage. Arched stone **gateway** and **gates** said to be from old Dumfries gaol, demolished 1802. **Back Lodge** is rustic Tudor, with large-diamond glazing.

Anderson

Auldgirth Bridge, 1782, David Henderson
Three segmental arches over the Nith; paired pilasters on cutwaters either side of arches support pedestrian refuges. Thomas Carlyle's father was employed as a *hewer* on its construction.

125 **Capenoch House**, 1847-68, David Bryce
Bryce greatly extended and remodelled a small, 1780, classical house, built for the Kirkpatricks of Closeburn, in successive phases, for James Grierson and then for Thomas Steuart Gladstone, a Liverpool broker. The 1847 work consists of the three-bay garden elevation with Bryce trademark crowstep-gabled canted-bay window corbelled to square at first; steps are 1855. Later work more strongly baronial; mock north tower topped with pepper-pot turret, girt with corbel courses and linked to the earlier

Capenoch House by David Bryce.

block by a balustraded balcony. Handsome stone-mullioned conservatory to west; single-storey service wings, 1868. Internally a galleried stair hall with turned timber balusters and pendant newel posts.

Estate buildings, 1860s, also Bryce, include **Capenoch House bridge**, single arch in red ashlar with rusticated voussoirs and contrasting pink ashlar parapet, and **lodge**, single storey, crowstep gables and diamond-laid slate roof.

126 **Blackwood House**, 19th century with earlier core

Sparse two-storey, seven-bay neo-Jacobean concealing laird's house origin. Paired projecting gabled bays near centre, hood-moulded windows, pedimented dormers, elaborate gargoyle rhone heads. Formerly surrounded by extensive grounds, walled garden with timber glasshouses. **Stables**, 1778; fine classical ranges around courtyard; tower over entrance houses intact **doocot**, cylindrical on internal plan. **Lodge**, probably late 18th century, piend-roofed with large central chimneystack. Porch surmounted by open-roofed structure and bull's-eye window.

Windsover Cottages, early 19th century Picturesque row of single-storey cottages; hood-moulds and lattice glazing; neat front gardens.

Below Blackwood House. Bottom Stables, Blackwood House.

Courthill Smithy.

Kirkpatrick McMillan was one of the first, if not the first, men to apply pedal propulsion to vehicles. He built a pedal-powered tricycle in 1834 and a bicycle in 1840.

Courthill Smithy, early 19th century
Small, single-storey, rubble, piend-roofed building with large hearth stack at one end. Its importance lies in the association with Kirkpatrick McMillan, who built the first bicycle here.

DUNSCORE

Small village in splendidly open and beautiful setting, best seen from the south, where the undulating road gives intermittent views of the 127 spiky *Heritors' Gothic*, towered **parish church**, 1823-4, James Thomson, which retains its largely unaltered interior. **Churchyard**, probably early 18th century, contains the burial enclosure of the Griersons of Dalgonar. Generally, the buildings are pleasing and, as at New Abbey (see p.78), the grouping is delightful. One odd little shed in the angle between two roads was built to house the village hearse.

128 **Throughgate**, on the approach to Dunscore, has two bow-fronted houses, one two- and the other three-storey, one converted from a toll-house. Between Throughgate and Dunscore is **Newton Farm**, with an unaltered circular horse-engine house and associated threshing barn.

Right *Dunscore*. Below *Bogrie*.
Bottom *Throughgate*.

Bogrie, probably 1860
Low two-storey rubble farmhouse, built from stones recovered when Bogrie Tower was demolished. Approximately symmetrical, apart from the arched entrance set between the centre and left bays, with two reset carved stones above.

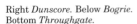

129 **Craigenputtock**, early 19th century
Typical plain two-storey, three-bay, rubble farmhouse occupied by Thomas Carlyle, 1828-34; U-plan steading to rear. Described by a biographer as *a melancholy building, gaunt, bare, cold and mean looking ... the ancestral home of Carlyle's wife*. Carlyle himself called it *the deil's den*.

Dalgonar Bridge, 1818, David Henderson
Rubble single-arch bridge over Cairn Water;
plain in detail save ashlar arch-ring.

Jane Welsh, Thomas Carlyle's wife,
inherited Craigenputtock from her
father. While resident there, Carlyle
wrote *Sartor Resartus*, one of his most
famous works. After Jane's death,
Carlyle gave the estate to the
University of Edinburgh to support 10
John Welsh bursaries, five each for
classical and mathematical students.

130 **Friars Carse**, 1873, James Barbour & Bowie
A chequered history: early illustrations show
16th-century three-storey tower complete with
parapet and caphouse. Adjoining the tower,
17th- and 18th-century thatched and
crowstepped lodgings all set within a walled
courtyard. This group mostly demolished and
metamorphosed into smart two-storey-over-
basement, Georgian, piend-roofed box, 1771. In
turn this house, in which Robert Burns and his
landlord Robert Riddell enjoyed drinking bouts,
subsumed into present Friars Carse, 1873. A
coarse-featured, ruddy sandstone edifice in
Barbour & Bowie's most lumpen baronial, built
for Dr Crichton of Crichton Royal.
 In the grounds **Burns Hermitage**, 1790,
restored and refaced, 1874; *a snug little stone
building 10½ft x 8ft with window and fireplace*
to which Burns and Riddell would repair for
the pouring of libations and the encouragement
of the poetic muse. The former **stable block** of
Friars Carse, early 19th century, extended
1905, is a quadrangular single-storey block,
with entrance tower and **doocot**, all in rock-
faced masonry with prominent eaves.

Left *Engraving of Friars Carse
(demolished 1773) from* The
Antiquities of Scotland *by Francis
Grose, 1789. Below* Ellisland.

131 **Ellisland**
Burns chose Ellisland from three farms
offered to him by Patrick Miller of Dalswinton
(see p.38), the factor shrewdly observing he
had made a poet's and not a farmer's choice.
The house, offices and field enclosures, 1790,
were constructed for £300 (at Miller's
expense). House is reported as demolished,
1812, to be replaced by current single-storey

From top *Lag Castle, 1788, drawn by Adam de Cardonnel; Stroquhan House; Chapel Farm, with drystane dyke typical of the area; Holywood Parish Church.*

L-plan rubble building but recent research suggests it was altered rather than demolished. Single-storey rubble steading, limewashed, like the house, also partly original, though **cart-shed** and **granary** are later. Recently conserved by Richard Jaques. Replacement recorded in the 1850s for the *Illustrated London News* and billed as Burns' Cottage ever since; now a **museum**. *Open to the public; guidebook*

132 **Lag Castle**, *c*.1526
Substantial ruin of a tower of the Griersons of Lag. Rectangular, with four storeys.

Sundaywell Tower Farmhouse
Three-tier range, with three-storey block at one end built as a vertically organised house, 1651; converted to farmhouse in late 18th century.

133 **Stroquhan House**
Pleasant but slightly awkward red sandstone house, about 2.5km south-west of Dunscore, with later 18th-century core, bowed end, *c*.1800, and three-storey extension, *c*.1845, with porch probably of similar date. Pleasing little piend-roofed Tudor **lodge**, *c*.1840-50, guarding contemporary gates with poppy-headed gatepiers.

Chapel Farm, a limewashed complex, with large all-iron overshot waterwheel which drove its threshing mill; the fireclay pipe lade carved on a drystone rubble wall.

Allanton House, built as a late Georgian laird's house, but baronialised, *c*.1870.

HOLYWOOD
The village owes its name to an abbey founded here in the 12th or 13th century, all trace of
134 which has now gone. The T-plan **parish church**, 1779, is dominated by a tall tower, the top stage dating probably from 1821. It has round-arched windows and was extended and recast, 1864, by Alexander Fraser. Former **manse**, Kirkland, 1773, adjacent. **Graveyard**, with 18th-century, ball-finialled gatepiers has adjoining hearse house. Some fine monuments, and an early 19th-century **mausoleum** of the Youngs of Lincluden.
South-west of the village is the **Twelve Apostles**, a Bronze Age stone circle, the largest in diameter in Scotland.

135 Fourmerkland Tower, 1590
Perfectly simple four-storey rectangular
tower bearing the Maxwell coat of arms,
slender turrets corbelled at two angles.
Rubble walls with red sandstone margins,
some roll-moulded; first-floor window
enlarged. Restored last century; turret tops
and dormers rebuilt.

Dalawoodie, 1840, ?Walter Newall
Italianate red sandstone villa; tight composition of
gabled elevations surmounted by a central square
bella vista tower topped with four lotus chimney
cans. Smooth red ashlar front, arched plate-glass
windows; overhanging bracketed eaves. **Lodge** in
similar style. Now a nursing home.

Above *Plans and section of
Fourmerkland Tower.* Left *East
Cluden Mills.*

136 East Cluden Mills, early 19th century
Two-storey, attic-and-basement red sandstone
water mill, probably the largest and finest in
south-west Scotland, on the banks of the
Cluden Water, retaining some internal
machinery and two low-breast paddle water
wheels; now converted to a house. Exterior now
harled on entrance front and windows
enlarged.

Isle Tower.

137 Isle Tower, 1587
Seat of John Ferguson of Isle. Three-storey-
and-attic rectangular structure, with
crowstepped gables and bartizans at opposite
angles; restored internally, 1891, Peddie &
Kinnear. Now attached to mid-18th-century
two-storey house, remodelled, 1882, Peddie &
Kinnear; service wing, 1806, to the west.

In this part of Dumfries and Galloway there are
several small Victorian mansions set in tiny
estates. **Steilston**, 1867, one-storey-and-attic

The creation of a new Portrack garden was one of the most elaborate landscaping schemes of the late 20th century. Designed by Maggie & Charles Jencks, the works have included the diversion of the river Nith to make inlets, and the creation of large grassed mounds, one in the shape of a spiral-ramped cone.

L-plan house with crowsteps and circular conical-roofed tower, built unusually of yellowish brick with red sandstone dressings. **Stepford House**, later 19th century, in contrast, also L-plan, 1½-storey, built of dark whinstone, with stucco dressings; prominent ground-floor bay windows and arched and columned porch.

138 **Portrack House**, early 19th century Two-storey villa, extended 1879, James Barbour, in mildly Italianate, with pyramid-roofed entrance tower. **Garden** being remodelled on a scale unique in late 20th-century Scotland. A feature is one of the former octagonal lodges to Mollance House, c.1770, moved here as a **summerhouse**, 1970. The other is at Glenkiln (see p.76).

Newtonards House has been demolished, but the grandiose former **stables** survive, a quadrangular block in baronial style, 1865-6, Peddie & Kinnear, with round stair-tower, open roundel, and arched carriage entrance with cable-work surround. Its dark whin and red sandstone construction give it a rather gloomy appearance.

Above Portrack House. Below Newtonards Stables. Bottom Cowhill House.

139 The picturesque **Cowhill House** dates in essence from 1788-9, when built for George Johnston, a Liverpool merchant, but was recast baronially, c.1867-71, W F Lyon. The 'tower-house', despite its antique appearance, dates from 1913-14, added by Peddie & Forbes Smith. Reconstructions after fires in 1948 and 1973. Former **stables range**, 1816, has a show front with central arched carriage entrance surmounted by a **doocot**, and flanking two-storey wings ending its Venetian-windowed end bays with former coach-house entrances below.

KIRKPATRICK IRONGRAY

Martyrs Monument, 1851, Hallhill, pedimented with flaming urn-finial, marks the site of a Covenanting graveslab, with the inscription:

*As Lagg and Blood[y] Bruce comman'd
We were hung up by Hellish hand
And thus their furious rage to stay
We dy'd near Kirk of Iron Gray:
Here now in peace sweet rest we take
Once murder'd for religeon's sake.*

Kirkpatrick Irongray Parish Church.

140 KIRKPATRICK IRONGRAY

Surprisingly from its present appearance the body of the **parish church** was built in 1803, but was radically altered, 1872-3, with new windows, square tower, new roof and ventilator in Romanesque. **Monuments** in the churchyard include one to Helen Walker, the model for Sir Walter Scott's heroine of *The Heart of Midlothian*, Jeanie Deans. Neat two-storey, attic-and-basement, three-bay, symmetrical **manse**, 1797, John McCracken, with tripartite windows at ground floor.

141 The Grove, 1825, Thomas Rickman

Red ashlar, two-storey, rambling Tudor-Gothic mansion by the Liverpool architect best known for his classification of architectural styles. Main elevation has imposing square entrance tower with machicolated embattled parapet, mullioned and transomed windows; balustraded conservatory. Additions, 1869, Peddie & Kinnear, to rear. Much-altered **stable block** with pretty gabled timber **doocot**.

Below *The Grove*. Bottom *Drumpark East Lodge.*

Drumpark East Lodge, 1860,

John Cunningham
Style of Sir James Gowans (see *West Lothian* in this series): picturesque single-storey L-plan lodge; distinctive polygonal rubble masonry with bull-faced band-courses; steep roofs with bands of fish-scale slates, guarding an elaborate set of wrought-iron gates and gatepiers; house demolished.

Lodges, Glenkiln
Set in a surprisingly wild landscape, immediately below Glenkiln Reservoir, one of these two identical octagonal buildings, with unusual wheel-glazed sashes, pyramidal roofs and central chimneystacks, was relocated, *c.*1970, from Mollance House (*c.*1770), and the 142 other is a clone. **Glenkiln sculptures**, bought by Sir William Keswick between 1951 and 1976, and sited at various points within the upland estate, comprise four works by Henry Moore, one by Jacob Epstein and one by Auguste Rodin.

TERREGLES
Small crossroads village, now expanding as a dormitory suburb of Dumfries. Originally an estate village for Terregles House, a pair of Tudor **cottages**, 1837, mark that function, as does the former **school**, also Tudor, *c.*1860. The most interesting building, tucked away behind street 143 frontages, is the **parish church**, the oldest part of which, the so-called *queir*, was built, 1588, by Agnes, Lady Herries, not, as its form suggests, as a chancel in the medieval manner, but as a burial aisle. Substantially altered to form a **RC burial chapel**, 1875-9, James Barbour for Captain Alfred Constable-Maxwell of Terregles. **Parish church** proper added, 1814; re-roofed and recast, 1900-2 (colour page 85). Fine monuments in the **churchyard**.

Terregles House, 1789 (demolished 1964)
Severe Palladian mansion for William Constable-Maxwell, enlarged with later porch in similar style by Sir Robert Smirke, 1831, for the 10th Lord Herries. Survived by **Terregles Stables**, 1831, Sir Robert Smirke; impeccable, classical red ashlar stable court; seven-bay showfront has pilasters dividing bays; tall corniced windows, all set on rusticated podium. Double pilasters flank arched pend to courtyard; now converted to housing. **Lodge** in chunky Gothic; three arched windows in centre bowed bay all under hood-moulds.

To outside view the *queir* of **Terregles Parish Church** looks like a medieval chancel, the resemblance being heightened by the buttresses added by James Barbour in 1875 for Captain Maxwell of Terregles. It was, however, built as a semi-detached mortuary chapel to comply with a Church of Scotland ban on burial within churches.

144 **Cargen House**, 1870, Peddie & Kinnear
Substantial baronial mansion, built for Patrick Dudgeon, mineralogist, every gable crowstepped. Three-storey block houses compactly planned main rooms with stair in square tower, service quarters in lower rear wing. Corbelled balustraded balcony links drawing room and dining room bay windows;

now ruinous. **Stables** in same style converted to housing.

145 **Dalskairth House**, 18th century
Two-storey, five-bay classical mansion, harled, with rusticated quoins. Additional wings and porch, 1899, John A Campbell in Queen Anne style. Campbell produced ambitious designs for a new Dalskairth, a large asymmetric Arts & Crafts/baronial house set in formal gardens; sadly never executed. Interior remodelled, 1899; now derelict. Odd little L-plan **lodge**, early 19th century, with open eaves at the outer ends and intersecting piended ends at the other; tall Tudor chimneystacks and lattice glazing.

Dalskairth Lodge, late 18th/early 19th century
Former stables of Dalskairth House, two storey, on a U-plan. Wings have pedimented ends and rusticated quoins. Large modern conservatory covers original entrance.

Cargenbridge is effectively a western suburb of Dumfries. Its major feature is a large works, built by Imperial Chemical Industries to make packaging film.

Dalskairth House.

Goldielea, 1785
Elongated three-storey, five-bay, rendered masonry mansion linked to swept roof pavilions, much modified, c.1857, with attic windows raised and pedimented. Picturesque backdrop provided by **Goldielea Viaduct**.

146 **Goldielea & Garroch Viaducts**, 1859
Built for the Castle Douglas & Dumfries Railway. Goldielea is tall and on a curve, with 10 semicircular arches, and Garroch a lower eight-span with segmental arches. **Carnichan**, mid-19th century, baronial H-plan building, with contemporary **stable block** in the same style.

147 **Kirkconnell House**, from 16th century
Rubble, three-storey and attic, L-plan tower of the Maxwells; roll-moulded windows, heavy corbelled parapet. Two-storey harled

Left *Goldielea with Viaduct.*
Below *Kirkconnell House.*

addition, mid-17th century, three-storey, five-bay brick range, with masonry quoins and lintels, 1755-60, and arched-windowed RC chapel of 1815, complete four sides of a courtyard. The 1755-60 addition, for James Maxwell returning from post-'45 exile in France, built *of bricks made on the property*, has original panelled library on ground floor, and Victorian dining room, with drawing room on first floor. **Chapel** has classical interior, with apse and family pew. **Castlehill House**, *c.*1800, two-storey-and-basement, three-bay laird's house, with Roman-Doric porch, fan-lit panelled door and rusticated quoins.

Mabie House.

148 **Mabie House**, late 18th century
Three-storey, three-bay house with piended and bellcast roof; porch and bay windows added, *c.*1900. Former **stables**, *c.*1800, now Forestry Commission offices, quadrangular, with two-storey front range, piend-roofed. Tall castellated centrepiece, with spired **clock tower**; central entrance blocked up. Very pleasing octagonal **lodge** has Gothic windows, depressed-arched door, oversailing eaves and central chimneystack.

149 **Shambellie**, New Abbey, 1856, David Bryce
Diminutive two-storey baronial/*Jacobethan* mansion in cherry-cocked granite with contrasting red sandstone margins. Bryce's original drawings posited a veritable sampler of baronial detail overstretching his client's purse and resulting in acrimonious wrangling over costs. Toned-down version built, though still with plenty of inventive corbelling, turrets and gables. Plain interior, perhaps showing the limited budget.
National Museum of Costume; open to the public

Shambellie.

NEW ABBEY
Perhaps Galloway's prettiest village consisting fundamentally of a single winding street and owing its existence to its situation near the mouth of the Pow Burn, which was navigable for small craft almost to the village. This, and its sheltered location in the lee of Criffel, made it attractive to the Cistercian monks who founded **Sweetheart Abbey** as a daughter-house of **Dundrennan Abbey**, in 1273, at the insistence of Devorguilla, widow of John Balliol of Barnard Castle. The Abbey (see p.80) still dominates the village.

The monastic fishpond by New Abbey Mill was used to keep carp to provide fresh fish for the monks' Friday day of abstinence from flesh meats.

Left *New Abbey*.
Below *New Abbey Mill*.

Approaching from Dumfries through Shambellie Woods, the first sign of the village is the **Woman's Guild Hall**, *c*.1890, beside a two-span **bridge**, 1715, over the Pow, then 150 **New Abbey Mill**, a late 18th-century corn mill, now in the care of Historic Scotland, and the **monastic fishpond**. The Arts & Crafts **Criffel Inn**, *c*.1900, faces the late 19th-century granite **Abbey Arms** across a small square with former smithy on the east side. **Main Street**, crossed by the **Abbey precinct wall**, has one- and two-storey vernacular buildings; **No 14**, single-storey cottage, has carved stones inset into its frontage, and **Abbey Cottage**, pretty, later 19th century, with wooden porch. Beyond the Abbey the built fabric becomes much more open, with **St Mary's RC Church & Presbytery**, 1824, Walter Newall, a simple Gothic building refurbished in the 1890s, and 151 **New Abbey Parish Church**, 1875-7, James Barbour, with leggy belfry; interior rebuilt, 1963-4, after fire. Behind the late 19th-century **primary school** is the present **primary school**, 1975, Stewartry County Council.

Kindar House, early 19th century Two-storey-and-basement, three-bay symmetrical villa, with iron-railed stair to the inset doorway; fanlight glazing, with ogee arch flanked by lancets, echoed in the tripartite window above. **Kindar Cottages** (so-called), now disused, two-storey, nine-bay range, with external stair in the centre, formerly part of a mill.

From the village **square**, a road runs off to the mill dam and the former **Masonic Lodge**, 1806, converted to **church hall**, 1887, now a 152 house. Beyond is the **Old House**, possibly 17th century bastle house, small, rubble, two-storey with forestair; and much-altered sawmill.

Old House.

Top *Glenharvie House.*
Above *West Shambellie Pottery.*

The name Sweetheart (Latin *Dulce Cor*) stems from Devorguilla's devotion to her husband, John Balliol. When he died in 1268 she had his heart embalmed and placed in a casket which she kept with her until her death, in 1290, when it was buried with her in the Abbey church.

Sweetheart Abbey from The Antiquities of Scotland *by Francis Grose.*

153 Glenharvie House, 18th century

Built as snuff mill on the New Abbey Pow, presumably in connection with Dumfries merchants' tobacco trade, and converted to house early 19th century; two-storey, five-bay, symmetrical, with prominent square-section chimneystacks. Small, two-storey **doocot** with pyramid roof, probably early 19th century, in the garden. **West Shambellie Pottery**, fine two-storey, 10-bay, rubble building, with slit windows at first-floor level, at some time used as a bacon factory. Plain two-storey-and-attic **Kinharvie House**, with open eaves and bargeboards, built as a shooting lodge, *c.*1850, has architectural interest in the **chapel**, with semicircular apse and windows with geometric tracery. Same open eaves as the house, but Gothic bargeboards and bands of fish-scale slating.

154 Sweetheart Abbey, 1273

Founded by Devorguilla, Lady of Galloway, in memory of her husband, John Balliol, the founder of Balliol College, Oxford. By the time of her death in 1290 the granite precinct wall, defining the limits of the community boundary, had been built, and most of the church had been completed. It seems to have been finished in the late 14th century, under the auspices of Archibald the Grim. After the Reformation the monks were allowed to stay in the Abbey until

they died, but a parish church was created in the refectory. This lasted until 1731, when a new **parish church** was built beside the nave. The ruin of the church was bought by a party of local gentlemen in 1779 to prevent it being

The conversion of parts of abbey buildings to reformed parish churches was common in Post-Reformation Scotland. Other examples include Paisley, Melrose and Jedburgh (see *Borders & Berwick* in this series).

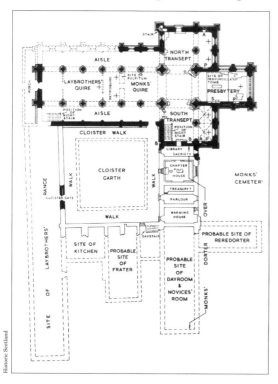

Historic Scotland

Left *Plan, Sweetheart Abbey.*
Below *Sweetheart Abbey east end, from the nave.*

Hume

used as a quarry. Repaired, 1862-3, Alexander Crombie, and taken into state care, 1928 (colour page 85).

Conventual buildings, used as a quarry, now much reduced, but east range relatively intact consisting of sacristy, chapter house, treasury, parlour and warming house, with granite-cored, red sandstone-faced walls. Church is remarkably complete, giving a clear impression of its original form; consistent with the philosophy of the Cistercians it is simply detailed, though the red sandstone gives the building a warmth lacking in Dundrennan. Geometrical Gothic, with rose window, and aisled nave, the eastern part of which was actually the monks' choir. There were small altars on the eastern walls of the transepts, with the high altar in the presbytery, which is the width of the nave less the width of the nave aisles. Squat tower, with the crowstepped gables of a saddle-back roof, above a corbelled parapet. General impression is of a broody hen, comfortably sheltering her chickens.

Historic Scotland; open to the public; guidebook

155 **KIRKBEAN**

Pleasant, mainly early 19th century and largely the estate village of Arbigland. Simple Jacobean **school**, 1885, and elegant **parish church**, 1776, a T-plan building attributed to William Craik of Arbigland. Two more stages added to the tower, 1835-6, Walter Newall, and interior recast, 1881-3, Samuel Hunter, who also added a porch (colour page 85). Prominent **gatepiers**, 1835, also by Newall. Fine tombstones. **Manse**, 1798, now **Woodside House**.

Below Kirkbean Parish Church. Right Carsethorn.

CARSETHORN

Founded early 19th century with a steamer pier for Dumfries, the village dates in essence from *c*.1815, with two-storey terrace of that 156 period including the **Harbour Master's House** with rusticated details. After the steamer service ceased the village became a centre for salmon fishing; now only residential.

SOUTHERNESS

Small maritime village established late 18th century, with the expectation of finding coal in the vicinity, by Richard Oswald of Auchencruive, with two L-plan ranges of low, single-storey cottages, now much altered. Focal point is a **lighthouse**, originally built as a beacon (landmark), 1748-9, by Dumfries Town Council, and heightened, *c*. 1785. Fitted with an oil light and reflectors on the pattern adopted by the Northern Lighthouse Board, 1790s; slate-roofed lantern. Further increased in height, 1842-3, Walter Newall, who added an iron-railed walkway. In 1894, after a period of disuse, a catadioptric lens system was installed, and when the light was finally

Southerness Lighthouse by G D Hay. 157

extinguished, its frame and burner were set in concrete on the seashore, much to the puzzlement of visitors (colour page 85).

Newmains Farm has good farmhouse with two-storey, three-bay central block and flanking single-storey bays with Venetian windows.

Newmains Farm.

158 **Arbigland House**, 1755, William Craik
Irresistible small classical house, two-storey over raised basement; five-bay central block; Ionic pilasters supporting pediment with urns and finials aplenty. Originally a curved perron stair rose to *piano nobile* entrance; alas removed and replaced by graceless Doric porch, mid-19th century. Polygonal pavilions with steep faceted roofs (colour page 85). Garden elevation plainer; early 19th-century curved bow window added off-centre. Interior has 18th-century doors, shutters and dadoes; simple cantilevered stair with iron handrail. Fine parkland and 18th-century polygonal **walled garden**. Rusticated ashlar **gatepiers**, 1805, Allan Cunningham, local mason and poet. **Stables**, 1755, also by Craik. Show front has high keystoned pend with **doocot** all under pediment with urns. In the grounds, **The House on the Shore**, 1936, by Kathleen Blackett-Swiny, who designed this rubbly Cotswold manor in miniature for herself as the dower house for Arbigland. A small cottage in the grounds is presented as the birthplace of John Paul Jones, founder of the United States Navy.
Gardens open to the public

John Paul Jones, 1747-92, the son of a gardener at Arbigland, was involved in the slave trade and in smuggling. He settled in Virginia and founded the American Navy in 1775, during the War of Independence, also serving in the French and Russian navies.

William Craik of Arbigland, 1703-98, was an agricultural improver and gentleman architect, who designed Mossknowe, Kirkpatrick Fleming (see p.103), and probably also Kirkbean Parish Church.

Arbigland House.

Below Langholm Town Hall. Bottom Eskdale Hotel. Right Townhead Bridge and West Presbyterian Church.

LANGHOLM

Grey, initially unassuming, town quite different in character to other burghs in Dumfries and Galloway, being closer in spirit to the eastern borders than to its peers to the west. An upland place, with the clear light that implies, and one is never far from the river Esk, with the freshness that open water gives to a place. Langholm is, in fact split into two by the Esk, with the older part on its east bank, and New Langholm on the west, in the angle between the Esk and **Wauchope Water**. Langholm proper was founded as a burgh of barony in 1621; its new neighbour laid out by the Duke of Buccleuch in 1778, though most of the buildings are 19th century.

Market Place

159 **Town Hall**, 1811, probably William Elliot of Kelso
On early 17th-century site, symmetrical three-bay, two-storey, with advanced central bay, pilastered at first floor, surmounted by three-stage clock and bell tower, with concave top. Sturdy, uncompromising character relieved by ornate lamp bracketed above the entrance (colour page 86). Behind, and in contrast, cheerful Jacobean **library**, 1875-8, James Burnet, with corner towers with leaded ogee roofs, shaped gable, mullioned and transomed windows. Interiors of both remodelled, 1970s.

Rather forbidding Gothic **Eskdale Hotel**, 1865-6, Habershon Spalding & Brooke, London, and behind, surprisingly light-hearted **Thomas Hope Hospital**, 1894-6, Wood & Ainslie, London, pleasing domestic-scale with crenellated square tower; post-modern glazed porch distinctly out of scale. The use of London architects is perhaps unexpected, but may well be owing to the Buccleuch connection.

Top left *Sweetheart Abbey looking towards the east end.* Top *Southerness Lighthouse.* Middle *Kirkbean Parish Church.* Above *Arbigland, Kirkbean.* Left *The 'queir', Terregles Parish Church.*

85

From top *Townhead Bridge, Langholm; Town Hall, Langholm; Lamp outside the Crown Hotel, Langholm; Riddings Viaduct.* Above right *Langholm Parish Church and its private bridge.* Right *Hollows (Gilnockie) Tower.*

From top *Craigcleuch; Detail of
Johnstone Mausoleum, Westerkirk
Churchyard; Local colour in
Langholm; Westerkirk Parish
Library and Telford Monument.* Left
Bentpath.

87

Left from top *Chapelcross Nuclear Power Station; High Street, Annan, with steeple of Old Parish Church; Cornerhouse Hotel, Annan; Robgill Tower.* Top *Town Hall, Annan.* Above *Stapleton Tower.*

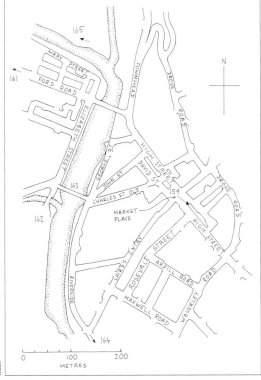

Hume

Below *Bank of Scotland*. Middle *Crown Hotel*. Bottom *Townhead Toll-house*.

Hume

High Street
Bank of Scotland, 1876, Wardrop & Reid
Italianate three-storey vying in scale, and
winning in smartness over **Royal Bank of
Scotland**, quirky baronial, with minute corner
turret with fairy-tale tall conical roof. Next,
Crown Hotel, three-storey, three-bay coaching
inn with pilastered doorcase, with concave-
curved pediment (colour page 86). **No 9**, early
19th-century villa with unusually fine doorcase.

Thomas Telford Road
Former **North UP Church**, 1867, Robert Baldie
Rather awkwardly detailed, but an effective
visual stop to Thomas Telford Road which leads
160 across **Townhead Bridge**, from 1775, Robin
Houston, widened, with iron-railed footpaths,
1880, and again, sympathetically, 1993-4, by
Dumfries and Galloway Council, to New
Langholm (colour page 86). Further north the
main road becomes Townhead, with **Clinthead**,
c.1800, delightful single-storey-and-basement
villa, its fanlight an original variation on the
usual Georgian theme. Similarly, one-storey-and-
basement **Townhead Toll-house** marks the end

Hume

Hume

of the burgh, its crenellated bowed front
unusual, but matched by its opposite number at
the south end of the town.

New Langholm

The most interesting feature is its planned-town
161 layout. At western end are **Langholm
Academy** and the town's primary school, the
Old Academy, 1854-6, in Buccleuch-estate
Tudor, single-storey, with central section rebuilt,
1984, as two storeys. Present **Academy**, 1962,
Dumfriesshire County Council, clean-lined,
three-storey international-modern block, with
strong horizontal emphasis. Elegant two-span
masonry **bridge** to parish church.

*Right Langholm Parish Church
and bridge. Below Ford Mill.
Bottom Housing, West Street.*

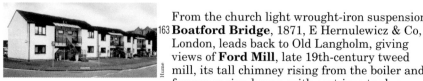

162 **Langholm Parish Church**, 1842-6,
William Burn and David Bryce
Strongly modelled Early English buttressed,
with large belfry. Inside, galleries and pulpit
are original, pews, 1915, by Peter MacGregor
Chalmers, the leading Glasgow church
architect of the day (colour page 86).

From the church light wrought-iron suspension
163 **Boatford Bridge**, 1871, E Hernulewicz & Co,
London, leads back to Old Langholm, giving
views of **Ford Mill**, late 19th-century tweed
mill, its tall chimney rising from the boiler and
former engine-house, with cast-iron tank on
the roof. Further south, and also by the river,
164 are the much larger **Waverley Mills**, 1865-7
and 1871, Thomas Aimers, Galashiels, built in
two sections with three-storey double-pile
spinning block. Modern **housing**, east of the
mill, of which the most attractive are six blocks
of four-in-a-block gallery access houses in **West
Street** and **Waverley Road**, 1960s,
particularly clean and crisp.

Langholm Lodge, 1786-7, James Playfair Classical Buccleuch mansion, rebuilt, 1790, after a fire; central section demolished, 1953, leaving two-storey piend-roofed wings as free-standing houses.

Ewes Bridge, 1784-6, and a clutch of **Buccleuch Estate** buildings in the grounds:

165 **Duchess Bridge**, 1813, William Keir Jun, early, fine and remarkably slender cast-iron arched footbridge; modest but well-proportioned timber **All Saints Scottish Episcopal Church**, 1887, James Burnet; and **Ewesbank House**, earlier/mid 19th century, a fairy-tale house, with its fretted bargeboards, two-storey, three-bay, asymmetric, with twin gables over the right-hand bays of the entrance front, and gabled porch.

South of the burgh the A7 passes the former **Langholm Distillery** before crossing

166 **Skippers Bridge**, 1693-1700, tall three-span, with triangular cutwaters, widened upstream, 1807. South side reveals its early date, with rubble arch rings and corbelled parapet.

Broomholm House, 1749
Charming two-storey, three-bay symmetrical, with pedimented central bay and doorcase, and bull's-eye window; later single-storey wings. Associated **steading** includes splendid two-storey barn, with slit ventilators at two levels.

167 **Gilnockie Tower**, mid-16th century Stronghold of the Armstrong family, by the River Esk, also known as Hollows Tower. Re-roofed, 1979-80, by W G Dawson and converted to a dwelling. Rectangular in plan, four-storey and attic (colour page 91). **Hollows Mill**, an early 19th-century water-powered grain mill, extended, 1867, after a fire, has internal waterwheel and machinery for feeding-stuff preparation.

Top *Duchess Bridge.* Middle *Ewesbank House.* Above *Gilnockie Tower before restoration.*

CANONBIE
Main street of this small village arches round a bend on the River Esk, with the massive

168 masonry **Canonbie Bridge**, 1752-4, Gideon Boyd & Andrew Mein, widened in 1899, at the north end. Focal points are the **Cross Keys Hotel** and the **Riverside Inn**, both late-Georgian fishing hotels (originally coaching inns) of note. Opposite is **Canonbie Parish**

169 **Church**, 1821-2, William Atkinson, rather heavy castellated Gothic with interesting

churchyard. **Primary school** and **schoolhouse**, 1860; extended 1989.

170 **Priorslynn Farm**, largely 18th and early 19th century, within which cruck-framed, clay-walled building with corrugated-iron roof, probably built as a byre and barn later 18th-century, is the best survivor of its type in Dumfries and Galloway.

171 **Rowanburn**, late 19th century
A curiosity for Dumfries and Galloway, built to house miners in the Canonbie coalfield, it consists of rows of miners' houses in the style of those in central Scotland. For many years in private hands, it is now difficult to trace their former uniformity. South of Rowanburn **Riddings**
172 **Viaduct**, 1864, Border Union Railway, nine-span viaduct on a skew, sharp at one end, and a curve; closed 1967 (colour page 86). The other two viaducts on the line, Tarras and Byreburn, were less well constructed and have been demolished.

Byreburn Limeworks, mid/late 19th century; limestone was mined here and burnt in a curious single-draw kiln, with triangular rusticated arch. Further up the B6318, where it crosses the Tarras Water is **Tarras**
173 **Tileworks**, c.1900, a late example of a drainage-tile works, on the Buccleuch estate, with single Newcastle kiln and L-plan range of drying sheds with louvred sides.

Top Canonbie Parish Church. Middle Priorslynn Farm, cruck-framed barn. Above Tile kiln, Tarras Tileworks.

Ewes Parish is mainly moorland and lies north of Langholm on the A7. **Arkleton** is the great house, begun 1860, extended 1884, in rather heavy baronial, appropriate for its Border setting. Little 1½-storey **gardener's cottage** in red and white brick with bargeboarded porch, is in much lighter mood; pleasant little crowstepped **stable block**. **Fiddleton Bar toll-house**, c.1820, is like the two Langholm toll-houses, with castellated semi-octagonal observation bay, and sunk
174 storey. Simple Gothic **Ewes Parish Church**, 1866-7, James Burnet, has lancet windows and gabled belfry.

Craigcleuch.

175 **Craigcleuch**, c.1874-5
Small Tudor mansion, with two-storey main block featuring central three-storey entrance tower and side bays with shaped gables and canted-bay windows (colour page 87).

Westerhall House, from 17th century
Circular stair-tower of the original L-plan

laird's house survives; extended to west early 18th century, and remodelled, 1783, possibly by Thomas Telford, with large three-bay bow. Repaired after fires in 1873, and 1955, Stanley Ross-Smith. Former **stables**, now part of steading, is quadrangular, single-storey with piended roof and central segmental arched entrance.

Thomas Telford was born at Westerkirk in the valley of the Esk where there is a monument to him (see below). He started out as a stone mason and became the greatest civil engineer of his time. One of the earliest contracts on which he worked was the construction of the Townhead Bridge at Langholm (see p.89).

Left Johnstone Mausoleum. Below *Westerhall House.* Middle *Westerkirk Parish Library and Telford Monument.* Bottom *Burnfoot Steading hay barn.*

BENTPATH

Scattered village in Eskdale (colour page 87) where the River Esk is crossed by a two-span **bridge**, 1734-7, leading to **Westerkirk Parish**

176 **Church**, 1881, James Burnet, but of a style current 50 years earlier, with pinnacled tower, lancet windows and a sufficiency of buttresses. **White House**, former manse, 1783, much altered early 19th century and again, 1910-11, R B Barnet. **Churchyard** has fine headstones, but

177 its glory is the classical **Johnstone Mausoleum**, 1790, Robert Adam, square on plan, with advanced central bays on all sides; round-arched entrance flanked by pairs of fluted Doric engaged columns supporting pedimented entablature; large, leaded dome, and frieze featuring Adam's favourite ox skulls (colour page 87).

North-west is the late 19th-century **primary**
178 **school** and **Westerkirk Parish Library**, looking like a church; present building dating from 1860. Boundary wall now features a **monument** to Thomas Telford, native of the parish, relocated recently, appropriately during road-widening. Built 1928 to designs by Curtis Gray, with bas-relief portrait plaque by D A Francis (colour page 87).

At **Burnfoot Steading**, generally rubble-built, with graded slate roofs, there is a piend-roofed hay barn bearing the inscription *He causeth the grass to grow for the cattle and herb for the service of man.*

93

Top *Eskdalemuir parish graveyard.*
Above *Eskdalemuir Observatory.*

The Eskdalemuir Observatory was built to complement the Royal Observatory on Blackford Hill, Edinburgh, 1892 (see *Edinburgh* in this series), which was suffering increasingly from light pollution.

The abiding impression of Annan is the richness of its stone, faded in some of the older buildings, which gives a warmth of feeling even in winter. It is a town that has lost some important, fine buildings in recent years: it should cherish what remains.

ESKDALEMUIR

179 Remote, scattered community, with **parish church**, 1826, probably by John Smallwood. The small stone octagonal steeple is a replacement of the original, by Walter Miller, 1853. Interior appears to be largely original with semi-octagonal gallery on slender cast-iron columns and pulpit with sounding-board. **Graveyard** contains an obelisk **monument** to Revd William Brown, died 1835. The little **school**, 1872, is by James Burnet, and the two-span **bridge** over the Esk was rebuilt in the same year.

DAVINGTON

Unexpectedly, for a tiny village in upper Eskdale, two nationally significant building complexes both sited here to take advantage of
180 remoteness. **Eskdalemuir Observatory**, 1904-7, built to designs by W T Oldrieve of the Office of Works, is in Jacobean style, with subsidiary buildings in Arts & Crafts; all rather clumsy in appearance.

181 **Kagu Samye Ling Tibetan Centre**, Garvaldwaterfoot, from *c*.1860
Based around a farmhouse, but hugely extended to include a **Buddhist temple**, 1979-88, Sherab Palden Beru, its balconies and pagoda roof look particularly exotic in this Scottish moorland setting.
Afternoon café; shop; guided tours on request

182 **Castle O'er**, Iron Age hill fort, now in forest, consisting of ditch-and-bank enclosure to which later sub-enclosure was made, to contain nine circular houses.

ANNAN

Annan owes its existence to its position as the river-mouth port on the Annan, one of the best harbours on the eastern Solway, with a rich hinterland and there may well have been a settlement here at a very early date. Constituted a burgh, late 12th century, by the Bruces of Annandale, an Anglo-Norman family granted land in the vicinity, who built a wooden castle to control the ford over the river; its earthwork *motte* survives by the river north of the present bridge. When Robert Bruce became King of Scots in 1306, Annan became a royal burgh. Layout reflects its medieval origins with broad central market-place with narrow roads leading off each end, and streets and wynds at right angles.

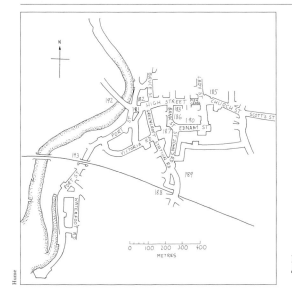

Below left Annan. *Below* Former Southern Bank of Scotland.

High Street

183 **Town Hall**, 1875-8, Peter Smith
Dominant red sandstone feature, with tall
baronial spire, in a manner fashionable in mid-
Victorian Scotland (others can be seen at
Lockerbie, Hawick, Renfrew, Dunfermline and
Huntly), with two-storey, three-bay entrance
front (colour page 88). Three-storey, five-bay
Buccleuch Arms, with columned porch, the
town's largest coaching inn. Behind, one of two
17th-century urban **doocots**, tall narrow red
sandstone towers with monopitch roof. **Royal
Bank of Scotland**, 1881, Sydney Mitchell,
typical bankers' Italianate, an unusual
treatment for this Edinburgh architect. Former
184 **Southern Bank of Scotland**, sternly
uncompromising three-storey, five-by-three-bay
block with Roman Doric portico looks somewhat
out of place. Two free-Renaissance three-storey
buildings, one the **Corner House Hotel**,
c.1900, dressed up with scrolled pediments to

Corner House Hotel.

its dormers and other extravagant details including prominent rounded oriel at the corner with slated dome and art nouveau finial (colour page 88). Its more restrained opposite number built as an **office block**, 1899-1900, T Taylor Scott, with circular ogee-roofed corner tower.

Further east some pleasing and unpretentious buildings, the most elaborate being the **Buck Inn**, French classical with shaped gablets and mullioned and transomed windows. Splendid
185 Georgian-steepled **Old Parish Church**, designed and built, 1789-90, James Beattie and John Oliver, joiners, and John Hannah, mason, all local craftsmen; tall round-headed windows with intersecting arc glazing, mostly *in situ*. Internally, a galleried rectangle, with fine canopied magistrates' pew in north gallery, with four Corinthian columns supporting an entablature with inset carved Georgian ceiling. Central entrance in base of tower, columned and pedimented. Large, impressive steeple, added 1798-1801, first of its kind in Dumfries and Galloway (colour page 88).

From top Annan Old Parish Church; Victoria Hall and former public library; Former British Linen Bank; Railway Station.

Bank Street
Most architectural interest here with discreetly
186 baronial **Victoria Hall**, 1882, and elegantly restrained Jacobean former **public library**, 1906, George Washington Browne. Four-square flat-classical former **Erskine Church**, 1834-5, William Gregan, built for a United Secession congregation, and two-storey, three-bay Georgian revival former **post office**, surmounted by the Royal Arms designed to
187 harmonise with the former **British Linen Bank**, c.1845, two-storey, three-bay Georgian, at the apparent end of the street, originally set back, but with single-storey flat-roof extension to the property boundary, c.1900, in Adam style. These apparently disparate buildings are tied together by the warm red of the sandstone to form a very attractive whole.

Station Road
Another good group of buildings round the
188 **railway station**, opened 1848 by the Glasgow Dumfries & Carlisle Railway, with two-storey Italianate building, with open eaves and low-pitched roof, now converted to a pub-restaurant. Grandiose Jacobean bulk of the **Central Hotel**, 1898, F J C Carruthers, on a triangular site with paired entrance towers *à la* Caerlaverock Castle. Open area round the station extends across the

Annan Academy.

189 playgrounds to **Annan Academy**, oldest part an extended single-storey plan with forward-facing gabled wings linked to two-storey entrance block with tall ogee-roofed ventilating tower, all Jacobean, 1894-6, J F C Carruthers, extended in Tudor, 1907, H E Clifford. Contrasting with the attractive but somewhat undisciplined Carruthers' frontage is the newer section, with elegant four-storey strip-glazed flat-roofed block, 1964-9, Dumfriesshire County Council.

Below *Old Grammar School.* Middle *Annan Bridge.* Bottom *Former cotton mill (demolished).*

Two earlier generations of school buildings survive in Annan: immediate predecessor of
190 the Carruthers' block is **Old Annan Academy** in Ednam Street, with flat-classical centrepiece, two-storey by five-bay, extended at both ends by two bays. Its precursor, handsome but plain three-storey and basement, five-bay
191 **Old Grammar School**, High Street, with rusticated quoins and pedimented porch, underused for far too long, is on the edge of the burgh, part of a close-knit group of mainly two-storey red sandstone buildings, including two inns, which form a satisfying entrance to the town from chunky three-span, segmental-
192 arched **Annan Bridge**, 1824-6, Robert Stevenson, the lighthouse engineer grandfather of Robert Louis Stevenson. Refinement of detail worth viewing from ground level, reached by a stairway on the north-west abutment.

Port Street leads to Annan's **harbour**, until early this century busy with small sailing ships and steam coasters, with Annan's **cotton mill**, 1785, later brewery and provender mill, demolished mid-1990s. Some warehouses built for grain and other trades survive south of
193 **Port Street Viaduct**, 1848, Glasgow Dumfries & Carlisle Railway, and give something of the feel of what was a bustling port.

Annandale Distillery.

194 Annandale Distillery, from 1830
Rebuilt 1887 and operated by John Walker &
Sons Ltd (*Johnnie Walker*) from 1896 to 1921,
when it was abandoned. L-plan group, still
with its pagoda-roofed kiln of the type
introduced by C C Doig of Elgin in the 1890s,
with an associated farm steading. Now used
for storage.

195 Warmanbie, *c.*1820
Tiny, two-storey, laird's house of red sandstone
ashlar with each of its four faces treated
differently. Entrance front has Greek Doric
portico, now a porch, garden front a full-height
central bow, and east front is pedimented. Good
interior with plaster-vaulted entrance hall,
coved ceiling over staircase with oval cupola,
and fine marble fireplaces. Now a **hotel**. Gothic
cottages in the grounds.

On the west bank of the Annan is
Blacketlees Farmhouse, *c.*1806, two-storey,
three-bay with rusticated quoins and
pedimented and swagged doorcase; original
nine-panel door with radial fanlight. Wire-rope
196 suspension **footbridge**, 1897, P & R Fleming,
Glasgow, built to celebrate the Diamond
Jubilee of Queen Victoria.

197 Chapelcross Nuclear Power Station,
1955-60, Merz & McLellan, engineers, and
L J Couves & Partners, architects
Dominates the landscape, with four
reactor/boilerhouse blocks, each with its own
chimney and cooling tower (colour page 88).

From top *Warmanbie; Suspension
footbridge; Chapelcross Nuclear
Power Station; Bonshaw Tower.*

198 Bonshaw Tower, from mid-16th century
Thick-walled, rectangular, rubble tower for
the Irvings of Bonshaw, three storeys and
garret. Vaulted basement at ground with
hall above, spiral stair in north-east angle.
Roll-moulded openings, windows with

mullions and lattice-pane glazing; squared letter-box cellar ventilation shafts to each elevation. To the north-east, smart 1770s two-storey Georgian villa with swept piended roof. Main front has three wide bays with central pedimented Doric porch; to garden front, full-height bow window, probably 1840s alteration. Mansion linked to tower since 1896 by single-storey wing; interior largely remodelled, but retains Georgian cornices and shutters.

Left *Brydekirk plan, from 1800 agricultural survey.* Below *Parish Church.* Bottom *Limekilns House.*

BRYDEKIRK

Grandiose plans for this village, drawn up in 1800 for Colonel Dioram of Mount Annan, show a horseshoe-shaped tree-lined boulevard with large windows fronting neat terraces on grid-iron plan. Amenities were to include mill and dam, caul with fish-gate, freestone quarry (to supply the building) and a woollen manufactory. Executed reality much more modest; simply **Bridge Street**, lined with much-altered single-storey cottages, leading to

199 **Brydekirk Bridge**, 1798-1800, Thomas Boyd & William Stewart, three arches over Annan Water, rubble-built with smart ashlar arch-ring and solid triangular cutwaters.

Parish church, 1835, formerly chapel of ease, *built entirely at the expense of Mrs Dioram of Mount Annan*, harled crowstepped rectangle with embattled pinnacled tower and lancet windows.

A minor road to the south-west leads past

200 **Limekilns House**, a small two-storey Georgian laird's house.

Interior and Belfast roof, foundry, Cochrane's boilerworks.

The Cochrane boiler had a one-piece hemispherical top, and was used as an auxiliary boiler on steamships.

Below *Dornock House Steading.* Bottom *Dornock Parish Church.*

201 NEWBIE

On the west bank of the River Annan, the village was built in 1898 to serve a boilerworks constructed to make, among other types, boilers to Cochrane's patent. The firm moved from Birkenhead, and built a quay to ship materials in and boilers out. To house key workers they constructed a very English-looking, two-storey terrace. The works itself was largely built of timber, with Belfast roofs, later extended by corrugated-iron-clad steel sheds. The earliest building has now gone.

DORNOCK

Very much an agricultural settlement, embodying two farm steadings and a former water-powered grain mill. Dornock House **steading** incorporates a somewhat altered early 18th-century mansion. T-plan **parish church**, 1793, with bellcote of 1855; interior remodelled, and porch added, 1884-5, by James Barbour. Former **manse** dates from 1844-5.

203 Robgill Tower, from 16th century

Mainly late 18th/early 19th-century, small two-storey and basement red sandstone mansion, with prominent canted bay, joined to 16th-century **tower**, refaced *c*.1870, built for Cuthbert Irving of Robgill (colour page 88).

204 **Stapleton Tower**, mid/late 16th century, for Edward Irving, incorporated in a 19th-century mansion, now almost completely demolished. Roofless, but otherwise well-preserved, four-storey tower, rectangular in plan (colour page 88). Early 19th-century **lodge** and **gates** survive, former with Doric portico.

Left Scottish Episcopal Church of St John the Evangelist.
Below Stapleton Tower.

EASTRIGGS

Built, like Gretna, to house munitions workers, to a plan by Raymond Unwin. The brick housing has been badly altered, and the only fine building is now the **Scottish Episcopal**
205 **Church of St John the Evangelist**, 1917, by C M Crickmer in **Ladysmith Road**; powerful, Early Christian style, with aisled nave and north transept; tower with bellcast, slated roof.

GRETNA, 1916-17

Grid-iron village with open central area built to house workers of Britain's largest munitions factory (now demolished), sited here for its good rail connections and distance from enemy action. Striking, incongruous, brick Byzantine
206 **St Ninian's RC Church**, Victory Avenue, 1918, Evelyn Simmons, is cruciform, with tall, narrow interior, and **All Saints Episcopal Church**, Annan Road/Central Avenue, 1917, Geoffrey Lucas, more conventionally Arts & Crafts, of sandstone rubble with bellcast roof; tower never completed. Cruciform **St Andrew's Church of Scotland**, Central Avenue, 1917, C M Crickmer, is harled brick, with exposed brick dressings and square tower with pyramid roof.

207 **The Institute** (now a **community education centre**), *c*.1916, the **cinema** (now a bingo hall), also 1916, and the **police station**, 1916, Henry G Paul, are all in the plain red brick neo-Georgian of most of the housing.

St Ninian's RC Church.

Gretna village was planned and designed by a government team, led by Raymond Unwin, with C M Crickmer as site architect, as a permanent settlement because the cost of doing so was not much greater than that of building temporary houses, and a full range of community facilities was provided in order to counter potential social unrest. The well-proportioned, simply detailed, brick terraced housing proved influential in the design of post-war public housing throughout Britain.

In recent years sale of the houses to individuals has reduced the uniformity of appearance of the community, but it is still a distinctive place.

Gretna Green became celebrated for runaway marriages after 1754, when secret marriages became illegal in England. As the Act did not apply to Scotland, English couples wishing to contract such unions fled there, and as Gretna Green was the community nearest to the border on either of the main north/south roads, it became the *resort of all amorous couples whose union the prudence of parents or guardians prohibits* (Pennant, 1771). Marriages were celebrated by laymen – blacksmith, tollkeeper or innkeeper.

RCAHMS

Primary school, Victory Avenue, 1981, Dumfries and Galloway Regional Council, has octagonal hall surrounded by single-storey classrooms, all in brick. Post-modern **Registration Office**, 1989-91, Peter Nelson of Dumfries and Galloway Regional Council.

Right *Interior, St Ninian's R C Church.* Below *Hunters Lodge Hotel.* Middle *Toll-house.* Bottom *Gretna Hall Hotel.*

Dumfries & Galloway Council

RCAHMS

D & G Council

208 **Hunters Lodge Hotel**, Annan Road, *c.*1917, ?C M Crickmer

Plain but accomplished Voyseyan English Arts & Crafts, 1½-storey house, with diamond-paned casement windows and swept eaves.

GRETNA GREEN

Celebrated for its runaway marriage facilities, just on the Scottish side of the border.

209 Marriages were conducted in the **toll-house**, a Telford bow-ended building, *c.*1820, and in the **Old Smiddy** (actually in Springfield Village) with Gothic front, probably mid-19th century. Gothic **Gretna Parish Church**, 1789-90, heavily remodelled, 1909-10, by James Barbour, who added the slender tower, with rosemary-tiled spire and caphouse.

210 **Gretna Hall Hotel**, 1710

Two-storey-and-basement mansion, built for Colonel James Johnstone, converted to an inn for the Anglo-Scottish stage-coach traffic, *c.*1792, when curious advanced end bays with large Venetian windows were added; early 19th-century box porch addition. Former **stables**, dated 1710 but probably later, have basket-arched entrance large enough to take a stage-coach.

Park Bridge, *c*.1810, probably Thomas Telford, over the boundary with England, two-span ashlar bridge with rusticated arch rings and pointed cutwaters. A modern steel-truss bridge, parallel to it, takes northbound traffic.

KIRKPATRICK FLEMING
Long and narrow, with the red sandstone **primary school**, 1881, and the mildly baroque **Victoria Hall**, 1898-9, George Dale Oliver.

211 **Parish church**, substantially rebuilt, 1775, but incorporating earlier masonry, including a bellcote of 1733; further alterations, 1892-3, J B Leslie. Fine **graveyard** includes two burial enclosures, one late 17th century.

212 **Mossknowe House**, 1767, William Craik of Arbigland
Unusual house, with narrow two-storey, attic and basement, three-bay pedimented centrepiece and two-storey end pavilions, attached to the centre by single-storey flat-roofed balustraded blocks. Between Kirkpatrick Fleming and Kirtlebridge, south of the old A74, are the remains of four-storey **Woodhouse Tower**, mid-16th century, rectangular on plan, consolidated and restored as a ruin, 1877. North, and west, is 15th-

213 century, wayside **Merkland Cross**, with tapering octagonal shaft terminating on cross-head consisting of four fleur-de-lys. Whole cross carved from single piece of stone, on later stone base. Legend associates the cross with the death in action of a military commander, but there is no firm evidence for this, and it may be simply a devotional cross.
Historic Scotland

Across the Kirtle Water from Bonshaw Tower (see p.98) is **Wyseby**, mid-18th century, good plain two-storey, three-bay farmhouse with central Doric pedimented porch and full-height bay to east, added 19th century. Interior preserves some original cornicing, panelled doors and lugged architraved fireplaces. **Stables** and octagonal vaulted **doocot**, from 18th century. Two-storey, three-bay **Langshaw House**, mid-18th century; much-altered and extended.

Merkland Cross is a rare survival of the type of isolated cross that served in medieval times both as a way marker and a focus for devotion.

Below *Mossknowe House*. Middle *Merkland Cross*. Bottom *Wyseby*.

KIRKPATRICK FLEMING

Fair Helen of Kirkconnel was the heroine of the ballad of that name, Helen Maxwell, who interposed herself between her lover, Adam Fleming and an assailant, being killed by a bullet intended for Fleming.

Kirkconnel Church.

214 **Springkell House**, 1734 onwards Medium-scale Palladian mansion, two storeys over basement, seven-bay front. Giant Ionic pilasters rise from the basement supporting mutuled pediment over three advanced centre bays; pair of oculi and family crest in tympanum. Nineteenth-century alterations include two-storey wings, 1818, Alexander Johnstone, in sympathetic style; central perron stair to south front, 1840; less fortunate 1894 *porte-cochère* obscuring much of the north elevation. All windows now plate-glass, astragals having been dispensed with a century ago. Balustraded terraced gardens to the south; 18th-century brick **walled garden**.

In the park of Springkell, beside the Kirtle Water, are the much-reduced remains of rectangular medieval **Kirkconnel Church** and **stones**. The **churchyard** contains some fine monuments, including two slabs said to mark the graves of 'Fair Helen of Kirkconnel', Helen Maxwell, and her lover, Adam Fleming.

North of Springkell is its home farm, **Burnfoot**, earlier/mid 19th century, with five rectangular cart bays, set within a U-plan range.

Above *Half Morton Parish Church before conversion*. Right *Springkell House*.

Half Morton parish is entirely rural, with one hamlet, **Chapelknowe**, a scatter of mainly 19th-century houses with Gothic former **United Presbyterian Church**, 1890, George Dale Oliver, and small, T-plan
215 **Half Morton Parish Church**, 1744, enlarged 1833, with belfry of 1839, renovated, 1889; now fairly sympathetically converted to a house.

Eaglesfield Primary School.

EAGLESFIELD

Long ribbon development, founded early 19th century, but mainly 20th century. Note the **hall-church**, 1953, buttressed Arts & Crafts
216 rectangle, the **public hall**, 1892-3, Peter Chapman, and the **primary school**, 1907, F J C Carruthers. Chunky two-storey, three-bay symmetrical piend-roofed **Sunnybrae House**, late 18th century, has blind window above the doorcase and prominent shouldered chimneystacks.

217 **Blacket House**, Eaglesfield, *c*.1835, Walter Newall
Small Tudor mansion house next to remains of L-plan rubble **Blacket Tower**, *c*.1600; stair jamb survives, probably owing to conversion to **doocot**, late 19th century; top-floor room made into **study**, *c*.1950; lintels on adjoining door bear the dates 1663 and 1714, with initials of members of the Bell family.

218 **MIDDLEBIE**

Built round the **parish church**, 1929, J M Bowie, tall, cruciform, with buttressed gable to the road and offset belfry, in very obviously snecked rubble. Good interior of the period; important because few churches were built at this time. **Graveyard** has fine carved stones.

Top *Broadlea farmhouse, c.1840, with pilastered doorcase.* Middle *Pennersaughs farmhouse, c.1840, with Roman-Doric portico.* Above *Middlebie Parish Church.*

WATERBECK

Pleasant little village, with some largely unaltered, mid-19th-century cottages and
219 some later villas. **United Presbyterian Church**, 1868-9, James Barbour, has broached spire and good interior; manse contemporary. **Village hall**, *c*.1900, with bellcote, is former primary school.

Lauriesclose has 1905, Arts & Crafts former **church**, with open-eaved roof and small tower; notable wrought-iron railings.

Immediately south of Middlebie village, on the banks of the Mein Water, is **Birrens Roman Fort**, originally known as Blatobulgium. The remains of the six outer ditches are visible on the ground. It was built in three stages during the second century AD, and has been extensively excavated. Finds are in the Hunterian Museum, University of Glasgow.

The Moffat Ram, or Colvin Fountain, gifted to the town by William Colvin of Craigielands, Beattock, was erected in 1875. By local tradition, the artist forgot to model the ears and consequently committed suicide. The facts were published in 1978 – the ram was a blackface, common locally before the Cheviot was introduced. The blackface, unlike the Cheviot, has very small ears. William Brodie RSA, who sculpted the bronze ram, was secretary of the RSA for five years from 1876 until his death aged 66.
The Moffat News, 2 Nov 1978

Right *Colvin Fountain, High Street and Moffat House Hotel.*

Star Hotel.

MOFFAT

Very pleasant, airy town, well deserving its reputation as a quiet resort and destination for coach tours, and one of the most distinctive and unusual of all the towns and villages in Dumfries and Galloway. It retains the character of a spa town and staging-post on the Edinburgh/Dumfries road which developed in the late 18th and early 19th centuries, reinforced by its role as a high-class commuter town for Edinburgh and Glasgow following opening of Beattock/Moffat branch of the Caledonian Railway, 1883. A burgh of barony from 1643, the virtues of the waters of the chalybeate (iron-infused) Moffat Well were recognised soon after, with another well, **Hartfell Spa**, discovered in 1748. From 1760s, probably with the development of coaching services, the town was remodelled, and the present layout of High Street dates from 1772-3.

Improvements in central Scottish roads made by Thomas Telford also increased trade, and a new **Assembly Hall** and **Baths** were built, 1827. The status of the town as a resort and commuter town in the Victorian period is reflected in the size and quality of the buildings of that period.

High Street

Spaciously laid out with, at its southern end, a series of wynds and streets, following the lines of old burgage plots to east and west, breaking up the street frontages into narrow strips (colour page 153). Most obvious is the **Star Hotel**, 1860, William Notman, with its attenuated gabled

MOFFAT

sandstone ashlar front, said to be the narrowest hotel in Britain. Opposite, more conventional and much larger **Buccleuch Arms Hotel**, c.1860, and earlier **Annandale Hotel**, c.1783, a coaching inn. Single-storey classical **Town Hall**, built as Moffat Baths, 1827, with Assembly Rooms in front and two **Provosts' lamps**, extended 1881, James Barbour, and front remodelled with central portico moved to the north end and matching feature created at the south end (colour page 153). **War Memorial**, 1919-20, Reginald Fairlie, and unique **Colvin Fountain**, 1875, William Brodie, surmounted by bronze ram (colour page 153). Pedimented **Old Court House**, 1772, with clock tower, and mid-19th-century **Bonnington Hotel**, with incised Greek detailing, **Dickson House**, late 18th century and **Balmoral Hotel**, c.1765, unusually of harled brick, and one of the first buildings constructed in the remodelling of the town. Late Victorian Italianate **post office**, and **Arden House**, 1861, former British Linen Bank.

Graveyard in south-east corner of High Street belonged to the medieval parish church, and contains a fragment of it. Some fine **monuments**, including the headstone of John Loudon McAdam the road-builder, and a stone marking the grave of a stage-coach driver who perished in a snowstorm.

The High Street, 300 yards long by about 40 yards wide 150 years ago, was a gravel bed close to the River Annan, freely draining. Moffat had been a burgh of regality since the mid-17th century, requiring a market cross for royal proclamations and acquiring a tolbooth about 1695. These and other central buildings, being obstructions to the market at the south end of the street, were demolished by the Earl of Hope, curator-in-law of his uncle the Johnstone 'mad marquis', around 1770 when he started to improve Moffat. The 1758 survey he commissioned shows 'the street' much as today.

Left *Moffat House Hotel*. Below *Town Hall*. Middle *Balmoral Hotel*. Bottom *St Mary's UF Church*.

Moffat House Hotel, 1762-7, John Adam The town's finest building; elegantly simple three-storey, five-bay house with concave quadrants linking to two-storey pavilions with blocked coach-house entrances. Twentieth-century additions on the garden front, which has bowed-end bays.

Academy Road
St Mary's UF Church, 1890-2, David Burnie Idiosyncratic Gothic, Early English, with tall tower, all executed in local whinstone with red

sandstone dressings, rivalling in scale and elaboration the parish church at the south end of town. Within, cast-iron columns supporting 228 galleries. Two-storey **Moffat Academy**, earlier part, 1932-3, John R Hill, red sandstone, with whinstone panels, extended 1958, George Bartholomew, also Dumfries County Architect. Beyond, non-uniform terraced **houses** facing parkland, and a series of villas. Pleasing mix of vernacular buildings on the left.

Church Gate leads out of High Street with the massive red sandstone **Bank of Scotland**, 1874, Peddie & Kinnear. Beyond, late Georgian **Black Bull Inn**, probably a traveller's inn catering for the less well-to-do.

From top Moffat Academy; St Andrew's Parish Church; Masonic Hall; Scottish Episcopal Church of St John the Evangelist.

229 **St Andrew's Parish Church**, 1884-7, John Starforth
Impressive, idiosyncratic in its treatment of Gothic, with central bell-tower flanked by bowed stair-towers, like his churches in Dumfries, Kelso and Nairn (colour page 153). Richly carved entrance; exceptionally wide interior with braced wagon roof, gallery carried on slender cast-iron columns and iron brackets; large central pulpit. A profusion of stained glass includes rose window above the pulpit, designed by Starforth. **Manse**, also by Starforth.

Station Park, c.1970, has pagoda-roofed pavilion and a **monument** to Air Chief Marshal Lord Dowding, 1972, by D Bruce Walker.

Well Street/Well Road
Wynd-like **Well Street**, almost medieval in character: **No 15-17**, late Victorian baronial; **No 2 Well Road**, late Georgian villa with 230 lying-pane glazing, and single-storey **Masonic Hall**, 1837, built as Morrison's School and converted for the Freemasons, 1892, F J C Carruthers, built in the distinctive local manner of narrow courses of whinstone with painted-ashlar and stucco dressings.

Burnside
231 **Scottish Episcopal Church of St John the Evangelist**, 1951-3, Ian G Lindsay
Original design concept – harled-brick with cement dressings and round-headed gable window with Georgian glazing – compromised by porch, added 1984. Although practical, this is unfortunate as the church embodied

Lindsay's interest in traditional Scots church design. Little wooden **RC Church of St Luke**, Mansefield Street, 1866, reclad c.1966, built as an Episcopal Church.

232 **Proudfoot Institute**, 1885-6,
Campbell Douglas & Sellars
Founded as working-men's institute.
Remodelled, 1893-4, Alan B Crombie, extended to rear, and enriched at the front with round-headed and pedimented rectangular windows. Doric portico added, with scrolled pediment surmounted by an aedicule with bronze bust of William Proudfoot, the founder, by J McLellan Arnott. Crombie also altered the north-west corner, creating an octagonal feature with lead dome and cupola.

233 **Langshaw House**, 1835, altered c.1890, probably J M Dick Peddie
Villa with prominent eaves and battlemented entrance tower. Up the road to Moffat Well is **Heatheryhaugh**, whose **stable block**, probably c.1828, is unusually small and rustic, with low-pitched piended roofs, rock-faced dressings and Gothic windows.

Ian Gordon Lindsay, 1906-66, was a pioneer of conservation in Scotland, and was also involved in the early days of statutory listing. He had a particular interest in 18th-century church architecture and wrote about it in his book *The Scottish Parish Church*. He was responsible for the design of Colinton Mains Parish Church, Edinburgh (see *Edinburgh* in this series) as well as the little Episcopal Church in Moffat.

Above *Detail, Proudfoot Institute.*
Left *Granton House.*

234 **Granton House**, 1830, probably Walter Newall
Three-storey classical mansion in local small coursed-rubble masonry with stucco dressings, with pillared and pedimented porch set in advanced and pedimented central bay; chimneystacks and stone stalks on transverse spine wall, which has low-pitched piended roof. Associated **steading** has unfortunately been allowed to decay.

Dumcrieff House.

Frenchland Tower, from 16th century
Ruin of three-storey and attic, L-plan laird's
house built by the Frenches of Frenchland and
remodelled early 17th century. T-plan
Craigieburn, also from 16th century, with
jamb founded on what was probably a 16th-
century tower. Main range added, *c.*1790;
further additions 1802 and *c.*1865.

235 **Dumcrieff House**, late 18th/early
19th century
Two-storey, symmetrical classical house, with
prominent projecting end bays, commissioned
by Dr John Rogerson, physician to the Russian
court. Three-bay central section dominated by
inset porch with Greek Doric columns and
tripartite window. For a time the home of John
Loudon McAdam, the road-builder.

*This is the night mail crossing
the border,
Bringing the cheque and the postal
order,
Letters for the rich, letters for the poor,
The shop at the corner and the girl
next door.
Pulling up Beattock, a steady climb –
The gradient's against her but she's
on time ...*
from W H Auden, **Night Mail** (1936)

Right *Beattock Station. Below Old
Brig Inn. Bottom Kirkpatrick Juxta
Parish Church.*

BEATTOCK
Small 19th- and 20th-century village,
originally a kirkton, but later a staging post on
Telford's Carlisle/Glasgow road. Solid five-bay
236 **Old Brig Inn**, 1822, probably designed in
Thomas Telford's office, with extensive
stabling an obvious reminder of its coaching
history (colour page 153). Telford **bridge** over
the Evan water replaced, 1951.

The building of the Caledonian Railway up
Annandale gave the village a new importance,
with impressive crowstepped **station**, Sir
William Tite; and locomotive depot established
to provide engines to help trains up to Beattock
summit. Both demolished but **lodge** at station
entrance, in similar style, remains. The single-
storey **cottages** in the centre of the village
were railway houses.

237 **Kirkpatrick Juxta Parish Church**, 1798-
1800, John McCracken, a Dumfries mason;
reconstruction 1875-7, James Barbour –

painting the whin-rubble in the walls has
brightened what was an oppressive building.
Single-storey, H-plan former **Beattock
School**, 1875, has twin-arched inset porch and
pyramid-roofed octagonal ventilator; now an
outdoor centre.

Lochhouse Tower.

238 **Lochhouse Tower**, 16th century; restored &
reroofed, 1973
Stranded on a motorway embankment, a
squat three-storey rubble tower-house,
originally built for the Johnstones of that ilk.
Stepped in over second floor as if in
preparation for great things, above; anti-
climatic upperworks shorn of parapet. Wide-
mouth gunloops cover all elevations.

Langshaw House, late 19th century
Suburban-style villa with broad-eaved gables
and rather too showy castellated entrance
tower with turret stair accessing roof-top
balcony. Contrasting dark-whin walling and
smooth-ashlar margins. **Coach-house** in
similar picturesque style.

239 **Craigielands**, 1817, William Burn
Striking, early Burn essay in Greek revival;
original single-storey house on sunk basement.
Five-bay front with giant Greek Doric
pedimented portico. Attic storey added, 1882, lit
by windows sandwiched between squat pilasters.
Interiors with cantilevered stone stair lit by tall
arched cupola. Masonry small-squared whinstone
blocks with painted sandstone dressings. **North**
and **South Lodges** also by Burn; single-storey,
chunkily detailed in classical style. Overhanging
shallow piend roofs, central paired stacks.

Above *Craigielands*. Left *Auchen
Castle Hotel.*

240 **Auchen Castle Hotel**, 1869
Large asymmetric picturesque country house,
roofline busy with campanile, gablets, French
roofs and emphatically placed stacks. Interior

satisfactorily ornate with rich plaster cornices and elaborate stair-hall. Fine ashlar balustraded demarcated terrace gardens, well-planted wider setting. Pretty pinned-whin single-storey **lodge** with gabled porch support on timber-die pilasters across the angle.

Beattock House Hotel, 1850, Walter Newall Picturesque gabled villa with asymmetric elevations. Richly decorated doorcase with consoled cornice supporting balustraded balcony. In grounds, square pagoda-roofed **summerhouse**.

241 **Auchencass**, 13th century and later Substantial remains of roughly square fortress, with outer bank-ditch-bank earthworks and inner masonry enclosure, originally with a round tower at each corner, reflecting English practice of the period. Built probably for the Kirkpatrick family, it controlled the route to the central lowlands through Beattock Pass.

JOHNSTONEBRIDGE
Very small village with the eponymous Telford **bridge**, 1820; widened in concrete, mid-1960s. **Primary school**, 1862-3, by Alexander
242 Morrison. L-plan **Johnstone Parish Church**, 1743-5, rebuilt 1818-19, John MacDonald; in the angle of the L is flat-roofed session house and porch. Interiors, 1881-2, James Barbour.

Raehills House.

243 **Raehills House**, 1782, Alexander Stevens jun
Most unusual house with Egyptian revival and
battlemented details for James, Earl of
Hopetoun; extended, 1829-34, William Burn, for
John James Hope Johnstone of Annandale.
North, entrance front has central three-storey,
three-bay section, with two-storey, two-bay
wings, with parapets and small corner turrets,
all crenellated; neo-Egyptian balustraded porch.
East front unique with three-storey, three-bay
central bow, flanked by two-storey, four-bay
wings, above a balustraded terrace with central
bowed bay. A colonnade runs above the terrace,
curved round the bay and extended to enclose
the first floor of the bay, with neo-Egyptian
columns at both levels. Below the house an
unusual three-way timber **bridge**.

244 **Applegarth & Sibbaldbie Parish Church**,
1762-3, Francis Patterson & James Bretton,
much altered, 1884-5, F J C Carruthers, and
now substantially of that period, with rose
windows in the gables. **Jardine Burial
Enclosure**, probably late 17th century, with
harled walls and lugged doorway with
curved pediment; good sandstone-slab
tombstones in **graveyard**.

Jardine Hall, 1814, James Gillespie Graham
(demolished)
Magnificent classical mansion, two storeys over
raised rusticated basement. Tall five-bay front
with steps sweeping up to pedimented portico
framed within giant paired Ionic columns.
Greatly extended, 1893, E J May; wings enlarged
and raised to three storeys, and vast *porte-
cochère* tacked on. Interior fabulous rococo of
1893; to rear of house, small railway to transport
coal to the cellars. Most satellite buildings
245 survive including the **stables**; same combination
of Gillespie Graham original and E J May
alterations. Courtyard plan block, symmetrical
entrance front, central pend surmounted by
baldachino clock tower. Converted to domestic
usage, 1985, Wheeler & Sproson.

From top *Applegarth & Sibbaldbie
Parish Church; Jardine Hall in 1892
(demolished); Jardine Hall Stables;
Balgray Home Farm Cottage.*

Balgray House, 1883-5
Symmetrical five-bay, red sandstone ashlar,
two-storey, attic and basement with prominent
balustraded *porte-cochère*; Italianate detailing.
Balgray Home Farm Cottage, early 19th
century, two-storey elongated octagon, piend-
roofed and rendered, with single-storey bays.
Unfortunate conservatory.

The Glasgow/Carlisle Road was rebuilt on an improved line, to designs by **Thomas Telford**, 1814-25. It was intended partly for stage-coach traffic, and partly to expedite troop movements, for the loyalty of the west of Scotland to the Crown was at that period somewhat doubtful.

246 **Dinwoodie Toll-house**, 1822-3, Thomas Telford
Best surviving example of a bow-fronted Telford toll-house in the area, constructed as part of the Carlisle/Glasgow road.

247 **Hewk House**, 1806
Handsome two-storey, three-bay, piend-roofed laird's house. Three-bay inset porch with Tuscan columns.

Fourmerkland Lodge & gates, early 20th century
Single-storey pyramid-roofed with banded central chimney and corner loggia. Imposing rusticated gatepiers with obelisk finials surmounted by balls.

Fourmerkland Lodge & gates.

Dumfries & Galloway Council

Millbank Farmhouse, 1839
Pleasing two-storey and basement, three-bay farmhouse with iron-railed staircase to central entrance.

Above *Hutton & Corrie Parish Church.*
Right *Wamphray Parish Church.*

Hume

Hume

248 **Wamphray Parish Church**, 1834, William McGowan
Rectangular with round-headed windows and Gothic glazing. Belfry tower with ball finial; vestry added, 1859, and storey put on, 1928. Some good headstones in the **churchyard** and a fine monument with garlanded column.

249 **Hutton & Corrie Parish Church**, Boreland, 1710
Converted to T-plan, 1764; the present windows may date from 1799-1800, apart from two flanking the pulpit, which may be 1871. Belfry probably *c.*1820. Fine 17th- and 18th-century stones in the **graveyard**.

Lockerbie High Street and Town Hall.

LOCKERBIE
Despite the irregularity of its plan, Lockerbie dates as a formal settlement from only about 1730, when the local landowners, the Johnstones, began to feu out plots along High Street and its southern extension, Mains Street, followed by expansion at right angles to the east. An important livestock market, especially for lambs, during 18th century, on Telford's Glasgow/Carlisle road and an important staging post until Caledonian Railway opened, 1848; locomotive shed built after the Lockerbie/Dumfries branch opened. Remembered for the terrorist bombing of an airliner, but more justly famous for its cheese, now made in a large new creamery outside the town.

Below *War Memorial.* Bottom *Former Commercial Bank.*

High Street
250 **Town Hall**, 1873, David Bryce
Not built until *c*.1880, and resembling the town halls in Aberdeen, Annan, Dunfermline, Hawick, Huntly and Renfrew, with its turreted clock tower and slated steeple. Elaborately baronial, two-storey and attic, crowstepped with eclectic range of details; large, three-light, mullioned and transomed council-chamber window, ogee-roofed cupola – an unusual feature (colour page 154). Inside, **memorial window**, 1991, John Clark, commemorates those who died in the Lockerbie terrorist disaster.

War Memorial, 1922, James B Dunn, has striking winged bronze figure by Henry C Fehr. Two Italianate banks, the former
251 **Commercial**, No 55, *c*.1870, now Abbey National, and **Royal Bank of Scotland**, No 47-49, late 19th century, Peddie & Kinnear. French Renaissance **Bank of Scotland**,

No 81-83, marred by inappropriate window replacement. Opposite is the three-storey, rendered **Blue Bell Hotel**, an 18th-century coaching inn at its core. South end marked by 252 spire of **Holy Trinity RC Church**, 1874-5, Ford McKenzie, built as UP church, with customary large rose window.

Behind War Memorial, pleasing mid-19th-century range of **shops**, with Venetian windows at first floor, in the end bays. Crowstepped, blocky **railway station**, built for Caledonian Railway, 1848, Sir William Tite, last of the pioneering Anglo-Scottish company's original stations, and **King's Arms**, refronted early 19th-century coaching inn, now magnificently Tudorised.

253 **Dryfesdale & Trinity Parish Church**, Townhead, 1896-8, F J C Carruthers Chunky, with battlemented corner tower and short spire, set in earlier graveyard. Galleried interior with panelled tunnel-vaulted nave, and semi-octagonal apse with organ of 1905; large marble pulpit (colour page 154).

Much simpler, lowered, church hall, built as **Mechanics Institute**, 1865-6, Alexander Fraser. Street ends with red sandstone twin gables of late 19th-century **Lockerbie** 254 **Academy**, concealing the international-modern, flat-roofed **Academy** of 1963, Dumfriesshire County Council.

Former **Lockerbie Free Church**, 1866, John Honeyman Red sandstone Gothic with tall broached spire. Hidden away to the east is **All Saints Episcopal Church**, 1901-3, in picturesque, modest Arts & Crafts, with altar-piece by J Ninian Comper.

West Lodge, Dryfesholm, c.1860, and its associated workshops and stores, have a double coach-house with central clock tower, unusually projecting from the face of the building. **Dryfesholm Farm**, mid-19th century, incorporates remarkably long, 18-bay barn with slated roof, unusually supported on tall cast-iron columns.

Top Holy Trinity R C Church.
Middle Lockerbie Academy.
Above Roberthill Steading.

255 **Roberthill Steading** includes a very fine, late 18th-century cartshed and granary range, forming an L with the farmhouse. The buildings are limewashed; four arched cart bays.

256 **Tundergarth Parish Church**, 1899-1900,
James Barbour
Rectangular with prominent and
uncompromising battlemented tower with
small belfry. Tracery freely interpreted late-
Gothic. Ruins of old parish church, 1771-2,
linger in the graveyard.

Single-storey piend-roofed parish **school**, in
the hamlet of Beckshill, with two-storey school
house at the front.

Castlemilk was built for Sir Robert
Jardine, Bt, at different times MP for
Dumfries and Dumfriesshire. Heir to
Dr William Jardine, he was described
by Benjamin Disraeli as *richer than
Croesus ... fresh from Canton, with a
million in opium in each pocket,
denouncing corruption and bellowing
free trade.*

257 **Castlemilk**, 1865, David Bryce
An ancient site, originally a Bruce stronghold
and later held by the Maxwells against attack
by Cromwell. A more gracious mansion
replaced the old house in 1796: a conventional
classical country house of two storeys over
raised basement with Doric porch and flanking
wings, demolished to allow Bryce to create one
of his largest baronial country houses.
Dominated by a huge drum tower, based on
Castle Fraser, the intricacies of its domestic
planning reflect the variety and asymmetry of
the exteriors. Three-storey wings house public
and family apartments with single-storey
service court. Lavish in details culled from
Billings with corbel tables, tourelles, dormers
and crowsteps; lead statues stand sentinel atop
turret roofs. Equally sumptuous interior in
Jacobean style; elaborately carved balustrading
to stair, pendant plaster ceilings and marble
chimneypieces. **Conservatory** Gothic
externally, but Tuscan-columned within.

Matching baronial **stable block** linked to
service wing. **Walled garden**, two Tudor
lodges and baronial **bridge** on south drive, all
*c.*1870.

Castlemilk.

Fireplace, Castlemilk.

117

258 KETTLEHOLM

Small estate village for Castlemilk, with **housing**, late Georgian, and later, rubble built and limewashed. Best range has pedimented doorcases of later date. **Village hall**, 1907-8, D W Campbell, in Wren style, with bowling green behind. **St Mungo Parish Church**, 1875-7, David Bryce, in Late Scots Gothic. Furnishings of that period, apart from pulpit and organ, inserted 1905. Beyond, former **parish church**, 1841-2, William McGowan, converted to **school** by James Barbour, following construction of the new church.

Ruins of even earlier church at Kirkland, **259** with good tombstones in the **churchyard**.

Top *Kettleholm Village Hall.* Above *Gravestone, Kirkland Churchyard.* Right *Lochmaben.*

LOCHMABEN

Founded 13th century, as a burgh of barony by the Bruces of Annandale; accepted as a royal burgh from 1440, gaining its charter in 1605. Best approached from the south, past the earth mound marking the site of the 12th-century **Castle** of the Bruces. Simple *Heritors' Gothic* **260** **parish church**, 1819-20, James Thomson, with, unusually, all its original gallery seating, named and gated pews. Rest refurnished, *c.*1880, F J C Carruthers.

Always a market town serving local interests, **High Street** is roughly triangular in plan, reflecting its earlier use as a market (colour page 154). Buildings are late 18th and earlier 19th century, and include the **Royal Bank of Scotland** and the **Old Schoolhouse**, *c.*1830, in the style of Walter **261** Newall, with Tudor detailing. **Tolbooth**, 1723, originally with a cupola, replaced by a steeple, 1741, remodelled and extended, 1867, David Bryce, including three Venetian openings, one with statue of Revd William Graham, a local historian. In front, statue of **Robert the Bruce**, 1879, J Hutchison, RSA (colour page

Hightae is the largest of the four villages which form, with the land round them, the barony of Lochmaben. The inhabitants of these villages held their lands direct from the Crown, by tradition from Robert the Bruce who, when he inherited the throne of Scotland, is said to have granted these lands to his retainers.

154). **Mercat Cross** contains pieces of 17th-
or early 18th-century date. Through a lane
west of the Tolbooth, **churchyard** of former
parish church, has some good monuments,
including one to Dr James Mounsey of
Rammerscales (see p.125), physician to the
Empress of Russia, mid-18th century.

Castle Street/Bruce Street
Bruce Arms, Castle Street, early 19th century,
with pedimented wallhead chimney. **Old
Manse**, Bruce Street, c.1838-40, style of Walter
Newall; the **Crown Hotel**, early 19th-century
coaching inn, and late 18th-century **Old Bank
House**, for Dr Clapperton, father of Thomas,
the explorer, converted to **National Bank**,
1847. Street elevation has giant Corinthian
pilasters flanking the bays, and lugged
openings. Garden front similar, but with
central Venetian window.

West of the town is the second of the two
Lochmaben Castles, built late 13th century
as a courtyard castle, with moat in front of
the main entrance, spanned by a drawbridge.
An important stronghold for the Scottish
Crown on the west border until the Union of
the Parliaments in 1603, but declined rapidly
and was used as a quarry. Most surviving
masonry is corework, the ashlar covering
having been removed.
*Historic Scotland; may be viewed from the
perimeter fence*

Lochmaben Hospital, 1908, F J C Carruthers
Two diphtheria wards of corrugated iron, with
standing seam roofs, on brick footings. Their
utilitarian character relieved by bell-cast roofs,
and by little lavatory pavilions with jaunty
pagoda roofs.

HIGHTAE
An early foundation, with narrow, curving
streets giving its origin away. At its heart the
Royal Four Towns Hall, 1910, John T
Laidlaw, harled with red sandstone dressings
and statue of **Robert the Bruce**, who
established four burghs nearby, hence the
name. **Church**, built as a Relief Church,
1796, and substantially altered for the
Reformed Presbyterians (Cameronians),
1865, when adjacent **manse** constructed.
Notable for the persistence of covenanting
loyalties in the area.

From top *Lochmaben Tolbooth; Old
Bank House; Moat, Lochmaben
Castle; Lochmaben Hospital
diphtheria wards.*

Jardine, Matheson & Co, one of the most successful merchant companies of the 19th and 20th centuries, was founded by Dr William Jardine who went to China in 1802 as assistant surgeon with the East India Company. Settling in Canton, he developed an agency business acting for others on commission, and in 1832, went into partnership with Sir James Matheson. After the firm was ousted from Canton, they settled in Hong Kong in 1841, two years before the territory became a British colony. They overcame many rivals to become the colony's leading merchant company and were instrumental in the success of the Hong Kong Bank (now part of HKSB bank). In 1866, when the London banking house of Overend and Gurney failed spectacularly, a Jardine Matheson steamship raced the mail steamer carrying the news to Hong Kong reaching the colony in time for the company to withdraw its balances with local banks in gold and jewels before its competitors could do likewise. The company was heavily involved in the opium trade from India to China and, later, were major players in the tea trade, all part of a complex web of interests, in which the company's reputation for acuity and probity played a very important part.

Right *Elshieshields Tower.* Below *Halleaths.* Bottom *Shillahill Bridge.*

The Corncockle Quarries exploited the Permian red sandstone, in which, from time to time, dinosaur footprints were found. The quarries were worked on a large scale in the late 19th and early 20th centuries, supplying stone for buildings in both Glasgow and Edinburgh. They were rail-connected from the mid-1880s.

Halleaths, rebuilt 1868, David Bryce (demolished)
Large baronial mansion, asymmetrical with square balustraded entrance tower with Jacobean-detailed doorpiece. Good range of contemporary estate buildings remain.
Halleaths Home Farm, Bryce farmhouse, 1½ storey with tall gabled dormers, bracketed eaves. Large **stable** court, 1843, perhaps by Walter Newall.

265 **Elshieshields Tower**, from 16th century
Oldest part of the house is a château of 1567, probably built up from ground floor of 15th-century tower; extended, mid-18th century, and, again, early and mid-19th century. Single-storey west wing added, 1848. Restored by Schomberg Scott.

266 **Shillahill Bridge**, 1867, George Cadell Bruce
Five-span masonry bridge over the river Annan, with segmental arches, increasing in size to the centre, and piers with moulded cutwaters.
Kinnel Bridge, 1723, John Frew, perhaps designed by William Luckup, and widened, 1821, John MacDonald; two main spans plus a flood-relief span, rubble-built, with massive cutwaters on the downstream (original) side.

Corncockle Farmhouse, early/mid 19th century
Unusual 1½-storey farmhouse, with castellated centrepiece. Doorcase has paired pilasters and semi-elliptical sculptured pediment, with flanking ground-floor windows set in shallow pilastered bays with quatrefoil panels below. Skew-puts with obelisk finials. Nearby
267 **Corncockle Quarries** were a major source of quality red sandstone in the late 19th and early 20th centuries.

RCAHMS

Spedlins Tower before restoration.

268 **Spedlins Tower**, *c*.1500
Fine tower-house of the Jardines of Applegarth, extended upwards, 1605, into a rare double-pile. As befits the date of the upper section, there is no wall-walk, but there are corner turrets, crowstepped gables and prominent wallhead chimneys. Restored, 1988-9.

HODDOM
269 **Knockhill**, 1777
Modestly scaled Georgian country house inscribed *too small for envy, for contempt too great*, and a little old-fashioned by time of building. Two-storey and basement, five-bay front with Roman Doric portico topped with steep, narrow, pediment (compare with Tinwald (p.37) and Craigdarroch (p.64)) and recessed tripartite doorway. Canted full-height bay on right, lower canted bay on left. Steep-swept piend roofs crowned with heavy stacks.

Knockhill House Stables, *c*.1780, neat, vernacular, with groom's cottage to the rear and flanking forward-facing wings, each with a coach-house at the front end.

Cleuchland House, *c*.1840, in the style of Walter Newall
Long low single-storey house with pedimented and pilastered doorway, timber-mullioned windows with lying-pane glazing.

270 **Shortrigg Farm**, late 18th or early 19th century
Typical improvement steading on a hill, with

Knockhill was built for Andrew Johnstone of Knockhill, who had been transported to the West Indies as a punishment for his involvement in the 1745 Jacobite Rising.

Below *Knockhill*. Bottom *Windmill, Shortrigg Farm.*

Hume

Hume

circular slated horse-engine house and slender three-storey windmill tower, both built to provide power for a threshing machine. Windmill tower has late-Victorian conical cap.

Some fine farmhouses and steadings in the parish: **Castlebank farmhouse**, early/mid 19th century, trim two-storey, three-bay sandstone ashlar with Roman Doric porch; 271 **Meinfoot farmhouse**, late 18th/early 19th century, unusually large, with three-bay central section, broad advanced wings and low-pitched roof.

ECCLEFECHAN

Ecclefechan's fame is tied to that of **Thomas Carlyle**, whose commanding reputation in his lifetime has not long survived it. However, the once-great man has been the excuse for a bronze **statue** on the Haggs, a replica by MacDonald & Creswick, 1929, of the Boehm statue of Carlyle in Chelsea, and for the 272 retention of his **birthplace**, a handsome *c*.1791 building in **High Street**, one of a pair of two-storey houses facing on to a pend, with arched entrance surmounted by Venetian window. Both houses together with wings added in the 19th and 20th centuries, now in the care of the National Trust for Scotland.
Open to the public in summer months

Above *Carlyle House*. Right *Ecclefechan, birthplace of Thomas Carlyle.*

Thomas Carlyle, 1795-1881, was one of the literary giants of the mid-19th century. His first significant publication was *Sartor Resartus* (1831) and he subsequently published major works on the French Revolution, Oliver Cromwell and Frederick the Great. *Sartor Resartus* – the tailor re-patched – is based on Carlyle's experiences in Ecclefechan and at Edinburgh University, cast in the model of German romantic writing.

Burnswark Hill is a landmark about 4km north of Ecclefechan. On its summit are the ramparts of an Iron Age native fort, with Roman forts to north and south of it, the southern one having three artillery platforms in front of its outer rampart. It is now thought that this was a training ground for the Roman army.

High Street/Church Street

Mainly late 18th or early 19th century: **Carlyle House** has pedimented Roman Doric doorpiece and rusticated quoins; **Ecclefechan Hotel**, late 18th-century coaching inn, remodelled late 19th century, two main blocks – three-storey, three-bay range, with tripartite windows on ground floor, and two-storey block to the north, with single tripartite window on first floor. **Carlyle Place**, single-storey part originally two cottages, one dated 1749 on an elaborate lintel. Two other early buildings survive in **Church Street**: **No 2**, single-storey cottage dated 1778, and **No 1**, two-storey house, with horse-tethering ring.

Though windmills were never as common in Scotland as they were in the Low Countries or in East Anglia, they were used where water-power was scarce in many parts of the country. Early examples seem to have been wooden post mills but, from the late 17th century, stone tower mills were built, initially for grinding grain, but from the late 18th century for driving threshing mills and pumping water.

273 **Hoddom Parish Church**, 1865, James Barbour
T-plan with simplified Gothic details and three-stage gabled tower, for UP congregation. Linked galleries internally, with cast-iron columns and panelled fronts; pulpit, with decorative cast-iron balconied front, set into an arch. Detached **churchyard**, enclosed by rubble wall, contains some fine 17th/19th-century monuments, as well as the site of **St Fechan's** church. **Thomas Carlyle** is buried here, in an iron-railed enclosure, as is **Archibald Arnott**, physician to Napoleon Bonaparte.

Mount Kedar, 1844
Two-storey piend-roofed former Free Church Manse, plainly detailed. In the garden **Mount Kedar Monument**, 1846, James Raeburn; tall ashlar obelisk mounted on corniced plinth commemorating Revd Henry Duncan, tending to both God and Mammon, founding a Free Church and School in Mouswald, and the first Savings Bank, in Ruthwell.

Below *Mouswald Grange.*
Bottom *Rockhall.*

274 **Mouswald Grange**, late 18th century
Extensive range of white-painted farm buildings dominated by large steeply tapering rubble tower of former **windmill**, probably late 18th century, now with conical slated cap. Built to grind oatmeal, and retaining adjoining low-gabled drying kiln (colour page 155). **Steading** is a good example of an improved farm.

275 **Rockhall**, early 17th century
Three-storey, painted rubble laird's house; originally simple rectangle with stair-tower projecting at east. Extended to form L-plan, early 18th century, by adding north-east wing. Windows enlarged, 1850s, door and armorial panel added, interior also largely refitted, 1915, J M Bowie. Barrel-vaulted ground floor to oldest part, main apartments on first floor. Recently reconverted from a hotel to a house (colour page 155).

Brocklehirst, mid-19th century
Large asymmetric picturesque ashlar-fronted country house with *porte-cochère* and balustraded outlook tower; barge-boarded gables. Large run of timber glass-houses to walled garden.

276 **Mouswald Parish Church**, 1816, remodelled, 1929, by J M Bowie, who heightened the walls, built the chancel and Gothicised the windows. Belfry rebuilt, 1929. **School**, 1866, Alexander Crombie, extended 1910, F Adamson, single-storey with over-sailing eaves and Venetian windows.

DALTON
Essentially a kirkton, where four roads meet, with cottages dating from 1760. Remains of a medieval church incorporated in the now-roofless 277 old **parish church**, 1704, in the graveyard; a sophisticated building, with rusticated surrounds to openings and moulded eaves-band, deserving proper consolidation. Present pleasantly simple Early Christian **parish church**, 1894-5, J M Dick Peddie, is one of the finest rural churches of its period. Brick **hall**, 1898, and former **school**, 1854-5, also of note.

278 **Hetland House**, 1868
Two-storey harled and whitewashed double-bow fronted neo-Georgian country house stretched by addition of two-storey bays at each end, altered roofline contributing to present streamlined appearance. Original 1868 centre block has shallow bow-windows flanking central door. Full-height bays added, 1925, roof continuous, now almost submerging paired stacks. Used as seminary with flat-roofed brick addition, 1965, Sutherland Dickie & Copland; now a **hotel**. Interior refitted, 1925, with timber panelling and elaborate plasterwork.

From top *Mouswald Parish Church; Dalton School; Dalton Parish Church; Denbie Doocot.*

Denbie House, from 1706
Two-storey, five-bay country house with steep-hipped roof, rusticated quoins and margins, pedimented Doric doorway with marriage stone *IC MC 6 April 1706* for its Carruthers builders. Principal rooms on ground floor. In detail it relates to Old Dalton Church, probably by the same hand. Original bolection moulded panelling and stone fireplaces inside. Extensive rear addition, 18th and 19th centuries. Nearby 279 **doocot**, 1775: octagonal whitewashed rubble tower contains two tiers of nest boxes; roof lantern pierced by flight holes.

280 **Rammerscales**, 1768

Three-storey, three-by-five-bay red sandstone ashlar, essentially plain, but with two-storey centrepiece, pilastered at first floor, with inset Roman-Doric porch below, built for Dr James Mounsey, formerly Chief Director of the Medical Chancery of Russia. Architect unknown, but may have been the designer of Knockhill (see p.121). Wallhead balustraded and unusually tall ashlar chimneystacks. Interior seems to have been remodelled early 19th century.

Neat octagonal wellhead and small **stable** and **coach-house** range of 1767 to the rear.

CARRUTHERSTOWN

Formerly a wayside village on the Carlisle/Portpatrick road, now bypassed. Old **Main Street** of 19th-century houses, with 20th-century development. Attractive modern
281 **primary school**, 1974, Alastair Macintyre, Dumfries County architect.

CUMMERTREES

In two sections, the old village to the west, mainly single-storey, 19th-century sandstone **cottages**, with single-storey former **railway station**, c.1848, for the Glasgow, Dumfries & Carlisle Railway; **primary school**, 1905, James Tweedie, enlarged, 1992, Dumfries and Galloway
282 Regional Council; and **parish church**, 1777, modified, 1875-6, by John Starforth, and again in 1924. Conspicuous lych-gate is a **War Memorial**, probably also 1924.

Left *Rammerscales.* Top *Well head, Rammerscales.* Middle *Carrutherstown Primary School.* Above *Cummertrees Parish Church and lych gate.*

Top *Queensberry Terrace.* Above
Powfoot. Right *Kinmount, as built.*

283 **Queensberry Terrace**, *c.*1900,
F J C Carruthers
Fifteen terraced houses, in Accrington brick,
part of a seaside development for General
Brook of Kinmount, widely varying in their
architectural treatment, like a cross between
Blackpool and Chelsea. Being more than a
kilometre from the Solway, hardly surprising it
was not successful for its intended purpose.

POWFOOT

Extraordinary seaside village, with range of
single-storey **cottages**, probably for fishermen,
and a very English development of red-brick
284 **houses**, with pleasure grounds. Pow Burn
dammed to form ornamental lake, now
drained. During the Second World War an
explosives factory was built east of Powfoot,
and managed by ICI.

Below *Converted stable, Kinmount.*
Bottom *West Lodge, Kinmount.*

285 **Kinmount**, 1812, Sir Robert Smirke
The young William Burn, thirled to Smirke's
office in London, was executant architect for
this astylar Greek revival mansion which cost
the young Marquess of Queensberry £40,000.
Ruthlessly unadorned originally, the design
relies upon the progression of cubic masses
culminating in a central square stair-tower,
flat lead roofs behind a plain parapet, and
unframed windows set in smooth ashlar walls.
Dubbed by Pugin *the square style*, the
uncompromising lack of detail appealed only to
the most ascetic of palates and quickly became
unfashionable. In 1899, James Barbour &
Bowie set about gilding the lily, adding roof
balustrades and urn finials creating a heavy
baroque feel quite at odds with Smirke's
original concept. Interior originally as refined
as the outside: three-stage atrium/hall with
Doric columns, coffered ceilings; 1899 intrusion
of oak-panelling. Large contemporary **stable
block** by Smirke, converted to **housing**, 1981,

Wheeler & Sproson. Range of estate buildings mostly late 19th century. Around the lake ornament-encrusted Northern Renaissance **bathing house**, Barbour & Bowie; by contrast, gently bio-degrading rustic timber **boat-house**. Picturesque **lodges**, with fine wrought-iron gates, Hannah & Hitchill; larger **west lodge**, F J C Carruthers, half-timbered Tudorish incorporating arched pend over main drive and octagonal stair-tower in re-entrant angle. **Motor house** like a miniature stables range, with pedimented Italianate pavilions linked by an open-fronted courtyard; probably 1907, James Barbour & Bowie.

Sir Robert Smirke, 1780-1867, was the son of an artist. He studied in London, and toured extensively in Italy, Sicily and Greece before setting up in practice. He became one of the architects attached to the Office of Works, and designed several major public buildings, including the British Museum. He built or enlarged about 30 country houses. Some of these, including Kinmount, are in a severe, simplified classical style, termed by Pugin *the New Square Style of Mr Smirke*. Other Scottish buildings by Smirke include Kinfauns Castle, Perthshire, Perth Sheriff Court, and Erskine House, Renfrewshire.

286 **Hoddom Castle**, *c.*1565-8,
Lord Maxwell of Herries
Taken by the Regent Moray in 1568, and again by English forces under the Earl of Sussex, who reduced the outer defences. Additions made late 1630s by 1st Earl of Annandale, and by John Sharpe, a Dumfries man, in 1690s. Further additions, late 18th and early 19th centuries. William Burn made substantial alterations and additions between 1826 and 1832, demolishing most of the courtyard, with circular guest tower and chapel, replacing it with Tudor ranges. Finally, between 1878 and 1890s, the then owner, Edward Brook, a Huddersfield mill-owner, made further large additions.

Above *Pier in the designed landscape of Hoddom Castle.* Left *Hoddom Castle.*

Between 1953 and 1975 demolitions left only the tower and Brook's extensions standing, looking very forlorn. Much altered in its long life, the tower is set in a courtyard, part 16th/17th century, part *c.*1830, and is essentially L-plan, four-storey, with handsomely corbelled wall-walk, with open roundels at the corners. Two-storey, turreted extension built on top of the parapet of the wall-walk, probably *c.*1636-40. North of the tower is a courtyard, with Tudor range on its east side, 1886-8, Wardrop & Anderson, with

The Five Red Herrings (1931) is one of the classic detective novels by Dorothy L Sayers. The protagonists are members of the Kirkcudbrightshire artistic community, and the plot depends on the peculiarities of the geography and transport systems of early 20th-century Galloway.

subsidiary flanking ranges. Baronial service court from 1891. In the grounds (now a caravan park), Jacobean piers, probably from the Burn period (1826-32). **East lodge**, battlemented, with rounded front, probably from earlier 19th century. Nearby, **Hoddom** 287 **Bridge**, 1763-5, Andrew Laurie, elegant, three-span masonry bridge with segmental arches and triangular cutwaters.

Right *Hoddom Bridge*. Below right *Repentance Tower*.

288 **Repentance Tower**

On hilltop overlooking Hoddom Castle, this rectangular watch-tower, *c*.1565, built by Lord Maxwell of Herries, has continuous wall-walk and stone-slabbed pyramid roof with stand for a beacon at the apex, probably 18th-century alteration; as is caphouse over stair to the wallhead. Tower set in burial enclosure, with some much-neglected headstones. *Repentance* inscribed on entrance lintel, and legends abound – but it may be simply, as John Gifford suggests, an admonition to burial ground visitors.

KIRKCUDBRIGHT

Justifiably famous as unusually attractive, a favourite with artists since the early 20th century, the county town of the Stewartry of Kirkcudbright was, in its day, a very significant port (colour page 156). Still an administrative and educational centre, and holiday resort. Because the estuary was important as a harbour, the place had a strategic role at an early date (like Dumfries and Annan), with a royal castle here by the end of the 13th century, and royal burgh status by 1330. Little trace remains of its medieval origins: the street layout visible today seems to be largely 18th century.

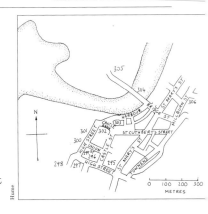

Bridge Street/St Mary Street

Best approached from the north, an outer layer of inter-war housing, is succeeded by Victorian villas, often with original cast- or wrought-iron railings and gates, as the town was far enough from the Central Belt to avoid the wartime drive for scrap. On the corner of Bridge Street, 289 former **railway station**, now a **tea shop**, with open eaves and twin gables to St Mary Street. Beyond are two-storey terraced shops and houses of early/mid 19th century, typical of much of the town centre. Opposite, **Johnstone** 290 **Primary School**, 1847-8, extended 1933, W A MacKinnell, its centrepiece an Italianate single-storey block with central tower, and advanced ends with tripartite windows. Steepled 291 geometric Gothic former **Kirkcudbright Free Church**, 1872-4, John Honeyman, sensitively converted to housing. Late 19th-century **Royal Hotel**, corner St Mary Street/**St Cuthbert Street**, followed by **Royal Bank of Scotland**, and the mildly Gothic **Bank of Scotland**, 1895, William McEwan, forming very solid approach 292 to the **Town Hall**, 1878-9, Peddie & Kinnear, tall two-storey Renaissance block.

293 **Kirkcudbright Parish Church**, 1835-8, William Burn
Large, red sandstone cruciform church, with lancet windows with zinc-lattice glazing, and octagonal stone spire, interior largely original.

294 **Stewartry Museum**, 1892, Robert Wallace
Rectangular block with central battlemented tower and galleried museum hall inside. Artefacts include the clockwork mechanism from the Little Ross Lighthouse and two cast-iron plaques from the old bowed-truss wrought-iron bridge over the Dee.

Below *Johnstone Primary School.* Middle *Interior, Kirkcudbright Parish Church.* Bottom *Cast-iron plaque from Old Kirkcudbright Bridge, Stewartry Museum.*

Parish Church Hall, 1892, Alan B Crombie
Red sandstone Gothic with octagonal cupola.

High Street

From top 117 High Street; Old Jail; Old houses next to Tolbooth; Tolbooth.

Creates an entirely different mood with the red sandstone and whinstone of St Mary Street replaced by colour-washed smooth render, a hallmark of the older part of Kirkcudbright (colour page 156). Uniformity of scale and variety of detail, together with a slight irregularity in street layout give a very attractive character, with most buildings late 18th or early 19th century. **Selkirk Arms Hotel**, old coaching inn with mid-19th-century doorpiece. **Nos 115, 117 & 119** are council offices with modern additions and **No 117** has flat bows flanking classical doorpiece. **Gordon House Hotel** and **No 110** are notable. Beyond **Castle Street**, the heavily impressive **Sheriff Court**, 1866-8, David Rhind, with the **Old Jail**, 1815, behind with tall tower, and octagonal caphouse (colour page 156); both castellated and distinctly out of place. A lane beside the court leads to simple Gothic **St Andrew & St Cuthbert RC Church**, 1886. **Nos 66-72**, two notable early 17th-century houses, with arched pends.

Tolbooth, 17th century
Formerly harled, the bulk of this three-storey, rubble building dates from 1625-7, but steepled **clock tower** (lower part originally harled) added, 1642, and one bay added to the west, 18th century. Forestair added, 1742, now supporting **Mercat Cross**, 1610. Altered to form **Visitor Centre**, 1992-3, Stewartry District Council.

Kirkcudbright Academy, from c.1815
Extended substantially, 1901, Alan B Crombie, in low-key classical, with **clock tower**; further extensions, 1958. To the right is the **Cochran Memorial Gymnasium**, 1930-1, W A MacKinnell, rather more boldly classical. West of the school, what is left of the old **castle**, a rectangular mound, with ditch, built late 13th century but abandoned soon after. Gothic, former **United Secession Church**, 1822, now an antique shop. **No 42**, Victorian, with minute turret.

Broughton House, 10 High Street, mid-18th century
Built as a town-house for the Murrays of Broughton and incorporating their earlier house; later the home of the painter E A Hornel, one of

the Glasgow Boys, from 1895 to his death in 1933. Vaulted cellars of the original lie beneath the area. Front rather severe, but behind are early 19th-century large bow, and broad-eaved extension, 1910, John Keppie, housing a gallery, with copy of the Parthenon frieze, and **studio** beyond. **Garden** is intimate, Hornel's own, with Japanese-inspired section.
National Trust for Scotland; open to the public; guidebook

301 **No 8**, though less interesting internally, has more obvious architectural refinement, and good wrought-iron railings; castellated bay at the rear, and circular-plan summerhouse and lookout tower at the end of the garden. Interest on the other side mainly in the Georgian doorcases, of which the double one at **Nos 23-25** is perhaps the most unusual. **Castle Bank**, with **warehouse**, 1880, converted to housing, 1983, and harled vernacular range, now **Harbour Cottage Gallery**.

Top *Doorway, Broughton House.* Above *Jessie M King and E A Taylor's house.* Left *MacLellan's Castle, engraving based on a drawing by A Reid.*

302 **MacLellan's Castle**, from 1581, Robert & Alexander Couper, masons Built for Thomas MacLellan of Bombie of materials from and on the site of former **Greyfriars Convent**, abandoned after the Reformation. Now ruined, it was one of the largest town-houses of its period, anywhere in Scotland, three-storey and attic, on an L-plan, with smaller three-storey jamb ending in a stair-tower and various other projections, including four rounded stair turrets corbelled out above ground level. House is liberally provided with gunloops and shot holes, with armorial panel above main entrance. Inside, a straight stair leads to the first floor, with a hall. Roofless at least since mid-18th century, but viewing gallery now installed.
Historic Scotland; open to the public

Jessie M King, 1875-1949, was the daughter of a minister in Bearsden. Despite parental opposition she studied at the Glasgow School of Art, where she was much influenced by the circle of Charles Rennie Mackintosh. She was primarily an illustrator with a very personal and decorative style, but also designed jewellery, fabrics and wallpapers. In 1908 she married **E A Taylor** and they spent some time in Paris before returning to Scotland in 1914 and setting up home in Kirkcudbright. Taylor was a year older than King and was, like his wife, involved in craft design as well as painting and etching. He was particularly noted for his furniture designs for Wylie and Lochhead of Glasgow. He died in 1951.

Ronald Searle in 1941 modelled his St Trinian's Girls on the daughters of Kirkcudbright artists, W Miles Johnston and his wife.

Kirkcudbright deserves its reputation for charm. It has been well looked after by its inhabitants and by successive local authorities. It is a shining example of a town which has made the best of a very mixed basket of assets.

Peter MacGregor Chalmers, 1859-1922, was one of the finest and most sensitive church architects in Scotland in the late 19th and early 20th centuries. He was an advocate of the Romanesque style, which he used extensively, as in Colvend (see p.138) and Urr (see p.141). At Ardwell (see p.213) he used a simple, dignified Gothic style.

Right *Greyfriars Scottish Episcopal Church*. Below *Kirkcudbright bridge.* Middle *Harbour*. Bottom *Former corn mill (now pottery)*.

Little **Greyfriars Scottish Episcopal Church**, remodelled 1919, Peter MacGregor Chalmers, has a complicated building history involving the adaptation of the Greyfriars Convent Church as the parish church, 1571, and the building of a burial aisle (complete with mural tomb of MacLellan and his wife, Grissel Maxwell) which now serves as the church. **War Memorial**, 1921, G H Paulin.

Castle Street, **Union Street**, and the eastern section of **St Cuthbert Street** are all pleasing rather than distinguished.

Harbour Square is on the site of a wet dock filled in when the present harbour was rebuilt, 1910, J & H B Eaglesham; **harbour** now used mainly by pleasure craft and fishing boats. 304 Upstream is the reinforced-concrete **bridge** over the Dee, 1924-6, Blyth & Blyth & L G Mouchel & Partners, with five bowed spans, echoing the form of its wrought-iron predecessor. At the 305 north end of the bridge is the **Kirkcudbright Creamery**, 1934-5, Alexander Mair, with notably elegant *moderne* front block.

Houses in **Millburn Street** and **Townend**, its southern extension, more vernacular in character, and later than those in the town centre, but the mixed whinstone colours and sandstone or stucco dressings have their own 306 charm. Former town **corn mill**, Millburn Street, *c.*1800, L-plan, with kiln at rear still with its ventilator; a studio pottery for many years.

AUCHENCAIRN
Founded as an agricultural village, with associated fishery and small port at **Balcary**. Vernacular buildings of that period include late 18th-century, two-storey, three-bay gabled former **Commercial Hotel**, with tripartite windows on ground floor, and **Craignair**, early 19th-century, double-pile house, two-storey, three-bay,

Stake net fishing for salmon and
sea-trout was formerly common on the
Solway Firth, and was also practised
in other parts of the Scottish coast. A
stake net is a *fixed fishing engine*, with
a line of nets supported on a line of
stakes, encouraging fish to swim into a
bag net at the end of the row of stakes.

Hume

Left *Auchencairn Church.* Below
from top *Solwayside Guest House;
Balcary Tower; Salmon stake nets,
Balcary Fishery; Auchencairn House.*

with gabled timber porch.

During the 19th century it became a watering
307 place and estate village for **Auchencairn
House**. Simple Gothic **church**, built as chapel
of ease, 1855, mainly granite, with red
308 sandstone front. **Solwayside Guest House**,
Main Street, the most striking building in the
village, very English two-storey and attic with
open eaves, red and white brick, above a range
of three former shops with timber fascias.

309   Three-storey, castellated **Balcary Tower**, later
19th century, picturesquely sited on a promontory,
with 20th-century tower on two-storey wing.
Idiosyncratic detailing: stepped castellation, rustic
quoins and window margins (colour page 155).

310 **Balcary Fishery**, mid-19th century
One of the few surviving centres of stake-net
fishing for salmon in south-west Scotland, with
single-storey cottage, store and net-drying
posts. The nets, unusually long, stretch out
into **Balcary Bay** towards Hestan Island.

311 **Auchencairn House**, *c.*1860
Rebuilt and extended, W R Corson, for Ivie
Mackie, Lord Mayor of Manchester. Two
vaguely Jacobean ranges: the taller, 1875,
two-storey and attic, with single-storey
canted bays and **tower** with oriel; lower
range, more domestic in scale, with
pedimented and advanced end bays. Striking,
tall, castellated **lodge**.

Collin House, earlier 19th century
Two-storey and basement, three-bay gabled
laird's house, with railed stair to inset entrance
with consoled cornice. Lower, set-back wings.

312 **Orroland**, from 16th/17th century
Two-storey, three-by-two-bay laird's house,
with 19th-century west wing, probably
remodelled, *c*.1800, from earlier house, with
bowed porch, *c*.1900.

DUNDRENNAN

Modest village set above remains of 12th-
century Cistercian abbey. Germanic Gothic
313 **Rerrick Parish Church**, 1864-6, W R Corson,
the dominant feature, with saddleback tower
and enormous rose window. Former **church
hall**, 1783, John McClure & Gilbert Liviston,
originally a school, probably the oldest school
building in Galloway. Present **primary school**,
1851-2, extended, 1911, Robert Wallace.

Top *Orroland.* Above *Dundrennan.*
Right *Dundrennan Abbey.*

314 **Dundrennan Abbey**, founded 1142,
by King David I and Fergus, Lord of Galloway
Consists of consolidated ruins of the Cistercian
house *which the brethren of Rievaulx built*, and
which provided Mary Queen of Scots with
shelter for her final night on Scottish soil. First
phase of building (transepts and presbytery)
completed 1165, and almost immediately
altered to provide three transept chapels to
each side. Body of the eight-bay nave
completed by the turn of the 13th century.
South of the abbey, mid-13th-century **cloisters**
and **chapter house**, with fine pointed-arch
portal. Partially ruinous by 1543, and further
pillaged after the Reformation, east end used
as church until 1742. Transepts are the most
intact portion, preserving round-arched

Chapter house, Dundrennan Abbey.

Romanesque openings from earliest phase of
building. Taken into state care, 1841, the work
of repair and restoration ongoing. Small
museum collecting together interesting carved
fragments and finds. Fine effigy tombs include
that of an unknown 13th-century abbot, who
had been murdered.
Historic Scotland; open to the public

315 **Orchardton House**, 1881, perhaps by
Wardrop & Reid
Asymmetrical baronial house for William
Robinson-Douglas encasing small, elegant,
classical house, 1761, only traces being some
pinned rubble among bull-faced baronial
granite. Roofline enlivened by corbelled turrets
with spiky finials, pilastered neo-Jacobean
doorpiece leads to entrance hall with inserted
medieval carved piscina, perhaps pilfered from
nearby Dundrennan. **Stables**, an interesting
group with some eccentrically applied classical
elements, columns and pediments, possibly
cannibalised from original house.

Top *Arch stones excavated during
consolidation work at Dundrennan
Abbey.* Above *Orchardton House.*

Port Mary House, later 18th century
Two-storey-attic-and-basement T-plan, with
Venetian windows, added 19th century, in the
front of the jamb.

316 **Buittle Old Church**, 13th–16th centuries
Most complete example of a medieval parish
church in the south-west: 13th-century nave
with round-arched openings; wider chancel
with three-lancet east gable probably 14th
century; small belfry atop west gable, 16th
century (colour page 156). Old church in use
until the building of the present **parish
church**, 1819, Walter Newall, in Gothic, on a
budget of £1000; windows have American
redwood tracery and leaded panes. James
Barbour added the chancel, 1902; stained
glass, 1920, by Douglas Strachan.

Choir, Buittle Old Church.

317 **Buittle Place** (**Old Tower of Buittle**),
16th century
Built for the Gordons of Lochinvar, apparently
ordinary L-plan tower with stair-turret
corbelled out over door in re-entrant, but
complex history of alteration and
reconstruction. Main block incorporates earlier
tower entered by (demolished) external
forestair to blocked first-floor door in north
wall. Jamb, therefore, is an addition, though it
contains no trace of the expected stone spiral

Buittle Tower.

stair; modern timber stair gives access to the hall. A 19th-century forestair abuts the south wall leading to an inserted door to first floor and has nothing to do with the 16th-century layout. Described as ruinous in 1789; restored late last century as farmhouse and roofline altered with all traces of the angle turrets adorning the corners removed, save the bottom row of corbels.

Buittle and the Balliols
Buittle was of immense importance from the 11th to 14th centuries as the stronghold of the Balliols, one of the Norman nobility encouraged to settle by David I in an attempt to develop a loyal countervailing power to the native warlords. A raised grassy mound near the farmstead is all that remains of the principal seat of the Lords of Galloway. From the 12th century a motte-and-bailey castle with earthen ramparts and ditches. By the early 13th century this was replaced by a stone castle built by John Balliol, husband of Devorguilla, and father of King John Balliol, all now vanished.

318 **Orchardton Tower**, late 15th century
A gem, this unique cylindrical tower sits amid gently rolling landscape with commanding view from its diminutive caphouse. Built by John Cairns, who may have had Irish connections, for these round towers are commonplace there. Family accommodation probably provided in the tower with more public spaces being in ancillary buildings, many of which survive (albeit fragmentary): bakehouse, brewhouse, cellars, kitchens and probably a more spacious great hall than that afforded within the actual tower. Interesting details include trefoil-cusped aumbry and piscina and delightful window seats (colour page 156).
Historic Scotland; open to the public

Right *Orchardton Tower.* Below *Palnackie Harbour in the 1960s.*

PALNACKIE
River port just off the Urr; in its 18th- and early 19th-century heyday the port of Castle Douglas. 319 Muddy estuary, with the present **harbour**, c.1850, built with wooden piles backed by wooden planks and branches (colour page 155). Small masonry **warehouse** close by, and some fine 19th-century **houses** built of local granite.

Barlochan House, late 19th-century baronial mansion, elaborately castellated.

320 Southwick Parish Church, 1891,
Peddie & Kinnear
Seizing on the rare opportunity to build a
Stewartry kirk on a greenfield site, the heritors
here rejected the run-of-the-mill Gothic
favoured throughout the district and opted for
a Romanesque design of considerable
sophistication. T-plan in coursed granite with
red sandstone dressings, the T extended by a
wide apse and firmly anchored by stocky
square tower with solid parapet, countered by
dynamic upward thrust of the steep pyramid
roof. Interior no less rewarding: chancel arch
with chevron detail, vaulted chancel and wagon
roof. Arts & Crafts light fittings.

Southwick Parish Church.

321 Southwick House, *c.*1750
Remodelled and substantially extended mid-
19th century with dominating wings with, at
its core, decent two-storey-and-basement, five-
bay, piend-roofed house. **Southwick House
Stables**, 1885, Peddie & Kinnear, two-storey,
rock-faced rubble ranges forming a courtyard,
with arched and gabled entrance surmounted
by slate-steepled **clock tower**; probably
contemporary with the house extension.
Southwick Lodge & Bridge, 1789, tiny
polygonal lodge with lattice windows, hard by
the narrow bridge, overhung by wonderful
beeches, and set to take the motorist by
surprise. **Shawfoot Cottage**, mid-19th
century, Tudor *cottage orné*, with leaded lights
and dramatic chimneystacks. **Southwick
322 Home Farm**, mid-19th century, well-preserved
testament to the expanding dairy- and cheese-
making practices of the time; two-storey
whitewashed dairy range with cottages to its
east end. Cheese lofts, located on first floor,
identifiable by slatted window vents and a run
of pipes connects to the boiler room below to
raise the required temperatures. Large granite
rubble piend-roofed threshing barn, internal
machinery long gone. Iron mill-wheel survives
as does the mill-pond and lade.

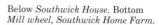
Below *Southwick House*. Bottom
Mill wheel, Southwick Home Farm.

323 Drumstinchall, 1832
Three-storey, three-bay symmetrical laird's
house; low attic storey has unusual oval
windows. Ground-floor windows enlarged into
canted bays, later 19th century, when house
extended to the rear.

Auchenskeoch Castle, *c.*1600, now
embedded in **Castle Farm** steading; all that

Colvend Parish Church.

Kipp Lodge (*middle*), earlier 19th century, two-storey, on elongated octagonal plan, with later single-storey extensions. **Kipp House**, mid-19th-century, two-storey, three-bay house with long single-storey recessed wings.

Boreland of Southwick (*above*), earlier/mid 19th century, splendidly vast group of limewashed rubble buildings with cobbled courtyard. Notable three-bay cart-shed.

remains is part of the east wall and the north-eastern tower. The steading also incorporates a circular horse-engine house and its associated threshing barn.

COLVEND

324 Small village with **hall**, 1933, and **school**, 1900. Early Christian **church** of note, 1910-11, Peter MacGregor Chalmers, with pyramid-roofed tower; interior ecclesiologically correct. Later stained glass.

325 **KIPPFORD**

Small village on the Urr estuary established as centre of granite quarrying, shipbuilding and ship-owning in the 19th century. Now a holiday village, though some older houses survive.

KIRKGUNZEON

Pleasant backwater village bisected by the burn, Kirkgunzeon Lane, spanned by single-arch rubble **bridge**, early 19th century. Single- and two-storey painted rubble, slated cottages; in 1844, a self-sufficient community with *a schoolhouse, a smithy, a joiner's shop, two small shops for groceries ... and an excellent mill [at Millhill], grinding meal and making pot barley.* White-painted simple Georgian

326 **parish church**, 1790, enlivened by 19th-century birdcage bellcote; interior recast, late 19th century, with communion table and font of plain oak; 18th-century pulpit retained. In churchyard **McWhire Monument**, 1831, tall red sandstone obelisk probably to Robert McWhire, late merchant in Halifax. **Manse**, 1804, commodious five-bay, two-storey with attic rectangle with single-storey flanking wings.

Kirkgunzeon Parish Church.

327 **Drumcoltran Tower**, *c*.1570
Plain and simple L-plan tower house; stair
contained in jamb to attics, vaulted ground-
floor kitchen, hall to first, paired chambers
above. Business-like parapet wallwalk sits on
single row of corbels. Guid Scots virtues are
prescribed in its Latin inscription: *Keep hidden
what is secret; speak little; be truthful; avoid
wine; remember death; be pitiful*. Oddly,
economy was not mentioned, though evidenced
by the lack of expensive dressed stone at the
quoins; instead the rounded corners are built in
cheaper rubble.

Corra Castle, probably early 17th century
Remains of a small rectangular tower, now
embedded in a much-altered 19th-century
steading.

Top *Drumcoltran Tower.*
Above *Lotus House.*

328 **Lotus House**
Two-storey-attic-and-basement, three-bay, early
19th-century mansion, with two-storey set-back
flanking wings, *c*.1840. Pedimented doorcase with
engaged columns approached by a perron, with
semicircular basement window in the centre. Now
home of the Camphill Village Community.

The hard light-grey granite from
the **Craignair Quarry**, first used on a
large scale for docks in Liverpool, 1826-
32, and later exported all over the
world, is the characteristic building
stone of the burgh giving a distinctive
crisp, if rather severe, appearance.

DALBEATTIE
Despite its apparent irregularity, a planned
village, laid out *c*.1780 by two local landowners
around **Dalbeattie Burn**, 1781, which
meanders through the town, and which
powered a series of corn and paper mills,
c.1790. Most important local industry was, and
remains, granite quarrying on the Urr.

Below *Bandstand, Colliston Park.*
Bottom *Round House and Town Hall.*

John Street
Colliston Park, laid out 1900, has three little
lattice-steel **bridges** over the Dalbeattie Burn,
329 cast-iron **bandstand** and **War Memorial** in
the form of a mercat cross. Two terraces of one-
storey-and-attic **quarrymen's cottages**, and
former **United Presbyterian Church**, 1860-
1, James Barbour, now a **boys' club**. **Bank of
Scotland**, Maxwell Street, faces bow-ended
Victorian **office**, known as the **Round House**
– the architectural focal point of the town.
330 Behind, two-storey **Town Hall**, High Street,
1861-2, with small **clock tower**.

Craignair Street
Fine, almost-unaltered terrace of Victorian
quarrymen's cottages, and, set back from the
331 road, **St Peter's RC Church**, 1814, the oldest

post-Reformation RC church in Galloway, **tower** added, *c*.1850. Large cruciform granite Gothic former **Craignair Church of Scotland**, now **Dalbeattie Parish Church**, 1878-80, Kinnear & Peddie, with broached stone spire. **Dalbeattie High School**, Haugh Road, 1953, Archibald T Caldwell, a low brick complex. **Port Road** leads to **Dubb of Hass**, the port of Dalbeattie on the Urr, busy in Victorian times with sailing vessels loading granite for export.

High Street
Leads south towards **Kippford** and the **Solway Coast Road** via **Southwick** and **New Abbey** crossing the **Dalbeattie Burn** on the steel-girder **Burgh Bridge**, with granite balustrades of 1930. **Post office**, 1902-3, J A Macgregor, and **shop and office block**, Mill Street, 1883, with fine cast-iron crown. Beyond the street becomes thoroughly vernacular in character, with two-storey terraced shops and houses. Episcopal **Christ Church**, Blair Street, 1875, Francis Armstrong, apse and vestry added, 1955. Pleasingly towered villa, **Alma House**, Mill Street, and former **cinema**, *c*.1930, in handsome *moderne*, now a furniture shop (colour page 189). **Alpine Street** leads from Mill Street past **Park Baptist Church**, built as **Dalbeattie Free Church**, 1880-1, Francis Armstrong, to **Southwick Road**, site of **Barrbridge Mill**, 1837, and H plan **Dalbeattie Primary School**, 1876, with octagonal belfry; east block, *c*.1900, and west block, 1912, James Barbour & Bowie, linked 1965.

URR
Crocketford or **Ninemilebar**
Founded, 1787, by the Buchanites, an apocalyptic sect and, as its name suggests, was a toll-bar nine miles from Dumfries on the Portpatrick Road. **Toll-house** with bowed front, set between two westward roads, still the most prominent feature of this small village, recently expanded by modern housing.

SPRINGHOLM
Planned village of *c*.1800, strung along main road, with some 20th-century housing behind. **School**, 1969, Stewartry County Council.

HAUGH OF URR
Really two villages, the other being **Hardgate**,

From top Shop and office block, Mill Street; Alma House; former cinema; Ninemilebar Toll-house at Crocketford.

with some 19th-century houses and 20th-century public housing. Antiburgher **Chapel**, in Hardgate, 1798, remodelled 1860, reroofed, 1910; now a house. **Hardgate School**, 1866, Alexander Crombie, with recent addition.

335 **Urr Parish Church**, 1914-15,
Peter MacGregor Chalmers
Late work, with tower, replacing earlier church; interior arranged ecclesiologically. Fine monuments in **churchyard**, including **Herries of Spottes** burial enclosure, 1793.

Rockliffe is a seaside settlement, south of Kippford, at the mouth of the Urr. Its most interesting feature is the Mote of Mark, a hilltop fortified settlement of the 5th century AD, originally defended by two concentric ramparts. The outer one was built of stone within a timber framework. When the wall was burned early in the 7th century AD, the stonework melted on the surface becoming *vitrified*. The Mark of the name is traditionally the King of Dumnonia, husband of Isolde, in the story of Tristan and Isolde. Artefacts discovered in 20th-century excavations, and now in the National Museum of Scotland, are consistent with royal occupation of the site.

Left *Aerial view of the Mote of Urr.*
Below *Urr Parish Churchyard.*
Bottom *Seed store, Chapelton Steading.*

336 **Mote of Urr**
Very well-preserved earthworks of 12th-century motte-and-bailey castle, probably for Walter de Berkeley, royal chamberlain – the finest monument of its kind in Scotland. Set in agricultural landscape, in the Urr River valley, it consists of oval mound, protected by bank and ditch, with, at one end, a 'pudding-basin' motte, itself surrounded by a ditch. Magnitude of earth-moving involved in its construction is astonishing.

337 **Chapelton**, 1865
Prosperous four-square farmhouse, two-storey, three-bay with central Ionic porch flanked by bay windows, large rear wing separates kitchens and offices from family apartments. Built for James Biggar who dealt in artificial manures and seeds from the large **steading** across the road. Rubble walled with sandstone dressings, long three-storey grain/seed store in U-plan range; internally floors supported on timber posts.

Spottes Hall, *c.*1784-9
Unusual small mansion, core apparently two-storey-and-basement, three-bay house, typical of 18th-century lairds' houses in Galloway. Imposing central bay added, 1826-8, Walter

141

Hume

Edingham Cordite Works.

Cordite was developed as a substitute for black gunpowder in guns, to reduce the smoke generated. It was patented in 1889 by Abel & Dewar, and became the standard *propellant* explosive in Britain. Edingham was one of a number of cordite factories built during the Second World War, and managed by the Nobel (explosives) Division of Imperial Chemical Industries.

Newall, with flat roof, central wallhead chimney and pilastered porch with flanking balustrade covering entrance stairway. Earlier wings rebuilt, 1873 (east wing), and 1887 (west wing).

Newbank Mill, Springholm, *c.*1804, Two-storey rubble L-plan, built as woollen mill.

338 **Edingham Castle**, probably earlier 16th century. Remains of three-storey tower on rectangular plan, for the Livingstones of Little Airds.

339 **Edingham Cordite Works**
Built during the Second World War for making cordite, a propellant explosive. Reduced remains contain artificial hills for making nitro-glycerine, buildings for mixing ingredients for the explosive, magazines for storing finished explosives and standard- and narrow-gauge railway tracks.

RCAHMS

Right Victoria Street. Below Beechgrove. Bottom Detail, St David's Masonic Lodge.

Dumfries & Galloway Council

RCAHMS

KIRKPATRICK DURHAM
Established, 1783, by local minister, Revd David Lamont, who used a legacy to acquire land and feu it on generous terms. Good example of late 18th-century planned village with two streets of one- and two-storey cottages, Victoria Street and St David's Street. The hope, fairly general in south-west Scotland at that time, was that cotton or woollen hand-loom weaving manufacturers would be attracted to the place.

340 **Beechgrove**, 20 St David's Street, late 18th/early 19th century
Delightfully idiosyncratic, 1½-storey, three-bay house, made notable by its curved and gabled porch, with elaborate fanlight.
   Village hall (former Free Church), 1843, remodelled, 1870, and former **St David's Masonic Lodge**, 1813. Notable houses at **Nos 7, 9 & 10**. Former **school**, 1885.

341 **Kirkpatrick Durham Parish Church**,
Church Road, 1849-50, Walter Newall
Looks older; like many Galloway churches, it
has pinnacled tower. Refurnished, 1949, and
jamb partitioned to form **hall**. **Graveyard**
contains 18th-century stones. Former manse,
Durham House, 1838, Mr Calendar, two-
storey, three-bay with pilastered doorpiece
flanked by slightly advanced tripartite
windows; lying-pane glazing.

342 **Durhamhill**, *c*.1820
Three-storey, three-bay laird's house flanked by
steading ranges. Front windows all three-light.

343 **Chipperkyle**, *c*.1810-15
Most idiosyncratic of the parish's mansions, for
Lt-Col Alexander Maitland, two-storey attic-
and-basement, three-bay symmetrical
platform-roofed. All interest crammed into
central bay: projecting porch with inset
depressed-arched entrance and broken
pediment, approached by railed stair. Small
tripartite window at first floor, and large
wallhead chimneystack with curved shoulders,
forming an attic thermal window. Left of the
porch, ground-floor window has been moved
giving an unbalanced look.

344 **Kilquhanity**, *c*.1820, Walter Newall
Started as calm and beautiful two-storey-and-
basement, three-bay with arched doorway set
in engaged-column architrave. Lower east
wing, added *c*.1840, still classical in detail, but
of markedly inferior quality. Now a **school**.

345 **Old Bridge of Urr**, probably 16th century
Hamlet round the two-span bridge, widened
1772, parapets rebuilt, 1843. Two weathered
carved panels of 1580. Upstream, small
whitewashed waulk mill, and downstream
decaying **Mill of Urr**, with waterwheel, stones
and kiln.

RCAHMS

Dumfries & Galloway Council

Dumfries & Galloway Council

Top *Durhamhill*. Middle *Chipperkyle*.
Above *Kilquhanity*. Left *Mill of Urr*.

Hume

Mill of Urr is unusual in the west of
Scotland in having its corn-drying
kiln separated from the rest of the
mill. This is much commoner in the
east of Scotland.

CROSSMICHAEL

Single street of 19th-century, one- and two-storey cottages (colour page 155) rising towards T-plan 346 **parish church**, 1749-51. Main section, probably 17th century, centrally sited round tower, with 19th-century conical roof. Interior largely early 19th century, retaining box pews. Spectacularly enriched classical **monument** to William Gordon of Greenlaw, 1757, *erected by his disconsolate widow*, built onto slightly earlier burial enclosure.

Auchendolly House

L-plan, rear wing apparently early 19th century, with pedimented Tuscan porch. Extended late 19th century, bow windows added at ground floor, and 1½-storey wing with prominent barge-boarded eaves and rustic veranda.

Glenlochar, late 18th/early 19th century Two-storey and basement, three-bay laird's house, with projecting corniced porch approached by railed stair.

347 **Greenlaw**, *c.*1741

Classical mansion for the Gordons of Greenlaw and Culvennan: well proportioned and devoid of frivolous detail; full-height bowed bays to side elevations soften the design. Ionic pilastered and segmentally pedimented portal providing dignified entry to the *piano nobile*. Alas, burnt out, 1970s, shell remains roofless but intact to eaves level and desperately seeking salvation.

From top Crossmichael Parish Church; The Gordon Monument; Greenlaw; Culgruff House.

348 **Culgruff House**, 1889

Built as wedding present by Robert Stewart for his bride Georgina Elinor, daughter of the 3rd Baronet Cardoness, Culgruff combines Free Style with a dash of baronial, clearly *new money* evidenced by the inscribed motto: *God's Providence is Mine Inheritance.* Splayed butterfly-plan entrance with steep barge-boarded gables; south elevation double-height canted bay window under tall arcade flanked by tall tower. Darkly Jacobean interior with panelling and strapwork ceilings; now a **hotel**.

Danevale Park Stables, mid 19th century Symmetrically planned quadrangular stable block, with central **doocot** tower over entrance to courtyard, and advanced pavilions, all with basket-arched entrances. House demolished.

349 **Glenlochar Bridge**, *c.*1790
Five-arched granite and rubble, spanning the
River Ken (colour page 190). Upstream,
Glenlochar Barrage, 1932, James Williamson of
Sir Alexander Gibb & Partners, vast mass-
concrete bulwark with steel gates, the penultimate
rung in the ladder of dams descending from Loch
Doon to the Solway powering the hydro-electric
scheme (see Tongland, p.165).

350 **Glenlochar Roman Fort**,
1st & 2nd centuries AD
On a site reckoned by 18th-century
antiquaries to be ancient Glenlochar Abbey,
Second World War aerial photography revealed
the extent of the typically grid-iron layout as
an important encampment with several
satellite fortlets; probably housing a large
cavalry and infantry garrison.

LOCHFOOT
Set in bleak moorland, an unpretentious
hamlet of single-storey cottages. **Lochrutton**
351 **Parish Church**, 1819, plain, whitewashed
rubble hall church on rising ground;
embellished, 1889, with red ceramic crest to
roof, bellcote and vestry. Fine tombstones
including twin Ionic aedicules to parish
ministers, father and son, both George Duncan.

Top *Glenlochar Bridge.* Above
Glenlochar Barrage. Left *Engraving
of Hills Tower, 1789.*

**The Galloway Hydro-Electric
scheme** was opened in 1935, with
Tongland and Glenlee power stations
commencing generation in March and
May respectively. The remaining
stations opened in October 1936. As
completed, there were stations at
Kendoon, Carsford, Earlstoun,
Glenlee and Tongland, Tongland
being the largest. A sixth station was
added at Drumjohn, between Loch
Doon and Carsphairn, in 1984. Apart
from the Drumjohn station, all the
others have associated dams, two in
the case of Kendoon. The dam on
Loch Doon is at the Ayrshire end.
The largest of the dams is
Clatteringshaws, which created
a new loch. The Glenlochar Barrage
regulates the level of Loch Ken,
allowing water to flow from storage in
the loch down to the relatively small
storage reservoir at Tongland.

352 **Hills Tower**, 16th century
Rectangular tower probably begun by Edward
Maxwell on taking possession of the lands in
1527. Spiral stair gives access to single
apartment of each floor and to parapet.
Embattled upper works, with chequered corbels
and cannon gargoyles, more flamboyant than
serviceable, probably later to match new
gatehouse, built 1598, by his grandson Edward

Maxwell. Two-storey, with low, gabled upper floor supported on continuous corbelling. Armorial panel with the royal arms of Scotland over outer, round-arched doorway. Abutting south-east gable, 1721, John Selchrig, mason, built *ane good and sufficient house* with kitchen and chamber to ground floor, opening a door into the tower cellar, and providing rooms and closets above. Materials partly recycled from older houses from *the east syde of the closs*; all to cost 900 merks Scots.

Drummore farmhouse, late 18th century
Two-storey, three-bay, symmetrical, with small vernacular pedimented wooden porch and flanking wings, both originally single-storey.

Below *Balmaclellan Parish Church.* Middle *Barscobe Castle.* Bottom *Holm House.*

BALMACLELLAN
Small, mainly 19th-century village on steeply 353 sloping site. T-plan **parish church**, 1753, jamb added, 1833, William McCandlish, and gabled centre of south wall dating from major recasting and re-roofing, 1886. Good 18th-century tombstones. Behind the church, well-preserved 12th- or 13th-century motte. One cottage built, or adapted, as **library**, 1878, by William Barbour of Barlay; now a house.

354 **Barscobe Castle**, 1648; restored, 1971-87, I G Lindsay & Partners
L-plan laird's house of three storeys, following general form of earlier tower houses but without even vestigial defences. Massive wallhead stack and kneeler skew-puts (more crow-slide than crowstep) give distinctive outline. Door remains in re-entrant with armorial panel dated 1648; inside, wheel-stair occupies the whole of the jamb. Restored 1971, by Sir Hugh Wontner (Lord Mayor of London) proudly displaying his initials in time-honoured tradition on spanking new dormer heads alongside those of the original builders William Maclellan (of Bombie) and Mary Gordon.

John Rennie, 1761-1821, started his working life with James Watt, and established his own civil engineering practice in 1791. He designed bridges, canals, docks and harbours, and the pioneering steam-powered Albion Flour Mills, London. Apart from Ken Bridge, built in the last year of his life, he also designed Bridge of Cree at Newton Stewart (see p.176), Threave Bridge (see p.164) and harbours at Portpatrick (see p.211) and Port Logan (see p.215).

355 **Holm House**, early 19th century (demolished 1970s)
Only single-storey U-plan service court of the long dour Doric mansion remains. Contrast could not have been greater; back premises completed in ebullient Elizabethan with extravagant curvilinear gables and barley-sugar chimneystacks. Diminutive **Holm Lodge** gives a good impression of these features; curlicue gables and snoozing lions atop the gateposts.

RCAHMS

356 **Ken Bridge**, 1820-1, John Rennie
Most elegant of Rennie's bridges in the south-
west; granite throughout, five graded
segmental arches leap the Ken's floodplain in
long low streamlined curve. Simple Tudor **Ken
Bridge Hotel**, *c*.1830, built as coaching inn;
chimneys removed, giving a bald appearance.

Ken Bridge.

357 **Ironmacannie Mill**, 19th century
Whitewashed whinstone rubble buildings on
much older mill site. Water-powered grain mill
with kiln building to east; two cast-iron water
wheels survive; larger overshot wheel to drive
three pairs of grinding stones, smaller one to
power kiln bellows.

Below *Ironmacannie Mill*. Bottom
Session house, Dalry Parish Church.

ST JOHN'S TOWN OF DALRY
Large village, on triangular plan above the
River Ken, extended from medieval hamlet,
and developed as planned village by the Earl of
Galloway from late 18th century. Original
settlement probably at the bottom of the hill,
where the mid-19th-century **Bank of
Scotland**, whinstone, with painted dressings,
358 the **Town Hall**, 1859, remodelled, 1895-7, with
curious slated spire with lucarnes, some shops
and the early 19th-century **Clachan Inn** are
gathered round a crossroads. **Main Street** is
lined with pleasing, generally 19th-century
houses. Large, creeper-clad **Lochinvar Hotel**,
with limewashed farm steading and Gothick,
359 cruciform **Dalry Parish Church**, 1830-2,
William McCandlish, with pinnacled tower
(colour page 189), approached through lime
avenue, past Gothic **session house**, 1880,
Thomas Bell, and crowstepped **Gordon Aisle**,
1546. Large arched recess, converted to glazed
porch, 1976, as at Glencairn Parish Church

Hume

Hume

147

(see p.64). Interior largely unaltered, with notable pulpit. Douce white-painted, two-storey and basement, three-bay **manse**, 1828-9, with Roman Doric doorpiece.

Southern Upland Way passes through the churchyard crossing the Ken on a timber-decked suspension **footbridge**.

360 **Earlston Castle**, late 16th/17th century
Bald L-plan, three-storey laird's house, probably for the Gordons of Earlston; spiral stair housed in the jamb up to first floor, thence clumsily corbelled out in re-entrant angle turret. Windows enlarged and fine Renaissance panelling (fragmentary survival), from 1655. By Chalmers' 1826 account *abounding in steep slated roofs, crow steps along the gables, and carefully provided with that indispensable appendage a dovecot. It is whitened and forms a conspicuous object from all parts of the glen.* Crowsteps gone, as are most of the mid-17th-century courtyard buildings. Two-storey addition, 1655, with initials of William Gordon and Mary Hope butted on east gable, demolished 1950; datestone re-set in original block.

Grennan Mill, mid-19th century
Grain ground at this site since 1506, though present whitewashed rubble buildings much later. Last used commercially, 1950, the mill machinery and cast-iron water-wheel driving three pairs of stones can still operate occasionally.

361 **Allangibbon Bridge**, c.1936, Blyth & Blyth
Reinforced concrete with four central arches flanked by pair of depressed-arch dry spans replacing 1816 masonry bridge. **Allangibbon Cottage**, c.1900, Arts & Crafts, with deep off-centre bow front and pend. Timber attic outshot over pend. An exotic sight in this upland Scottish setting.

Top *Earlston Castle*. Middle *Allangibbon Cottage*. Above *Kendoon Power Station*.

Milton Park Hotel, early 19th century
Two-storey cottage extended twice, last, and most elaborately, early 20th century, with half-timbered first floor and veranda.

The Galloway Hydro-Electric scheme was one of the most distinctive, and in its day significant, groups of buildings and structures in Galloway is this important pioneering hydro-electric scheme. It is a tribute to the care that went into its design, by Merz & McLellan and Sir Alexander Gibb & Partners, that its power stations still look modern more than sixty years after they were built, and that the dams and reservoirs they impound are now attractive landscape features.

362 **Kendoon Power Station**, Merz & McLellan & Sir Alexander Gibb & Partners, opened 1936, part of Galloway Hydro-Electric Scheme. One of the larger power stations in the scheme, with a large riveted steel surge tank.

CARSPHAIRN

Staging post on the main road from Dalmellington, consisting mainly of one- and two-storey, 19th-century cottages. Coaching inn, a popular haunt of motorists, now **flats**. **Visitor centre**, 1990, in the form of small three-bay cottage. Also of note are Georgian **primary school**, 1861, and the harled rectangular 363 **parish church**, *c*.1815, altered to 'nave and aisles' layout, 1931-2, when apse added. Long communion table, probably a feature of the original church, survives in the nave. Fine monuments in the **graveyard**, including one to Roger Dunn, Covenanting martyr.

The Galloway Hydro-Electric scheme seems to have originated in the concept of using Loch Doon as a source of power for the Ayrshire side of the catchment, first mooted in 1900, and revived in 1922-3 when the Ayrshire Joint Electricity Authority secured a Parliamentary Order to construct a scheme based on water from Loch Doon. Also, *c*.1922, three residents of the Stewartry, including William McLellan of Merz & McLellan, came together to look at a hydro-electric scheme for Kirkcudbrightshire. McLellan brought Sir Alexander Gibb & Partners in to look, with Merz & McLellan, at possibilities. The outcome was that though the river Dee had potential, large storage reservoirs would be necessary, and these would be prohibitively expensive. The passage of the 1926 Electricity Act, which set up the National Grid, and the failure of the Ayrshire authority to use its powers to develop Loch Doon altered the position. The 1923 scheme was revived, on the basis that a Kirkcudbrightshire scheme could be used to provide 'top-up' electricity to that produced by coal-fired stations, to cope with peak loads, using the Grid to feed Galloway power into the Central Belt of Scotland, where demand was greatest. Eventually, a bill was presented to Parliament in 1929, and despite opposition from coal-mining interests, was passed in May of that year. The first contracts were let in 1931, beginning with the Glenlochar barrage. Great care was taken to minimise the impact on scenery and fishing, and both dams and power stations were attractively designed. Loch Doon Castle was removed from its island site in Loch Doon and re-erected on land overlooking the loch.

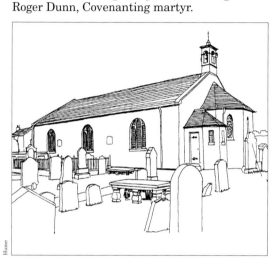

Hume

Dalshangan Stables, earlier 19th century Quadrangular block of one-storey-and-attic buildings, with ball-finialed tower, 1865, over entrance pend. Small, circular, rubble **doocot**, later 19th century, with conical roof.

Left Carsphairn Parish Church. Below Dalshangan Stables. Bottom Suspension Bridge, Kendoon.

Bridge, Kendoon Loch, *c*.1936
Two-span steel-truss bridge built when loch raised to serve as reservoir for Kendoon Hydro-Electric Power Station. **Suspension Bridge**, 364 **Kendoon**, *c*.1936, gives access to the power station and associated houses, on Galloway Hydro-Electric Scheme. The bridge is of the wire-rope type with steel pylons.

RCAHMS

365 **Lead Mines, Woodhead**,
mid/late 19th century
Significant remains of large lead-mining complex; smelter with long flues leading to chimneys, and other buildings including housing.

Hume

Engraving of New Galloway from Scotia Depicta 1804. Note pack horses.

Below Detail of Town Hall, burgh crest (with Belted Galloway cow) and jougs. Bottom St Margaret's Scottish Episcopal Church.

NEW GALLOWAY

More ancient than it appears to be. Established as a burgh of barony, 1630, but failed to grow and, by default, became one of Scotland's smallest burghs. Consists fundamentally of a north/south **Main Street**, with **West & East Ports** leading off.

High Street

Built of distinctive local grey granite, most buildings are one or two storey, with three-storey hotels at the centre (colour page 189). 366 **Town Hall**, remodelled, 1875, and many pleasant vernacular buildings. Opposite, range of three single-storey **cottages**, one with roll-moulded openings, suggesting it was among the first buildings in the new burgh. To the south the tightly terraced character of the town breaks up, with villas in their own grounds, including **Meadowbank**, *c*.1800, and Edwardian **Ardlaggan**, with short terraces climbing the hill.

Small group of Victorian buildings at the north end: mid-19th-century Jacobean **Clydesdale Bank**, **St Margaret's Scottish** 367 **Episcopal Church** and **Rectory**, and two or three large villas. Strikingly sited **War Memorial**, 1922, John W Dods, in the form of a cenotaph. **St Margaret's**, 1904, W M Harrison, picturesque Arts & Crafts with open-eaved rosemary-tiled roof. **Chancel**, 1908, and **lych-gate**, 1912, are ashlar, also by Harrison.

In the garden of **Overton House**, *c*.1900, is an early 19th-century, octagonal **doocot**.

368 Cruciform **Kells Parish Church**, Kirk Road, 1822, William McCandlish, in spectacular rural setting above the town with battlemented tower; altered, 1910, by James Barbour & Bowie, who inserted organ chamber, and renewed the roof and furnishings. Fine monuments in the **churchyard**.

369 **Kenmure Castle**, 16th – 20th centuries
Palace-wise seat of the Gordons of Lochinvar, on man-made mound of medieval origin, with long history of habitation and probably fortification, Kenmure took shape under James Gordon, 1st Viscount Kenmure in 1630. Roofless, derelict (burned out 1950) and encroached on by scrub woodland, it is difficult to gain any sense of the grandeur and drama of the site, save by viewing the roofline across Loch Ken. Thankfully Francis Grose recorded the scene in 1790 before demolition (1817) of the towers and the walls which enclosed the large courtyard. West range, 1630, three-storey with canted stair turrets and squat buttresses to ground floor added, 1879, M R Hatfield. South range largely 1840 on site of 18th-century range, rope-moulded doorway retained from 1630. Close to, flashes of the original shine through in elaborate string-courses, ropes of granite winding in lovers' knots around doors and windows, sadly now smothered in the worst kind of monotone 20th-century cement harl.

370 **Glenlee Park**, 1822, Robert Lugar
Remodelling of small 18th-century house, retained as service wing for picturesque Italianate house. Lugar had to restrict his initial scheme, which included a round tower and circular library. Instead, rather plain, current roofline missing overhanging eaves, the hallmark of the style. Internally, not much of Lugar remains, the house being more lavishly refitted, *c*.1860. **Glenlee Park Bridge**, late 19th century, in bull-faced ashlar with decorative balustraded parapet, is worth a look.

371 **Forrest Lodge**, 1910, G Ramsay Thomson
Wonderful remote setting for this symmetrical Scots Arts & Crafts house; harled with crowsteps and granite string-courses, cosily baronial.

William McCandlish, *c*.1779-1855, was an architect-mason, born in New Galloway. He designed, apart from Kells, the parish churches of Dalry (see p.147), and Glencairn (see p.64) and was also responsible for alterations to Kenmure Castle. He is buried in Kells churchyard.

From top *Kenmure Castle, from* The Antiquities of Scotland *by Francis Grose, 1790; Plan of Kenmure Castle; Glenlee Park, as built; Forrest Lodge.*

RCAHMS

RCAHMS

Dumfries & Galloway Council

Dumfries & Galloway Council

Top *Knocknalling barn*. Above *Old Garroch*.

Right *Clatteringshaws Dam*. Below *Balmaghie Parish Church*.

S R Crockett was born at Balmaghie in 1860 and died at Avignon in 1914. The son of a farmer, he studied at Edinburgh University on a bursary and worked as a journalist while studying at New College for the ministry. The enthusiastic reception of *The Raiders* (1894), with its Solway Firth setting, led him to leave the ministry and live by writing.

372 Knocknalling, *c.*1840
Gabled country house in mild Tudor manner. Two-storey with ball-finialed dormers cutting eaves; all windows basket arched. **Stable block** in chunky granite baronial, *c.*1880, with ball-finialed gablets and clock tower. Marvellously perforated 18th-century barn, each wall punched through with triangular vents; probably for hand threshing and winnowing grain, and drying hay; all activities requiring healthy draughts.

373 Clatteringshaws Dam, 1936
Largest dam on the Galloway Hydro-Electric Scheme, a gravity structure 476m long and **Earlstoun & Glenlee Power Stations**, both 1936, all by Merz & McLellan and Sir Alexander Gibb & Partners.

Old Garroch, late 17th century
Two-storey laird's house with roll-moulded openings, extended at both ends 19th century.

374 LAURIESTON
Picturesque village of mainly 19th-century, white-painted houses, generally pleasing. Former **Free Church**, 1845, now a house, **Beechmount**, where the novelist S R Crockett was educated; monument to him in the form of a tower with domed top, 1932, J Jeffrey Waddell. Present **school**, 1879; enlarged, 1965.

375 Balmaghie Parish Church, 1794; later alterations
T-plan kirk with octagonal tower midway along the long elevation, a pair with its neighbour Crossmichael; both sited on hillocks, their tall towers saluting each other across Loch Ken. Sadly, this visual link severed, 1893, when a full storey was lopped from the tower by James Barbour, one more act of *Barbourism* from the architect responsible for ruining many a good Galloway building (colour page 189).

Top *High Street, Moffat.* Middle *The Colvin Fountain, Moffat.* Above *Provost's lamp outside the Town Hall, Moffat.* Above left *St Andrew's Parish Church, from the old churchyard.* Left *Old Brig Inn, Beattock.*

153

Top *Dryfesdale Parish Church, Lockerbie.* Above *Town Hall, Lockerbie.* Top right *High Street, Lockerbie.* Middle right *High Street, Lochmaben.* Right *Rainwater head, Townhead Street, Lockerbie.* Far right *Statue of Robert the Bruce, Lochmaben.*

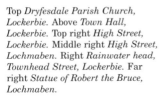

154

Top *Rockhall. Middle Mouswald Grange Windmill.* Above *Palnackie Harbour.* Top left *Balcary Tower, near Auchencairn.* Left *Seashore Roses by Edward A Hornel.* Below *Crossmichael from Balmaghie.*

Top *Kirkcudbright Landscape by Charles Oppenheimer.*
Middle *High Street, Kirkcudbright, with the tower of the Old
Jail.* Above *Orchardton Tower.* Above left *A close off High
Street, Kirkcudbright.* Left *Buittle Old Church.*

Left *Hensol House*. Top *Livingston*. Above *Gordon Chapel*.

376 **Hensol House**, 1822, Robert Lugar
Tudor mansion executed in sparkling grey
granite for John Cunninghame of Lainshaw.
The hammer-dressed granite gives a rougher
texture than Lugar's original drawings imply,
and more chimneys appear than were planned
in his more streamlined vision. Apart from the
recent re-siting of the porch to the service wing,
the house is, inside and out, much as Lugar
intended. Interior continues the *Old English*
theme, ribbed hall ceiling with Tudor arches.
Gardens include **Lainshaw Sundial**, late 17th
century, brought here from Ayrshire. This
magnificent piece of carving has numerous
dials and bears the arms of Sir Alexander
Cunninghame and Margaret Steuart, married
in 1673. Probably also by Lugar are **Hensol
Lodge** & **Bridge**, providing a suitably
impressive prelude to the house.

377 **Livingston**, mid-18th century
Epitome of the smaller classical mansion with
all the usual features. Two storeys with five
bays, central three bays advanced and
pedimented; rusticated quoins and raised
window margins. All standard details but
nonetheless attractive and comfortable for the
modest landowner anxious to upgrade from
tower or castle. Porch added 19th century, but
reuses original architraved door surround.

378 **Gordon Chapel**, *c*.1840
Private Gothic mortuary chapel, despite its
small size with nave and chancel, both
buttressed. Burial place of Admiral Gordon.

379 **Threave Castle**, tower 1369, curtain walls
1447
The tall forbidding tower takes on the
characteristics of its builder Archibald The Grim,
3rd Earl of Douglas. Set on a lonely islet in the
River Dee, Threave was built to withstand all-
comers: five storeys high, simply rectangular on

The history of the **Black Douglases** is
one of shifting alliances. The earldom
was conferred on Sir William Douglas in
1357 by a grateful David II for services
rendered against the English and their
Balliol allies. Threave Castle was
therefore built for Archibald, 3rd Earl of
Douglas, with the blessing of the Crown
to keep the unruly Gallovidians in
check. Archibald's cognomen *The Grim*
coined by the English *becaus of his
terrible countenance in weirfair ... he
tuke grit trawell to purge the country of
Englis blude* (1560, Sir Richard
Maitland MS).
  Clearly not a family to be trifled with,
Douglas influence grew beyond the point
of acceptability leading to the murder of
William, 8th Earl, by James II at
Stirling in 1452. His widow, Margaret,
the *Fair Maid of Galloway*, vowed
vengeance and wed her brother-in-law to
keep the Douglas lands intact. In 1453,
Threave withstood a 13-month siege
against James II's artillery and was
taken only after the garrison succumbed
to bribery. The Douglas lands were
forfeit and the power of the Black
Douglases extinguished. Following its
capture, Threave remained in Crown
hands; it was again besieged in 1640 by
Covenanters and again surrendered
without incurring serious damage. It
was afterwards partly dismantled and
the stones taken away; scavengers
account for its present appearance
rather than the ravages of war.

Threave Castle.

Below Detail, Glenlair. *Bottom* Corsock House.

plan with thick walls and few windows. The 14th-century defences chiefly focused at wallhead where timber rampart supported on corbels allowed unimpeded firing range for archers. The curtain-wall with its round towers was probably the creation of the 8th Earl in 1447 and denotes the shift from man-powered missiles into the gunpowder age (colour page 189).

Inside, tall stone barrel-vault houses two levels; storage for victuals and prisoners below and kitchens above. First-floor **Great Hall** has large mullioned and transomed windows overlooking the river and vast fireplace; second floor contains private chambers and third unheated quarters for the garrison.

To provide additional accommodation for the noble family, and to service the retinue, the island would have been built upon with workshops, kitchens and stores – now only discernible as humps and bumps. Harbour on the west side for communication.
Historic Scotland; open to the public (ferry crossing)

CORSOCK
Straggling village with, at its summit, **hall**, 1889-90, and mid-19th-century harled **school**.

380 At the bottom, **parish church**, built as a Free Church, 1851-2, William McCandlish, extended and recast, 1912, J A Macgregor. Pleasing little **Kirklynn**, 1838-9, built as chapel of ease, possibly Walter Newall; now a house. Former **manse** below.

381 **Old Temperance Inn**, mid/late 18th century Coaching inn, with two-storey, three-bay symmetrical gabled central block, and single-storey piend-roofed wings, left-hand probably contained stables and coach house; now a garage.

382 **Glenlair**, *c*.1830 and later, Walter Newall Small two-storey, double-pile house; later 19th-century Peddie & Kinnear wing now largely roofless. Important as the country home of James Clerk Maxwell, Scotland's greatest scientist.

Corsock House, late 18th century; extended, 1853, David Bryce; 1910, C S S Johnston Rambling baronial, two-storey attic-and-basement, with usual embellishments of crowstepped gables, bartizans, pedimented dormers and bays corbelled out from semi-octagonal to square. Main entrance, probably 1853, has octagonal cast-iron Gothic gatepiers and gates, with unusual cruciform rotating pedestrian gate.

Barwhillanty, 1886, A Thompson Vaguely French mansion, with central pyramid-roofed tower, timber lych-gate porch and eclectic range of Victorian mannerisms.

James Clerk Maxwell, 1831-79, was born in Edinburgh, and held Chairs in Aberdeen, London and Cambridge. His work on electrical theory predicted the existence of electromagnetic waves – later discovered by Herz – the basis of radio and television broadcasting. He has been described as the greatest scientist of the 19th century.

Left *Parton*. Below *Barwhillanty*.

383 **PARTON**
Estate village for Parton House (demolished 1964), built by B Rigby Murray consisting of L-plan terrace of Arts & Crafts houses, 1901, with octagonal communal lavatory (now **summerhouse**) and laundry. **Village hall**, 1908, with corrugated-iron roof.

Parton Parish Church, 1832-3, Walter Newall Simple *Heritors' Gothic*; interior recast late 19th/early 20th century, but some earlier box-pews survive. Remains of **old parish church**, 1592, with 1635 belfry, in **churchyard**; pulpit now in National Museums of Scotland. Recent **monument** to James Clerk Maxwell in front of the churchyard wall.
    Well-defined **motte**, 12th or 13th century, south of the parish church.

Above *Plaque commemorating James Clerk Maxwell*. Left *Loch Ken viaduct*.

384 **Loch Ken Viaduct**, 1861, B & E Blyth
Three long wrought-iron, bowed-truss spans over the loch, with masonry approach spans, for Portpatrick Railway – oldest surviving bridge of its type in Scotland.

Before 1756 Castle Douglas was a tiny hamlet, **Causewayend**, but with the vogue for agricultural improvements, its deposits of marl (a limy gravel) were exploited successfully, and the village of Carlinwark grew up. In 1792 it was purchased by Sir William Douglas of Gelston, who renamed it Castle Douglas, and made it a burgh of barony. Under his auspices a cotton-spinning mill was constructed, but, like all its Galloway contemporaries, it did not survive competition from urban steam mills in Glasgow and Lancashire. The town centre is substantially as laid out by Sir William Douglas, on a grid plan. With its development as a trading centre came administrative, religious and educational importance and it is now a sub-regional centre of considerable significance with bustling streets that contrast with many other burghs in Galloway.

Below *King Street, Castle Douglas.* Bottom *Public library.*

CASTLE DOUGLAS

The most regularly arranged and commercially successful of Galloway's planned towns, like Gatehouse of Fleet and Newton Stewart, intended as a factory town, but like them has proved its worth as a centre for the surrounding area, richer, for the agricultural land is better in the centre of the Stewartry. Simple plan: three parallel streets, with cross-links and outliers, but, unlike its relations, much better architecturally, with good vernacular, badly affected by window and door replacement, and Victorian buildings of some pretension, including churches, commercial buildings and the largest of the Galloway clock towers.

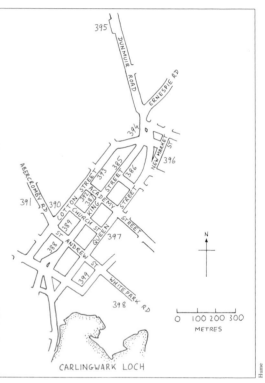

King Street

Original late 18th- and early 19th-century buildings survive only in patches and, as in many a market town, its best buildings are hotels and banks. From Dumfries the first is 385 two-storey Georgian **Crown Hotel**, with later oriel, then **Imperial Hotel**, early 19th century, with Tudor details. Red sandstone **public** 386 **library**, Market Street, 1902-4, Sir George

Washington Browne, with circular **tower**, and
art gallery extension of 1938.

Banks include imposing Jacobean
Clydesdale Bank with **No 61**, former **Union
Bank**, also Jacobean. Granite **Royal Bank of**
387 **Scotland**, 1864. **Post office**, 1969-70, one of
the town's better modern buildings, and beyond
Jacobean **office** block, *c*.1890 (colour page 190).
Douglas Arms Hotel and former **Merrick
Hotel**, both built as coaching inns, earlier 19th
century. Urban character ends with tall
388 octagonal **clock tower**, 1934-5, W F Valentine,
replacing late 18th-century town house and
steeple destroyed by fire (colour page 190).

Abercromby Street
389 Italianate **Town Hall**, 1862-3, James Barbour,
extended to the west, 1902, and large Gothic
390 **RC Church of St John the Evangelist**, 1867-
8, George Goldie, with small spire. Former **UP
Church**, 1870, James Barbour, its gable
unusually treated with recessed arch and
containing rose window – a badge of this
denomination. Joyous pair of Victorian semi-
391 detached **villas**, with wooden porches, opposite.

Cotton Street
Notable buildings include two schools:
392 **St John's**, 1872, single-storey, first-generation
Board school, and former **Higher Grade**
393 **School**, 1910, J A Macgregor, stark two-storey,
mildly classical, now **community centre**.
Other interesting buildings include **police
station**; two-storey and attic double-gabled
villa; and romantic red sandstone baronial
394 **villa**, Dunmuir Road. Three-storey
international-modern **Castle Douglas High**
395 **School**, Dunmuir Road, 1958, Stewartry
County Council.

Pleasing two-storey granite terraced houses in
Queen Street. **Castle Douglas Auction**
396 **Mart**, New Market Street, *c*.1900, has octagonal
yellow-brick auction room with pyramidal roof.

From top Clydesdale Bank, King
Street; Villa, Dunmuir Road; Castle
Douglas High School; Auction Mart,
New Market Street.

397 **Castle Douglas Parish Church**, 1801
Started life as a Relief church, acquired,
c.1870, by Reformed Presbyterian Church,
when the United Presbyterians moved to their
new church in Abercromby Street, and
substantially remodelled, with curious spire
that overhangs its supporting tower. In 1923,
when United Free Church, transepts and
chancel were added.

The town gained much from the coming
of railways. A branch from Dumfries
was opened in 1860, and in the following
year this was extended to Stranraer and
Portpatrick. Three years later a branch
to Kirkcudbright was opened. These
lines reinforced the role of Castle
Douglas as a trading centre, especially
as a cattle market, and as a shopping
centre for the farms and villages round
about. Though by the 1890s there were a
tannery, an agricultural implement
works and a mineral water works,
manufacturing was never anything
other than peripheral to the success of
the town.

St Andrew Street
Sequence of large 18th- and early 19th-century terraced houses and villas ending at **St**
398 **Ninian's Episcopal Church**, 1856-61, E B Lamb, chunky, robust, whinstone with granite dressings, squat with massive tower, formerly with spire.

Lochside Road leads to **Lochside Park**, a suitable setting for the shallow but very picturesque **Carlingwark Loch**.

399 Former **Castle Douglas Parish Church**, Lochside Road, 1869
Simple Gothic, with tall castellated tower with Gothic cap-house on one angle. Much enlarged, 1881, James Barbour, who also built the **tower**, 1890. **Chancel**, 1931, J Jeffrey Waddell. Converted to **theatre**, 1992.

Top Doorway of villa, St Andrew Street. Above St Ninian's Episcopal Church.

400 **Threave House**, 1872, Peddie & Kinnear Scots baronial red sandstone villa for William Gordon, a Liverpool businessman, now **National Trust for Scotland School of Gardening**. Usual range of devices culled from antiquarian source books: Castle Fraser drum tower, flat-roofed with balustrades and ogee-roofed cap-house; mullioned and transomed windows, triangular or segmental pedimented dormers, angle turrets. **Stables**, 1872, smaller-scale baronial and more enjoyable than the house. U-plan block with central gabled **carriage house**; taller round turret to left with fish-scale slate roof. **Lodge** loosely Gothic with timber porch. L-plan **visitor centre**, 1975, Bill Murphie, with central octagonal pavilion; timber-boarded walls, slate roofs.
National Trust for Scotland; open to the public

Below Threave House. Bottom Douglas Mausoleum.

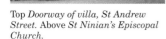

KELTON
Scattered hamlet forming a kirkton, with fragmentary remains of **old parish church**, 1743, and two Georgian burial enclosures in the
401 **churchyard**. Present **parish church**, 1805-6, remodelled, 1879, R Rowand Anderson, who lined the walls internally with the red tiles of which he was so fond (see also Holy Trinity Scottish Episcopal Church, see *Stirling & The Trossachs* in this series). Further additions, 1895 and *c*.1930.

402 **Douglas Mausoleum**, *c*.1820
One of Dumfries and Galloway's most extraordinary buildings, in a wooded setting

north of the church. Fabulous Aegypto-Grecian mausoleum of Sir William Douglas with deep pagoda roof, ramped Doric portal and exquisitely carved frieze. Magnificently theatrical, though the bowler-hatted supporters of the Douglas crest strike a note of farce. Architect unknown, the most likely candidates are Walter Newall whose sketch-books contain similar designs, or a collaboration between William Douglas (Sir William's nephew) and the landscape painter Hugh *Grecian* Williams with whom Douglas *did* the Grand Tour (colour page 190).

403 **Gelston Castle**, *c*.1805, attributed to Richard Crichton
One of the unsung heroes of south-west architecture, a romantic Adam-style castle built of the finest red sandstone as the seat of Sir William Douglas. Strictly symmetrical square plan, round towers at the corners, crenellated parapet with the central bay a sophisticated balance of triple-arched openings and rather light-hearted arrow slits. Curved perron stair (now demolished) formerly ascended to the *piano nobile*; a touch too baroque for the desired martial effect. Garden front gentler with double bows flanking a taller canted central bay. Sadly now a roofless shell.

Sir William Douglas, 1745-1809
Son of the impecunious Laird of Balsalloch, William Douglas amassed a fortune through judicious investment and trade with the Americas to the extent that he retired from business under 50 and devoted himself to life as an improving landowner in his native Galloway. Founder of Castle Douglas and Newton Douglas (later Newton Stewart), Douglas was not inclined to let such civic virtue go unnoticed, his shameless canvassing being finally rewarded with a baronetcy in 1801. His love for Galloway was never in doubt, though; he was buried at Gelston *in earth brought from Balsalloch, at his own request.*

Left *Gelston Castle*. Below *Gelston Stables.*

404 **Gelston Stables**, *c*.1805, attributed to Richard Crichton
Symmetrical stable-block well converted to holiday accommodation. Central pend to courtyard with impressive ashlar hexagon tower; the slightly taller end pavilions are former carriage houses. Early 19th-century **coach-house**, less well known than the stables, has pointed-arched windows, a later box porch; extended by two bays, late 20th century.

Old Bridge of Dee.

When completed, **the Galloway Hydro-Electric scheme** was the largest integrated hydro-electric installation in Britain. It did not, however, meet with universal approbation. One local man wrote:

*A raider comes today who kills
The glories of our glens and hills
With unheroic Acts and Bills
And 'private legislation':
The company promoter's pen
Will dam the Deugh and dam the Ken
And dam the Dee – oh damn the men
Who plan such desecration.*

As befitted a major public works scheme of this period, the architecture and engineering were clean-lined and had *moderne* overtones. The dams were largely of concrete construction, in some cases being arched on plan to resist water pressure. Flood-gates (sluices) were provided, of suitably monumental scale and design. At Kendoon and Tongland large riveted-steel tanks, on arched reinforced concrete bases, were provided to take the water in the turbine pipelines in the event of a sudden shut-down of the power station, preventing damage to the pipelines from the energy contained in the moving mass of water.

Hume

405 Old Bridge of Dee, 1737
Previously known as *Granny Ford* bridge, this rubble-built four-archer is the best-preserved 18th-century bridge in the area. Carriageway, still perilously narrow, escaped *improvement* thanks to bypass by John Rennie's **Threave 406 Bridge**, 1825, further upstream; 1986 widening, Barr & Co, doubled the width of the carriageway to the south and involving re-cladding new south elevation with the original granite masonry, though the original slightly curved profile has been straightened. In contrast, one is hardly aware of having crossed a bridge.

RHONEHOUSE OR KELTON FELL
Small 19th/20th-century village of one- and two-storey houses, many now much altered.
407 Buildings of note are **Hall**, *c.*1900, looking like a church, with pointed windows, and **Millhill**, early 19th-century, two-storey, three-bay house with rusticated quoins and pedimented and pilastered doorway.

Airieland House, 1895
Two-storey, four-bay, near-symmetrical, with mullioned and transomed windows, and projecting pedimented Ionic-columned porch.

Ingleston Farmhouse, 18th century
More pretentious than most, three-storey, three-bay, with tripartite windows on ground floor flanking pedimented and columned porch. Later additions to rear.

408 Dildawn House, 1813, Walter Newall
Handsome two-storey-and-basement, four-bay mansion, with piended roof and spine-wall chimneystacks. Advanced central bays extended at ground floor to form pilastered three-bay porch, 1852, with Roman Doric-columned entrance. Earlier 19th-century

Below *Billies Farmhouse.*
Bottom *Dildawn House.*

Dumfries & Galloway Council

Dumfries & Galloway Council

409 Billies Farmhouse has its wide-eaved Italianate form contradicted by its Gothic centrepiece in the style of James Gillespie Graham.

TONGLAND
Curious collection of buildings on the banks of the River Dee, with small Tudor **parish**
410 church, 1813, with tower, now disused.
Churchyard has remains of **old parish church**, 1773, incorporating doorway from Tongland Abbey, founded probably, 1218, as Premonstratensian house. Granite **mausoleum** of the Neilsons of Queenshill contains busts of James Beaumont Neilson, inventor of the hot-blast system of iron-smelting, his wife, and his son Walter Montgomerie Neilson, founder of Neilson & Co, locomotive builders in Glasgow.

Across the river, First World War concrete-framed factory of **Galloway Engineering Co**, built to make aero-engines, adapted after the war to make *Galloway* motor cars. Victim of 1920s recession, but has found new use as store, with most of its glazing bricked in.

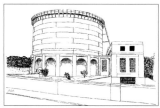

411 Tongland Power Station, 1936, Merz & McLellan and Sir Alexander Gibb & Partners, engineers
Built as the lowest and largest station in the Galloway Hydro-Electric Scheme, art deco concrete station complemented by riveted steel surge tank, on reinforced-concrete arches, to relieve pipeline pressure in case of sudden switch-off of water turbines. Power station supplied with water from reservoir impounded by concrete arch and gravity dam with monumental floodgates. Old two-span **bridge**, 1737, behind.

From top *Neilson family mausoleum, Tongland Parish Church; Galloway Engineering Co; Surge tank, Tongland Power Station; Tongland Bridge, engraving by P Nasmyth.*

412 Tongland Bridge, 1804-8, Thomas Telford
A Telford masterpiece spanning the Dee, the unusual rustic appearance of this bridge, with its triple flood-relief arches on each side of the large central span and castellated parapets, was apparently due to Alexander Nasmyth, the landscape painter. As with other large Telford bridges, the roadway is carried on spine walls rising from the arch rings, said to be the first bridge in Britain to use this technique.

RINGFORD
Small village of 19th- and 20th-century houses, now bypassed.

James Beaumont Neilson, 1792-1865, born at Shettleston, Glasgow, was the first manager of the Glasgow Gas Works, and a scientific consultant. His discovery that the use of heated air in blast furnaces for iron smelting reduced fuel consumption and improved the output of iron revolutionised the Scottish iron industry. His *hot blast process* is still universally used in the modern iron industry.

The last abbot of Tongland was Damian, an Italian alchemist, who tried to fly from the battlements of Stirling Castle, in the presence of James IV. He landed in a dunghill, breaking his thigh bone, a failure attributed by him to the use of the feathers of a dunghill cock in his artificial wings.

Lodge, Argrennan House.

Bogra House.

Barwhinnock House.

413 **Argrennan House**, 1818, attributed to James Gillespie Graham
Two houses in one, with later 18th-century house now relegated as rear wing of Graham's magnificent neo-Greek mansion. Front so similar to Graham's Mount Melville, 1821 (see *The Kingdom of Fife* in this series), that no other architect is likely. Long severe seven-bay front with central Tuscan-columned porch giving onto elegant Doric-screened hall. Interior preserves much original timber and plasterwork of both builds, recently well restored. East elevation of old house relatively intact preserving central bow with delightful Venetian window. **Walled garden** and rose garden with fountain, 1821.

Argrennan Lodge, probably also by Graham, a pretty cottage with lattice windows and spindly Gothic porch.

414 **Bogra House**, *c.*1920
Interesting rather than immediately appealing two-storey, three-bay symmetrically fronted house, with low-pitched piended roof, built as fishing lodge for the Neilson family. Advanced central bay has rounded corners, corbelled to square above eaves' level, and is flanked by one-storey canted bays tucked in to the angles of the bay. Doorway with broken pediment, central window with low-relief arched head and two-storey rounded bay on west end.

TWYNHOLM
Large village of mainly 19th-century vernacular houses, with former **school**, possibly 18th century, extended 1844-5 and 1862-3, present **primary school**, 1911, J A Macgregor, added 415 to, 1954, and Tudor **parish church**, 1818, re-roofed and remodelled, 1913-14, but retaining two earlier box-pews, porch added, 1963.

416 **Cumstoun**, 1827-9 and later,
Thomas Hamilton
Tudor mansion-house striving for romantic
silhouette and using determinedly Gothic
asymmetry of surface detail to disguise
basically symmetrical classical tripartite
ground plan. Shallow U-plan north (entrance)
front had recessed central bay with projecting
porch flanked by taller projecting gabled
bays. Variety of traceried window shapes and,
up top, all angles clasped by spindly turrets.
All Hamilton's good intent knocked wildly off
balance by 1896, Peddie & Kinnear,
enlargement of east wing, broadening it and
adding large bay windows. Porch shifted
unceremoniously to west gable and replaced
by single-storey addition to the centre.
Similar havoc wrought internally with much
of the original delicate filigree Gothick
detailing lost in favour of darkly Jacobean
baronial styling.

Ruin of **Cumstoun Castle**, possibly 16th
century, in the grounds, and early 19th-
century, 1½-storey, three-bay **Garden House**,
with Gothic semi-dormer windows,
crowstepped gables and porch with concave
leaded roof.

417 **Barwhinnock House**, early 19th century
Soigné Regency cottage/villa, architect
unknown. Double-pile plan; front elevation
appears single storey though is in fact two
storey to rear. Squared dark-whin walls with
contrasting white-painted smooth margins and
quoins. South front has central three-bay block,
bowed end bays with tall Venetian windows
flanking wide Tuscan-columned porch. Lower
single-storey, bow-ended wings. Garden
elevation two storey with centre canted full-
height bay. A stunner inside: double-height hall
with paired stairs ascending in horseshoe curve
to fluted Doric-screened landing. Beneath the
meeting of the stairs, Tudor-arched glazed door
leads to library. Oval rubble-walled garden to
south west. At main drive single-storey whin
lodge with Tudor-style leaded octagonal small-
pane glazing and deeply overhanging eaves.
Double bowed ends.

Top *Cumstoun*. Middle *Entrance
Hall, Barwhinnock House*. Above
Interior, Kempleton Mill.

418 **Kempleton Mill**, 1785
Two- and three-storey rubble mill, formerly
with internal low-breast wheel driving three
pairs of stones, now at the **Mill on the Fleet**
(see p.171) in Gatehouse of Fleet.

Bronze panel commemorating **William Nicholson**, 1783-1849, the Galloway Poet. Born in an *auld clay biggin*, he published collections of poetry and became a noted figure at local weddings and celebrations. Later *he fell into dissipated habits, playing at fairs and markets as a sort of gaberlunzie, the grave at last closing in gloom over the ruins of a man of real genius.*

BORGUE

Small village, mostly 19th century in construction, dominated by late 19th-century 419 **hotel**. **Parish church**, 1814, Walter Newall, a conspicuous landmark and early example of *Heritors' Gothic*, substantially rebuilt and extended, 1897-8, both internally and externally. Fine, late 19th-century Gothic **mausoleum** of the Gordons of Earlston in the **churchyard**. **Village school**, 1803, much altered, 1911, James Barbour & Bowie.

420 Borgue Old House

Roofless remains of substantial later 17th-century Y-plan mansion possibly incorporating earlier fabric. Two-storey-and-attic main range, with three intercommunicating rooms on each floor. Two projecting wings on the south side had one room on each floor; third wing, on the north side, probably contained the stair.

Strung along the sandy coves of the Carrick shore are the idiosyncratic buildings of the 421 **Knockbrex Estate**. Wealthy Manchester cloth merchant James Brown acquired the estate in 1895 for his retirement, beginning an ambitious building programme. His first project was **Knockbrex House**, relatively sober in comfortable Edwardian classicism with luxurious Arts & Crafts interiors. Radiating outwards fantasy triumphs: the garage block becomes **Knockbrex Castle**, 1906, a toy-fort based on Warwick Castle. On the shore, a mass-concrete **bathing house** disguised as a mini-Moorish castle; at the **harbour** mouth twin drum towers topped with leading lights guided pleasure yachts into the port. The whole estate ringed by rustic coped stone walls with inset panels of pebbles in geometric arrangement.

Top *Knockbrex Castle, the 'toy-fort'.* Middle *Chapel, Kirkandrews.* Above *Corseyard.*

422 At **Kirkandrews**, 1906, small rubbly rectangular **chapel**, top-heavy with battlements and buttresses, round-arched doorway with portcullis. Entry through elaborate timber lych-gate with red-tile roof. Pair of Arts & Crafts houses opposite are probably also his.

423 Corseyard, 1911-14

Pièce de résistance model dairy known locally as the *Coo Palace*; Italianate milking-parlour in the form of nave with side aisles, white tiled within. Campanile is part water tower, part grain silo. Never a commercial success, the decaying buildings await rescue. Some charming details

The Braes o' Gallawa'

Oh! Gallawa' braes they wave wi' broom
 And heather bells in bonnie bloom
There's Lordly seats and livin's braw
 Among the braes o' Gallawa'

such as the Egyptian concrete drinking trough, and the keyhole-shaped gateway to the vegetable garden (colour page 191).

424 **Castle Haven**, 1st century BC – medieval; restored, 1905
James Brown of Knockbrex had archaeological interests which found an outlet reconstructing this Iron Age fortified homestead. D-shaped on plan, walls rebuilt above excavated foundations giving a good impression of how the site may have looked. *Accessible to the public*

425 **Rockvale Pier**, Brighouse Bay, late 18th century
Short rubble pier with battered sides and rounded end, with small warehouse at the landward end, built for coastal trading vessels.

Top *Castle Haven*. Above *Rockvale Pier*. Left *Plunton Castle*.

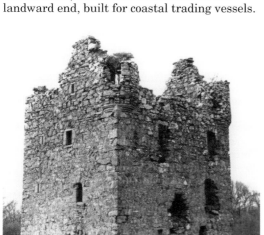

426 **Plunton Castle**, mid-16th century
L-plan tower-house built for the Lennoxes and passing by marriage to the Murrays of Broughton, late 17th century. The Revd Symson notes it as *a good strong house* in 1684, now roofless with much dressed stone from window jambs robbed leaving gaping holes at upper levels. Angle turrets at three corners supported on neat corbel courses with top row of dentils. Stair occupies whole wing accessing usual first-floor hall and paired chambers above. Only unusual feature is that the two vaulted cellars do not interconnect; the northern apartment being accessed directly from the courtyard, a situation extremely rare in a tower of this type. A high courtyard wall did exist to compensate for this breach of security.

Gatehouse of Fleet was founded in the 1760s by James Murray of Broughton as the estate village for Cally, and as a focus for industry. Tanning was an early trade, and brewing followed, but the village could have remained modest if the cotton industry had not been introduced in 1785, when the village was given burgh status. By the mid 1840s there were four mills, but their comparatively small size and remote location led to their early demise. After the closure of the mills the lower group was converted into a bobbin mill, which lasted into this century. The Fleet was made artificially navigable to a timber quay to the south-west, **Port McAdam**, which was restored in the 1970s.

Below *Clock tower, High Street*. Middle *Aerial view*. Bottom *Angel Hotel*.

GATEHOUSE OF FLEET

The Water of Fleet divides the village into two sections, the parish of Girthon, being older and larger, and Anwoth parish, containing most of the

427 more modern housing; **toll-house**, *c*.1823, later extended to form a school, marks the entrance.

428 **Clock tower**, 1871, F T Pilkington signposts the **Murray Arms Hotel**, Ann Street, probably from 1766, David Skimming, a coaching inn (colour page 191). Across **High Street** are former **stables**. Villa-style **Bank of Scotland**, Church Street. High Street runs south-west to the Fleet, with mainly two-storey terraced houses and shops, and red sandstone **Town Hall**, 1884-5, J Robert Pearson, remodelled, 1993-4, Stewartry District Council, set back on the south side;

429 **Bank of Fleet Hotel**, the best 18th/19th-century frontage building in the street. Another coaching

430 inn, **Angel Hotel**, *c*.1800, with Venetian-windowed frontage, faces single-storey-and-basement building, now part of a supermarket, traditionally a tannery. Its juxtaposition with a smart hotel suggests, however, that it was stabling and coach-houses for the hotel. Former

431 **brewery**, 1784, massive brick bulk recently converted to **housing**, though the office/house on the street frontage has been retained unaltered. Below, former **Girthon & Anwoth Free**

432 **Church**, 1844, echoing the *Heritors' Gothic* churches of the establishment.

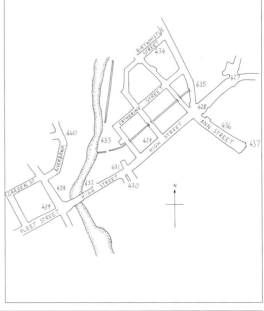

433 **Mill on the Fleet** visitor centre (formerly Birtwhistle Cotton Mills), *c*.1790, rebuilt after fire, 1841; converted early 1990s, Stewartry District Council

Tucked in behind church and brewery, converted from the larger of the two mills. Upper mill survives as a shell. Waterwheel on downstream end from Kempleton Mill, 1824, much smaller than the original. The lade taking water to the mills runs parallel to the High Street, and between it and **Catherine Street**, the cross-streets, **Victoria Street** and

434 **Digby Street** both bridge it. **Birtwhistle Street** contains ranges of very English two-storey brick cottonworkers' housing, their uniformity broken by individual alterations.

435 **Girthon Parish Church**, 1817-18, remodelled, 1895-6, Thomson & Menzies, dominates the streetscape, with its quirky tower.

Ann Street

Entirely different in character to the rest of the burgh, with the 18th-century frontage of the

436 **Murray Arms**, the **Masonic Arms**, 1812, and pleasing two-storey granite terrace, **Nelson Square**, also 1812, and late Georgian **Cally Estate Office**. Tucked in the south-east corner is Gatehouse's other cotton mill, **Scott's**,

437 *c*.1790, long a sawmill but now **housing**.

Western extension of Gatehouse reached by crossing the Fleet on a bridge with an early core, 1661, subsequently widened at least twice, *c*.1820 and 1965. Simple Gothic

438 **Scottish Episcopal Church of St Mary**, attractively set overlooking the Fleet, built as United Secession church, 1840, remodelled, early 20th century. **Fleet Street**, lined by terraced two-storey granite houses, well-proportioned and relatively uniform, with

439 mid-19th-century **Anwoth Hotel** marking the approach from the east. **Secondary school**, 1964, Stewartry County Council, and **RC**

440 **Church of the Resurrection**, 1971, Sutherland Dickie & Copland.

Girthon has little single-storey cottages set at odd angles either side of its winding road, a sure sign of pre-*improvement* origin. **Old**

441 **Church**, 1620 (now roofless), has round-arched simply moulded doors and windows; set high in the north wall, a door indicates gentry access to the gallery. Note Renaissance wall monument,

From top *Mill on the Fleet; Cottonworkers' housing, Birtwhistle Street; Scottish Episcopal Church of St Mary; Shop, High Street.*

Top *Cally House before conversion to hotel*. Middle *Cally Mains haybarn*. Above *Cross Cottage, Cally Mains*.

reused piscina and good collection of 18th-century gravestones. Former **manse** has earlier 18th-century appearance and is likely to have earlier origin; extremely thick walls, narrow windows and awkward juxtaposition of a window with the internal flue-bearing gable indicate a 17th-century house regularised.

442 **Cally Palace Hotel**, 1763-5, Robert Mylne
Country seat of James Murray of Cally, Mylne's original conception was a rather compact house of three storeys and basement with single-storey projecting pavilions. After a series of alterations and expansions effect now decidedly wide-angle. Mylne's block solidly constructed in polished Kirkmabreck granite with contrasting red sandstone window surrounds. Unusual six-bay arrangement of entrance front, lacking the conventional centre-bay emphasis (compare with Galloway House, see p.193). Flanking wings heightened and extended, 1795, Thomas Boyd, producing a more sprawling building; unfortunate modern extensions to garden elevation of the wings.

Megalithic Doric *porte-cochère*, 1833, J B Papworth; stark and overbearing in polished granite it is difficult to love, but encases sumptuous marbled interior. Garden elevation now altered to accommodate hotel use; glazed dining room and lift tower, 1955; large **bedroom extension** to west wing, 1975.

Surrounding parkland laid out, late 18th century, by James Ramsay; many wooded walks and follies, notably the **Temple**, a Gothic tower and a brace of 19th-century baronial **gate-lodges**.

443 **Cally Mains steading**, late 18th century, has fine one- and two-storey limewashed main range, and spectacular later 19th-century, 10-bay, piend-roofed hay barn, with roof-ridge ventilator. Roof carried on granite and whinstone piers. Attractive minor building, **Cross Cottage**, rebuilt 19th century, originally a chapel, with basket-arched door and lancet window turned into *Venetian* by added side lights. **Walled garden**, *c.*1800, unusually large brick-walled enclosure with later 19th-century hot-house range.

444 **Enrick**, *c.*1830
Two-storey, three-bay farmhouse; low *basket handle* arches indicate that beneath harl lies brick walling, probably from the Gatehouse

works. Front elevation aggrandised by late 19th-century bays; rear preserves Gothic detailing oddly married with quite ordinary Doric porch.

445 To the north-west is the 20-span **Big Water of Fleet Viaduct**, built for the Portpatrick Railway, 1861, B & E Blyth, of the poor-quality local stone. Piers encased with brick, mid-20th century, making it a striking and unusual feature in its moorland setting.

ANWOTH

Off the beaten track, the only remains of this little clachan are the neat granite rubble former **schoolhouse**, late 18th century, and the ruinous

446 **Anwoth Old Church**, 1626. Visiting in June 1826, Robert Chambers remarked *the Church, Pulpit and all the curious old fashioned seats were seen in an entire state; but cannot remain so much longer, as a new church is on the point of being erected*. Inside, magnificent Early Renaissance **Gordon Tomb** with finely wrought inscriptions in praise of the women in the life of Laird John Gordon: his mother and first and second wives. In the graveyard a fine collection of **gravestones** including table stone, 1685, for John Bell, and granite mausoleum, 1878, of Sir William Gordon of Cardoness. Close by, the successor **parish church**, 1826-7, Walter Newall, Gothic box with tower and hood-moulded windows.

The Portpatrick Railway, opened in 1861, ran between Castle Douglas and Portpatrick. Originally independent, it secured running powers to Dumfries, and was then effectively taken over by the Caledonian Railway, which had reached Dumfries from Lockerbie in 1863. Eventually, in 1885, the line became jointly owned by the Caledonian, the Glasgow & South Western, the Midland, and the London & North Western Railways, and was run jointly until all these companies disappeared during the grouping of the railways in 1923.

Left *Anwoth Parish Church*. Below *Big Water of Fleet Viaduct*. Bottom *Gordon Tomb, Anwoth Old Church*.

Samuel Rutherford, *c.*1600-1661, is commemorated by the 56ft-high granite **obelisk** erected, 1842, on a hill above Fleet Bay, and rebuilt nine years later after being struck by lightning. Dismissed from his teaching post in Edinburgh for *falling in ante-nuptial fornication*, he turned to religion, ministering at Anwoth, 1627-39, and spent his life in constant conflict with the establishment for his non-conformist ideals. A charismatic preacher, religious and political tracts issued from his pen; he became Principal of the College of St Mary, St Andrews, and was twice offered chairs at Utrecht.

447 **Ardwall House,** 1762
Modest classical mansion; original two-storey over basement, five-bay centre block, simply detailed with Doric porch, bracketed window sills and good deep-hipped roof. Projecting wings added 1875, Leadbetter & Fairley, transform the house to an H-plan, preserving 18th-century good taste inside and out, though Venetian windows do rather over-egg the pudding. Inside a mix of original 18th-century work in the main block and pastiche classical in the wings.

448 **Cardoness Castle,** late 15th century
Five-storey tower, stronghold of the McCullochs, standing sentinel on a rocky outcrop above Water of Fleet: sheer walls, few windows, parapet walk and keyhole gunloops for defence. Ground-floor entrance into tall vaulted basement with timber entresol floor carried on stone corbels; to the east, trapdoor to pit prison. Spiral stair in south-east corner runs the height of the tower, opening at first into large hall, the baronial fireplace adorned with carved cluster shafts, ogival aumbry and salt box. Second floor has two rooms entered from short corridor; possibly 16th-century refinement of domestic planning.
Historic Scotland; open to the public

Below *Ardwall House.* Middle *Cardoness Castle.* Bottom *Rusco Tower.*

Cardoness House, 1889, Kinnear & Peddie
Built as large baronial mansion, but cut down to much smaller dimensions, 1959-60. Baronial **lodge,** with circular-section tower, constructed *c.*1900.

Cardoness Chapel
Minute gabled rubble building, almost on the seashore, with cross-finials and triangular-headed windows. Must be one of the smallest chapels in Scotland.

449 **Rusco Tower,** *c.*1500, extended 17th century
Substantial rectangular tower-house, with a corbelled wall-walk. The **extension,** 16th century, was of three storeys and probably included a gallery to judge by engravings of an array of chimneys, but now survives in a fragmentary condition. Restored, 1975-9, by W Murray Jack.

Barlay Mill, probably 18th century
One-storey and attic whitewashed range, home of the Faed family of painters; now a **garage.**

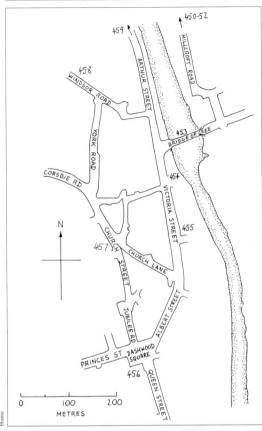

The ancient community at the head of the Cree estuary was probably **Minnigaff**, on the east bank of the river. Newton Stewart was given burgh status in 1677 by the Stewarts of Castle Stewart, up the valley (see p.178), and feuing began in 1701. The first bridge was built in 1745. Sir William Douglas of Gelston took over the feudal superiority in the 1770s, changed the name of the burgh to Newton Douglas, and built a cotton mill, which did not survive competition from urban steam-powered mills. The town now functions as an administrative and educational centre and as a market town for eastern Wigtownshire.

Below *Minnigaff Mill before conversion.* Middle *Monnigaff Parish Church.* Bottom *Bridge of Cree.*

NEWTON STEWART

The old road from the east is the most attractive way to reach the first part of the town, Minnigaff. The terraces of Creebridge
450 lead to former **Minnigaff Mill**, Millcroft Road, 1823, large four-storey, piend-roofed **corn mill**, possibly built as woollen mill, now **sheltered housing**.

451 **Monnigaff Parish Church**, Old Minnigaff, 1834-6, William Burn
Perhaps the finest *Heritors' Gothic* church in Galloway, the buttress pinnacles surmounted by flaming urn finials. In the **churchyard**, well-preserved remains of former **parish church**, part probably medieval, but mainly 17th-century, long rubble rectangle with birdcage belfry, and two burial enclosures. Beyond, a right fork leads to an old bridge and the three-storey-and-attic former **Cumloden**
452 **Walk Mill**, *c.*1800, now a house, retaining internal waterwheel.

Victoria Street

453 **Bridge of Cree**, 1812-13, John Rennie, with four segmental arches in granite ashlar, leads into Newton Stewart proper. Tall Gothic **monument** to the 9th Earl of Galloway, 1874-5, Richard Park, with sculpture by John Rhind, in the angle between it and the bridge. Beyond, **Clydesdale Bank**, mid-19th century, and

454 **Town Hall**, *c*.1800, two-storey with three-bay frontage, tall Venetian windows at first floor and tower with ogee cap (colour page 191).

The street opens out to form a market place with **Galloway Arms Hotel**, 18th/19th-century coaching inn, and three-storey, red sandstone **Royal Bank of Scotland**, 1873, James M Thomson. **No 69**, **Galloway Gazette** building, probably 18th century; its doorpiece

455 certainly is, and 1920s **cinema**, recently refurbished. Pleasing vernacular-classical buildings, the best being **Nos 30-32** with central pedimented chimney gable and columned doorpiece.

Victoria Street becomes **Albert Street**, appropriately of lesser importance, but note late 18th-century, two-storey, **Masonic Lodge**, with fine doorcase, and bow-ended **Central Bar**, on the corner of **Church Lane**. **Bank of Scotland**, remodelled 1879, Wardrop & Reid, from early 19th-century building. At the top of the hill is **Dashwood Square**, dominated by

456 **McMillan Hall**, 1884, Richard Park, large and unprepossessing, with French detailing.

Queen Street, broad with two-storey buildings on both sides, a relief after the ominous bulk of the McMillan Hall. **Auction Mart**, 1894, William Agnew, dominated by the octagonal auction room.

Top Town Hall. *Above* 30-32 Victoria Street. *Right* Auction Mart, Queen Street.

Churches include: gabled former **Reformed Presbyterian Church**, Princes Street, 1833, with Georgian pointed windows and later porch; and large steepled Gothic parish church,

457 **Penninghame St John's**, Church Street, 1834-40, William Burn, one of the earliest of its type in Scotland; interior, little altered.

York Road
Museum, a treasure-trove of local bygones, housed in simple but large Gothic former **Newton Stewart Presbyterian Church**, 1877-8, Richard Park, with spire. Gothic **Ewart Institute**, 1862-4, Thomas Cook, Liverpool, with tower, 1869, Heath Wilson & Thomson, Glasgow, built as school, now housing. In **Windsor Road**, slightly
458 cumbrous, vaguely Arts & Crafts **Our Lady & St Ninian's RC Church**, 1875-6, Goldie & Childe, London.

Arthur Street
Main route north leading past 19th-century, one- and two-storey vernacular houses and abandoned single-storey former woollen mill to
459 former **Samuel Douglas Free School**, **King Street**, front 1834, John Henderson, monumental classical, with central belfry. Immediately beyond, footpath to **George V Suspension Bridge**, 1911, D H & F Reid, Victoria Bridge Works, Ayr, built to mark the coronation; wire-rope bridge with lattice truss sides and lattice towers, recently overhauled by Crouch & Hogg, Glasgow, leading to **Old Minnigaff** (see p.175).

Top *Penninghame St John's.* Above *Former Samuel Douglas Free School.*

PENNINGHAME
Corvisel, early 19th century
Fine, two-storey-and-basement gentry house, with Roman-Doric doorpiece, south of A75 bypass on the Wigtown road.

Interior, All Saints Scottish Episcopal Church.

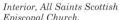

460 **All Saints Scottish Episcopal Church**, Challoch, 1871-2, W B Habershon & Beresford Pite, London
Strikingly sited geometric Gothic, built as private chapel by Edward J Stopford Blair of Penninghame House, with richly decorated interior, almost all as built, including elaborate Gothic pulpit, stencilled ceiling panels, stained glass windows and fine wrought-iron chancel screen.

461 **Penninghame House**, 1864, attributed to Brown & Wardrop
Main body in imposing Jacobean, with castellated corner tower, single-storey canted bays and gableted dormers with kneelers and finials. At the rear, two-storey Tudor range, with hood-moulds over the openings, apparently mid-19th century. Modern additions; now an open prison.

Top *Castle Stewart*. Above *Merton Hall*.

The inscription on the Bruce Memorial reads: *In loyal remembrance of Robert Bruce, King of Scots, whose victory in this glen opened the campaign of independence which he brought to a decisive close at Bannockburn on 24th June, 1314.*

Below *1930s postcard view of the Bruce Memorial, Glentrool.* Bottom *Bargaly House.*

462 **Castle Stewart**, *c*.1500
Ruin of four-storey tower on rectangular plan, with rounded corners and corbelled wall-walk. Some repair work in recent years.

Challoch, mid-19th century
Mildly Tudor, L-plan farmhouse, with mullioned and transomed windows, castellated entrance and scrolled barge-boards. **Steading** has four-bay cart-shed with depressed-arched bays.

463 **Merton Hall**, from 1767
A complex house with a three-storey core, 1767, with two-storey piend-roofed and urned pavilions. Twin semicircular bows added, with tripartite windows and first-floor balconies; heavily sculptured and columned porch added, *c*.1900, probably when conical roofs added to bays to give vaguely French appearance to the side of the house. The 18th century is much more in evidence in the garden front, apart from Victorian ground-floor bays and large timber-and-lead sun porch at first floor, approached by broad flight of railed stairs.

Balterson steading, earlier to mid-19th century
Large vernacular range with segment-headed cart entries. Concrete **silo**, *c*.1970, James Scott & Son, Aberdeen, in north range.

464 **GLENTROOL**
Like Ae, a Forestry Commission village, in the heart of a gigantic upland forest. One-storey-and-attic harled houses, 1952-4, laid out, with picturesque intent, round village green with **primary school**, 1954-6, Archibald T Caldwell, Stewartry County Architect.

MINNIGAFF
465 **Bargrennan Church**, 1838-9
Small rectangular building with round-headed windows with later glazing, and gabled belfry, built as chapel of ease of Minnigaff. Interior, 1909, P MacGregor Chalmers. **Bargaly House**, begun 1691, remodelled *c*.1800, has swept roof and both triangular and semicircular pedimented dormers. West wing from early 18th century, subsequently
466 remodelled. **Garlies Lodge**, 1910, Humphreys Ltd, corrugated-iron bungalow, with wood-framed veranda all round; an unusual sight in its upland setting.

Cumloden House.

Below from top *Glencaird;
Kirroughtree House before conversion
to hotel; Machermore Castle; Glen
Trool Lodge.*

467 **Cumloden House**, *c.*1875
Extraordinary Gothic confection, for Sir William
Stewart, five-bay, with projecting gabled bays,
all with pointed-arched windows and prominent
eaves supported on timber posts. Sections of
veranda continue the line of the posts, with
Swiss-style balcony in the centre. Summer
retreat of the Earls of Galloway.

Glencaird, 1930s, Roger Pinkerney
L-plan Arts & Crafts, two-storey-and-attic
house; entrance, in the angle, is in quarter-
round bay flanked by sub-Mackintosh
projecting chimney; doorway has subdued
Gibbsian surround.

468 **Kirroughtree House Hotel**, from 1719
Complex building history reflected on its
wedding-cake exterior. Core is two-storey-and-
basement house, built for Patrick Heron,
remodelled, *c.*1775, and again *c.*1890 and 1907,
Peddie & Washington Browne. Now two- and
three-storey-and-basement, rendered with full-
height canted and semicircular bays and
piended roof; Corinthian porch with ball finials,
probably *c.*1890. **Ice house**, **doocot**, 1719,
octagonal, and former **stables block**, now
housing, in grounds.

469 **Machermore Castle**, 16th/17th century
Four-storey tower, remodelled, 1884-6, Richard
Park, with castellated entrance front,
bartizans and bay windows on the garden
front; 20th-century, flat-roofed extension.
Now a nursing home.

Glen Trool Lodge, mid-19th century
Deliberately informal 1½-storey rock-faced
granite house, with open eaves and single-
storey mullioned bays on entrance and garden
fronts, retaining diamond-frame glazing.

The Battle of Glentrool, effectively,
was a skirmish between a company of
Robert the Bruce's troops and an
English band. Bruce's escape from this
encounter, and another at Loudoun
Hill in Ayrshire led Edward I to try to
counter Bruce in person. The effort was
too much. He died at Burgh-on-Sands
on 7 July 1307, and his successor
Edward II was no match for the Scots.

Murray's Monument, 1835, John Parker, Edinburgh, commemorates Alexander Murray, 1775-1813, local shepherd lad who became a minister and professor of oriental languages; 24m-high obelisk, whose designer was a lawyer.

Auchinleck, 1863
Two-storey, whin and sandstone baronial farmhouse with circular stair-tower featuring cannon gargoyles and arrow slits. Part of the 9th Earl of Galloway's estate improvements.

470 **Whitehills**, 1912
Unusual for Galloway, charming English Arts & Crafts, long and low, with small-paned timber-mullioned casement windows, complex low-pitched roof with overhanging eaves; garden layout contemporary.

Right *Cairnsmore House*. Top *Whitehills*. Above *Cairnsmore hay barns*.

Cairnsmore House, c.1740
Two-storey attic and basement, piend-roofed centre; basement fully exposed on entrance front, with grand staircase to Roman-Doric portico. Round-headed windows in *piano nobile*, Victorian attic bay dormers and flanking bay-windowed wings. Associated **stables**, two-storey, quadrangular, with crowstepped, three-storey-and-attic centrepiece with arched entrance; end bays slightly advanced, with coach-houses on ground floor.
471 Remarkable pair of open **hay barns**, with monolithic stone pillars supporting piended slate roofs.

472 **Kirkmabreck Granite Quarry and pier**, 19th and 20th centuries
Very large hole in the ground from whence came both building stone (evident in Creetown and Newton Stewart) and crushed stone aggregate for roads and concrete.

CREETOWN
Laid out as planned village, 1785, its real popularity came with the opening of the large granite quarry at Kirkmabreck, mid-

19th century, hence the very plain granite rubble one and two-storey houses in its single main street, **John Street**, clean but rather bleak in character. **Adamson Square** has, in true Galloway fashion, chunky
473 granite **clock tower**, 1897, for Queen Victoria's Diamond Jubilee (colour page 191), and **Ellangowan Hotel**, 1898, George W Webb, which tries to blend the local granite with English Arts & Crafts, expressed in balconied veranda – granite wins.

High Street here is descriptive: it runs uphill from Adamson Square, leading to very plain
474 Gothic **St Joseph's RC Church**, adapted 1876 from a Free Church, 1859, Peter McKie. T-plan former **parish school**, Chain Road, 1857, Peter McKie, with open eaves and lying-pane glazing, now **Gem Rock Museum** of minerals from around the world.

Harbour Street
Mostly granite vernacular, but with curious
475 English **seaside terrace** of two-storey, stucco-fronted houses, now much altered, and singularly out of place as it looks out over the muddy Cree estuary.

476 **Kirkmabreck Parish Church**,
Church Street, 1831-4, John Henderson
Large, typical Galloway *Heritors' Gothic*, with pinnacled tower and perpendicular tracery; centre section of roof raised above sides, increasing the impression of height disproportionately. Rather daunting externally, with its dark whinstone rubble with red sandstone dressings. Inside, unexpectedly, plaster-vaulted ceiling.

477 **Creetown Station**, *c.*1860, Sir James Gowans
Distinctive single-storey station office and waiting room for the Portpatrick Railway in advanced disrepair. Polygonal masonry with Locharbriggs red sandstone ashlar horizontal and vertical band courses and copings. Currently roofless and in coal merchant's yard; planning application to convert and extend station to dwelling.

From top *Creetown clock tower, Adamson Square; Terrace, Harbour Street; Kirkmabreck Parish Church; Creetown Station.*

Sir James Gowans, 1821-90, was an advocate of a scientific approach to the use of masonry, with rectilinear panels defined by bands of freestone, with whinstone or other stone, in irregular shapes, filling in the spaces. His highly idiosyncratic 2ft modular grid and masonry expertise had been first employed for his own house, Rockville, 1858 (see *Edinburgh* in this series), for Gowanbank, 1842-62 (see *West Lothian* in this series), and at Lochee Burns Club, 1860-1 (see *Dundee* in this series).

Glebe House, mid-19th century
Two-storey, piend-roofed former manse, with curious inset central bay, with plastered architrave, flanked on ground floor by tripartite windows.

Top and above *Kirkdale House.*

478 Kirkdale House, 1787-8, Robert Adam
Elegant and aloof, Adam's only major surviving
work in the shire, for Sir Samuel Hannay of
Mochrum, a Wigtownshire laird who made a
fortune as a London merchant. Two-storey-and-
attic centre block flanked by lower wings
linking end pavilions. Severe lines emphasised
by ashlar granite masonry, nowhere more so
than in the monolithic Doric columns of the
porch. Garden front marginally softened by
central canted bay with steps sweeping up to
French doors in drawing room. Central block
gutted after fire, 1907; little of interest
internally.

Full complement of Adam-inspired estate
buildings include **icehouse** and **Kirkdale
Bridge**, planned as neo-Egyptian
extravaganza complete with swags and
sphinxes; as built, the result distinctly plain
and workmanlike, though handsomely
proportioned and doubtless easier on Sir
Samuel's purse.

Below *Kirkdale Sawmill.*
Bottom *Carsluith Corn Mill.*

Kirkdale Mains, *c.*1790, perhaps by
Robert & John Adam
Octagonal steading: four sides of two-storey
piend-roofed blocks, and four of single-storey,
with segmental arched cart bays. Two of the
latter have gone; one being rebuilt.
479 Kirkdale Sawmill, one of the best-
preserved in Galloway, retains its waterwheel.
Carsluith Corn Mill, 1817, much altered,
retains some machinery, and **round-ended
barn**, early 19th century, set into hillside, a
fine example of its type, unusual in Scotland.
Kirkdale Churchyard contains remains of
small medieval church of the Parish of
Kirkdale, abandoned when parish assimilated
into Parish of Kirkmabreck. **Mausoleum**,
1787, perhaps Robert & John Adam, to Sir
Samuel Hannay of Mochrum.

480 **Cassencarie House**, late 16th century
Complex building, now largely ruinous.
Earliest part four-storey, L-plan tower,
extended by late 18th century to give near-
symmetrical, three-storey, five-bay front with
advanced end bays. Part-baronialised, c.1880,
for James Caird; mid-19th-century service
wing now an **inn**.

481 **Cairn Holy Chambered Cairns**,
3rd and 2nd millenniums
Of all Galloway's prehistoric relics, **Cairn
Holy** is the most dramatic; the site, high on a
hillside, consists of two exposed chambered
cairns, apparently consisting of two chambers,
perhaps indicating two phases of construction.
Cairn Holy I, the southern cairn, a vast
mound (43m by 10m) of loose stones once
covering the inner burial chamber with
formalised central entrance emphasised by
monolithic pillars set out in horseshoe
formation. Area of level ground in front forms a
forecourt: surely a performance space for ritual
gatherings. All covering cairn stones robbed
during 18th century for dyking, leaving the
upright stones and inner burial chamber
exposed to view. **Cairn Holy II** is stripped
bare; its forecourt curtailed by the sloping site,
but massive portal stones still stand upright.
Historic Scotland; open to the public

482 **Barholm Castle**, late 16th century, with
earlier origin
Ruin of L-plan tower house which, like
Carsluith, began life as rectangular tower,
civilised c.1580, by addition of the stair-jamb.
Entry formerly by forestair to first-floor hall;
later by smart round-arched cable-moulded
doorway at foot of stair-jamb. As further
evidence, quoin stones change from rubble to
dressed pink sandstone indicating rebuilding
from first floor upwards. **Barholm Farm**, mid-
18th-century, plain four-square; its boulder
footings and narrow windows giving the lie to
its age.

483 **Carsluith Castle**, 1568, with earlier origin
Much the same development as Barholm, an
armorial panel dates the changes to 1568.
Further similarities are the simple row of
corbels supporting angle turrets and cap-house
and the charmingly carved gargoyle through
whose mouth the hall sink discharges. On
north front, a second-floor timber gallery

From top *Cassencairie House before
damage; Cairn Holy II; Barholm
Castle; Carsluith Castle.*

Carsluith Castle belonged to the Browns of Carsluith, and one of its owners was the last abbot of Sweetheart Abbey.

linked the jamb to the main range; removed 17th century, but position indicated by holes for floor joists, and corbels for ridge-beam of lean-to roof. Utilitarian gunports, probably 1568, proclaim a weather-eye be kept against raiders. Adjoining piend-roofed steadings, *c.*1800, contribute handsomely to the composition. *Historic Scotland; open to public; information boards*

Glen Farmhouse.

484 **Glen Farmhouse**, 1734
Up-to-the-minute laird's house: two-storey, with long five-bay frontage enhanced by rusticated quoins and moulded cornice; inscribed *Founded 1734 by IMCD* (John McDouall of Logan). Internally, ground plan unaltered with basic rectangle divided into three. Paired front and back rooms flank central hall with wide stair to rear; at least one original chimneypiece.

North-east of Creetown is the best-preserved 485 lead mine of the area, at **Pibble**, with remains of mid-19th-century Cornish pumping **engine-house**. Mining here, a short-lived venture.

Ruined engine-house, Pibble Mine.

WIGTOWN
Medieval burgh, founded 12th century, with triangular market place, wider and shorter than many, and its own harbour on the Cree, which, when sea transport was vital in Galloway, gave it a competitive edge over other towns and villages in the area. County town for Wigtownshire for many years, with architectural flourishes that hint at past distinction. After the coming of the railway it lost out to Newton Stewart and Stranraer, and has that deserted feel, as though life has passed it by.

Mercat crosses, The Square, Wigtown.

The Square
Originally the market place, triangular despite its name, now with park and bowling green where sheep, cattle and horses were once sold. 486 Original function marked by two **mercat crosses**, symbols of the burgh's right to hold a market: the earlier, 1783, a simpler, slender sandstone Roman-Doric column with cubic sundial. The later, with octagonal buttressed base, terminating in a cross, dwarfs the earlier.

487 **County Buildings & Town Hall**, 1862-3, Brown & Wardrop
Out-of-proportion to the rest of the town; red and yellow sandstone, with piended roof, in

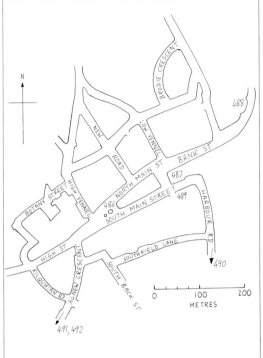

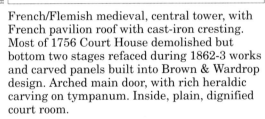

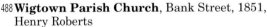

French/Flemish medieval, central tower, with French pavilion roof with cast-iron cresting. Most of 1756 Court House demolished but bottom two stages refaced during 1862-3 works and carved panels built into Brown & Wardrop design. Arched main door, with rich heraldic carving on tympanum. Inside, plain, dignified court room.

488 **Wigtown Parish Church**, Bank Street, 1851, Henry Roberts
Large, but very dull, Gothic with tower terminating in slated pavilion roof. **Graveyard** contains fragments of old **parish church**, now seriously ivy-grown. Of much greater interest are the **gravestones**, *c.*1720, of the martyrs. In Windyhill, off High Vennel, monument to them.

The Square, mainly two-storey, terraced houses, mostly vernacular, but with some classical detailing generally at odds with the simple designs of the rest of the building. Grandest is the **Old**
489 **Bank**, with large Ionic doorpiece on front elevation, and better one on the east side. **Nos 18 & 22 South Main Street**, and **No 11** all have classical doorpieces or porticoes (colour page 191).

Top *County Buildings.* Middle *Sheriff Court, County Buildings.* Above *Wigtown Parish Church.*

The Wigtown Martyrs were two local women, Margaret MacLachlan, in her 60s, and Margaret Wilson, 18 years old, who, in 1685, were sentenced to be drowned by the incoming tide for refusing to recognise the King as head of the Church, a Covenanting viewpoint. Whether or not they were in fact drowned is disputed.

Old Bank, Wigtown.

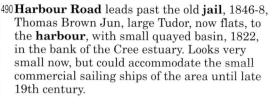

490 Harbour Road leads past the old **jail**, 1846-8, Thomas Brown Jun, large Tudor, now flats, to the **harbour**, with small quayed basin, 1822, in the bank of the Cree estuary. Looks very small now, but could accommodate the small commercial sailing ships of the area until late 19th century.

Wigtown is now a *book town* with several good second-hand bookshops, bringing life back to an essentially very pleasing place.

Bladnoch

Part of Wigtown, though really self-contained community with its own industries. A bridge-**491** town, present **bridge**, from 1866, D & T Stevenson, engineers, two-span structure with **492** semi-elliptical arches. Upstream, **Bladnoch Distillery**, probably founded 1817, Thomas McClelland, rebuilt 1878 and later, mostly whinstone rubble, with pagoda-roofed kiln. Village itself consists of single street of mainly mid-19th century, one- and two-storey houses; grandest, **No 33**, with Roman-Doric piers flanking its door.

Top *Classical doorpiece, off The Square*. Right *Bladnoch Bridge*. Above *Bladnoch Distillery*.

493 Torhouse (or Torhousekie) **Stone Circle**
Well-preserved Bronze Age circle of 19 granite boulders, about 20m in diameter, with setting of three stones in the centre. Finest stone circle in south-west Scotland.
Historic Scotland; open to the public

Kirkinner Cross.

KIRKINNER

Pleasant little village with curving main street and one- and two-storey houses mostly **494** Victorian, some recently altered. **Parish church**, 1828, usual towered *Heritors' Gothic* so popular in Galloway at that time, refurnished late 19th century, though pulpit may be original. Inside, **Kirkinner Cross**, 10th century, with disc head of Whithorn type – a very good example – in graveyard until

1967. Late 18th-century classical **mausoleum** of the Van Agnews of Barnbarroch, in the **churchyard**. Cruciform, Tudor **school**, *c*.1880, marred by plastic replacement windows.

495 **Milldriggan Mill**, rebuilt early 19th century, as woollen mill, later converted to corn mill, now decaying. Three-storey-and-attic, eight-bay rubble, formerly with large internal high-breast wheel by J & R Wallace, Castle Douglas Foundry.

496 **Baldoon Castle**, 16th century
Only one fragmentary wall remains. Seat of the Dunbars and inspirational setting for Sir Walter Scott's *Bride of Lammermoor*. Fine pair of mid-17th-century **gatepiers** testify to the profits of the beef trade and are the most accomplished pieces of Renaissance work in the area.

Baldoon Mains, *c*.1830
Unusually large and elaborate, 1½-storey, six-bay farmhouse, with off-centre tetrastyle Roman Doric portico. Four gableted dormers, also off-centre, reinforce the informality. Farmsteading includes reinforced-concrete drum **silo**, *c*.1920.

497 **Barwhanny Windmill**, late 18th or early 19th century
Slender tapering rubble tower, which had on top a cap and sails making it a wind engine used to power a threshing mill.

498 **Barnbarroch House**, 1780, ruinous since 1942
Original house two-storey attic and basement, five-bay, with full-height bows on outer bays, Doric portico added, 1806-8, J C Loudon, who also added west wing. Even in decay a handsome building. Former **stables** a plain buttressed quadrangle, mildly Gothic. Grand scheme of formal gardens, lake and fountains, also by Loudon, now reverted to farmland.

From top *Milldriggan Mill; Baldoon Castle gatepiers; Barwhanny Windmill; Barnbarroch House.*

SORBIE
Well-developed planned village, founded late 18th century by the 7th Earl of Galloway. L-plan, its cottages mainly 19th century and single storey.

499 Simple former **free church**, 1843-4, and nearby ruin of T-plan former parish church, 1755 and **mausoleum** of the Earls of Galloway, 1735.

Sir David Dunbar of Baldoon, prototype cattle baron, kept within his walled park *ane thousan bestiall* for export to England presumably by sea. Disaster befell him in 1682; 59 cows impounded by English authorities were mistaken for illegal Irish imports and all *knocks on the heid and kill*.

500 Old Place of Sorbie, late 16th century
L-plan tower house of the Hannay family, four-storey with door in re-entrant and corbelled stair turret. Instead of usual corkscrew ascent, generous scale-and-platt stair leads to first-floor hall. As at Castle of Park, hall is forcibly foreshortened to accommodate, in north gable, the enormous kitchen flue leaving room each side for a mural chamber. Turrets to three sides; ground-floor windows enlarged; consolidated 1970, for Clan Hannay Society. *Open to the public*

501 Cruggleton Church, 12th century
Probably built for Fergus, Lord of Galloway, most complete Romanesque church in the area. Simple two-cell plan of nave and chancel, extensively rebuilt, 1890, under Robert Weir Schultz as part of the 3rd Marquess of Bute's restorations. Chancel arch has most original features; moulded shafts support simple cushion capitals, and unmistakably chunky medieval stonework. Work of 1890 delineated by inserted row of tiles above which all is new, including narrow round-headed windows, timber roof and studded doors.

Poulton Mains farm steading, later 19th century, has unusually fine cart-shed range, piend-roofed and whitewashed, with four depressed-arch cart entries.

GARLIESTON

Geometrically planned village, founded *c*.1760, and designed as an improved port for the Machars by the then Lord Garlies, later 7th Earl of Galloway. Also estate village for Galloway House (see map p.5). Maritime industries – rope and sail-making, shipbuilding, sawmilling and fishing – successfully introduced; grain and other agricultural produce exported and coal, lime and manure imported. With the advent of steamships the place assumed greater
502 importance; **harbour** enlarged, *c*.1855, regular steamer sailings to Glasgow, Liverpool and the Isle of Man, and railway link from the Whithorn branch. Small water-powered grain mill, replaced 20th century, by concrete-and-brick building, on larger scale, by the harbour.

North Crescent and South Crescent

From top *Sorbie; Old Place of Sorbie; Cruggleton Church, chancel arch; Poulton Mains.*

Two single-sided streets facing the sea, with curved ends, with late 18th- and early 19th-century houses, mainly two-storey, three-bay.

Top *Threave Castle.* Middle *Tower of Dalry Parish Church, St John's Town of Dalry.* Above *Former cinema, Dalbeattie.* Above left *Balmaghie Parish Church.* Left *High Street, New Galloway, with the spire of the Town Hall.*

Top *Clock Tower, Castle Douglas.*
Middle *Detail of office block, King
Street, Castle Douglas.* Above
Ornamental slating, Castle Douglas.
Top right *Douglas Mausoleum,
Kelton.* Middle right *River Ken at
Glenlochar.* Right *Post office, King
Street, Castle Douglas.*

Hume

Historic Scotland

Hume

Hume

Hume

Hume

Top *Corseyard steading.* Middle
Murray Arms Hotel (right) *and
Clock Tower, Gatehouse of Fleet.*
Above *Window of Town Hall,
Newton Stewart.* Above left *Castle of
Park.* Left *Doorcase, New Road,
Wigtown.* Far left *Clock Tower,
Creetown.*

191

Hume

Hume

Hume

Hume

Hume

Top *Portpatrick from the north.*
Middle *The Pend, George Street,*
Whithorn. Above *Old Town Hall,*
Stranraer. Above right *Corsewall*
Lighthouse. Right *Craigcaffie Castle*

503 **Lincoln Cottage**, 15 Culderry Row
Remarkable Tudor confection with complex
glazing pattern, altogether surprising among
the Galloway vernacular of the rest of the
village. Brick **mill** dominates the harbour, but
note earlier two-storey stone **warehouses** and
offices, and open-sided transit **shed** on pier-
head, used by steamers. Principal features in
504 the village are the **mill wheel**, J & F Wallace
of Castle Douglas, and late 19th-century Tudor
505 village **school**. Gothic **Sorbie Parish
Church**, 1873-6, David Thomson.

506 **Galloway House**, 1740-50, John Douglas
architect; John Baxter site architect
Built as main residence of the Stewarts of
Garlies, Earls of Galloway, it cannot fail to
impress, if only by its gargantuan proportions:
four-storey front with giant pilasters and
pediment, curving wings linking piend-roofed
pavilions. Testament to the determination of
an architecturally insensitive patron to realise
the house he required (four full storeys and 18
bedrooms) against the better judgement of his
architects, while declaring *I must have
cheapness primarily in view*. Douglas
produced the basic design leaving Baxter to
cope on site with Garlies' parsimony. Excellent
carved red-sandstone decoration to entrance
front with deeply undercut egg-and-dart
moulding: garden front unadorned in interests
of economy. Landscaping of parkland left to
next generation with the 7th Earl planting as
many as 200,000 trees per annum.

In 1841 William Burn added upper storeys
to the pavilions and infilled to the rear of the
curved corridors greatly enlarging the garden
front. Robert Lorimer added bathrooms in
1909 and remodelled much of the interior in
his best 18th-century style. Scattering of
pretty lodges adorn entrances to the park;
stables much altered; **Park House**, 1848,
the most attractive estate building, gabled
Gothic with mullioned windows.

Top *Garlieston, harbour and
cornmill.* Middle *Garlieston, South
Crescent.* Above *Interior, Galloway
House.*

Galloway House.

WHITHORN

A name known round the world as the site of **St Ninian's Mission Church**, *Candida Casa*, dedicated to St Martin. There was a church at Whithorn when the Saxons of Canterbury were still pagan and Iona was an uninhabited rock. The cult of St Ninian made it a place of pilgrimage, and a succession of phases of occupation – British, Anglican and Irish – have been identified. It featured in the Normanisation of Scotland in the 12th century, when the church became a **cathedral** and **priory**. It was a favourite place of pilgrimage of Robert Bruce and the Stewart kings, and became a burgh in 1325 and a royal burgh in 1511.

George Street

Centre of the main street, and medieval market place, lined mainly with two-storey 18th- and early 19th-century houses. Highlight

507 is the **Pend**, former gatehouse of the priory, with semicircular arch supported on columns bearing arms associated with the Vaus family, two members of which were bishops here in the 15th century. Above the arch, armorial panel bearing the Royal Arms of Scotland, probably in recognition of royal pilgrimages to the shrine of St Ninian (colour page 192).

Below Pend, George Street.
Bottom St Ninian's Priory.

508 **Town House**, 1814

Two-storey, three-bay L-plan, with coved-ceilinged council chamber at first-floor level above shops. In the angle of the L, town **steeple**, five-storey tower, with clock and belfry stages, topped by stone conical steeple, and with balustraded parapet contains two cells in the ground floor and prison room on the first floor. Two further prison rooms contained

509 in rear wing of the L. **No 29 George Street** is a two-storey, three-bay villa, unusually well built of whinstone, with painted dressings, and round-headed doorway with fanlight of unorthodox design.

Returning to the Pend, and turning left through it into **Bruce Street**, following the route traversed by countless pilgrims since the Middle Ages, we see ahead of us the site of the

510 **cathedral** and **priory**. Very difficult now to envisage what it would have been like before the Reformation. Two rectangular fragments, the most obvious the former **nave** of the priory church, founded by Fergus, Lord of Galloway, in

the 12th century; extended in the 13th century by Premonstratensians. After the Reformation the derelict nave was rebuilt to serve as the parish church, the walls being lowered, and a tower being built at the west end, which collapsed late 17th century, west gable subsequently rebuilt. Nave abandoned as parish church, 1822. Unroofed, it became a burial ground.

The other fragment comprises the **crypt** which underlay the east end of the priory church, altered probably 15th century, refaced late 19th century, when remains (including nave walls) consolidated for the 3rd Marquess of Bute by William Galloway, architect. This consists of four interconnecting rubble vaults, probably originally used as stores for the priory. *Historic Scotland; open to the public*

511 Present **Parish Church of St Ninian**, reached by a path through the site of the transepts and crossing of the priory church, plain gabled rectangle, 1822, constructed by Jones Laurie, James McQueen and Authy McMillan. Tower later; pulpit and communion table, Peter MacGregor Chalmers.

Town House.

512 **Museum** displays Early Christian grave markers and sculptured stones, including several disc-headed crosses characteristic of Whithorn area, including the **Monreith Cross**, tallest of the group. To the south, site of excavations carried out since 1986, revealing a complex of multi-period settlements. Findings now interpreted both on site and in a **visitor centre** in early 20th-century commercial building in **George Street**. The excavations and the visitors they attract have brought new life to this rural community. *Open to the public*

St Ninian is recorded by Bede as the first Christian Missionary to Scotland. He is supposed to have been a Briton, instructed in Rome, and to have converted the southern Picts from a base at Whithorn, where he was bishop, and where he is supposed to have built a church known as *Candida Casa* – the white, or shining, house.

Because the town is on a through road, and because of its pilgrimage and archaeological interest, **Whithorn**, though sometimes quiet, has a lively feel: perhaps the spirit of that daring pioneer, Ninian, still inhabits it.

Left *Early Christian sculptured stones, museum.* Below *Excavating the site of Early Christian Whithorn.*

513 St John Street
Main road to Wigtown and Newton Stewart
with **New Town Hall**, 1885-6, David Henry,
disappointingly gloomy, dark whinstone, with
mullioned and transomed windows. More
cheerful **St John's Garage**, formerly Arts &
514 Crafts Gothic **Whithorn UP church**, 1892,
Thomson and Sandilands, with filling-station
paybox set in main entrance. Church has been
a fine building and its off-beat conversion has,
if anything, given it extra charm.

Top *St John's Garage*. Above
Tonderghie farm steading.

515 Castlewigg has at its oldest section a tower,
1593, built by Archibald Stewart of Barclye
and Tonderghie, extended *c*.1800, with its
show-front on the north featuring flattened
bows flanking the entrance; now roofless
516 ruin. **Tonderghie**, late 19th-century, two-
storey attic and basement, three-bay laird's
house, with curved wing walls ending in

Below *Isle of Whithorn harbour.*
Bottom *St Ninian's Chapel.*

single-storey gabled pavilions; altered at the
rear, 20th century. Two notable mid-19th-
century estate farm steadings: **Tonderghie**,
fine single-storey piend-roofed range, with
raised pyramid-roofed section over main flat-
arched entrance to the centre court, and
circular conical-roofed horse-engine house;
Arbrack, similar in construction, but lower,
with three cart bays.

Isle of Whithorn, an evocative place, where
the land runs into the sea, owes its existence
to its natural harbour, at the southern edge of
the Machars. Its early importance in the Irish
Sea economy is marked by the siting of **St**
517 Ninian's Chapel on the headland looking
across to Ireland, the start of the pilgrimage
route to St Ninian's Church at Whithorn. The
chapel, small single-chamber church, *c*.1300,
substantially restored, 1898, Peter
MacGregor Chalmers.
Historic Scotland; open to the public

Present form of the village dates from the *improvement* movement of late 18th and early 19th century. Focal point is 16th-century, L-plan harbour, modified, 1790, and *c*.1900, with boat-building yard; and much-altered range of warehouses along **Harbour Street**. **Steam**
518 **Packet Inn**, reminder of the importance of steamships in mid-19th-century economy of Galloway. Mainly 19th-century terraced housing strung round the harbour, mostly on single-frontage streets.

519   **Isle of Whithorn Church**, former Free Church, 1843-4, and group of buildings on **Main Street** projecting into the harbour, with their castellated sea wall, give point and sparkle to the village. Also tucked in behind, **Isle of Whithorn Castle**, small tower-house, unexpected in this context, with the tops of the corner turrets trimmed to fit under later slate roof, and **Bysbie Mill**, small, formerly water-powered, grain mill.

Top *Isle of Whithorn Church*. Above *Isle of Whithorn Castle*. Below *The third Glasserton House (demolished)*. Middle *Butler's Lodge*. Bottom *Physgill House in 1949, before remodelling*.

Glasserton
Today, no trace remains of the three successive residences of the Earls of Galloway. The first was *consumed to ashes* in 1734 when her ladyship was careless with a candle whilst turning out the linen cupboard. The loss nearly ruined the family and the replacement **summerhouse**, 1737, proved unsatisfactory: damp, draughty and cold, and fell into oblivion. Very smart classical house, *c*.1790, Robert Adam, within extensive parklands, alas demolished, 1948. Fortunately extensive **stable block** and 18th-century **doocot** survive along with picturesque **Butler's Lodge** and **Posting House**, with distinctive large-diamond glazing.

520 **Glasserton Parish Church**, 1732 and later
Original rectangular box-kirk, rubble walling with dressed stone for the round-arched windows. Blocked door to south provided direct access to the pulpit and a chance for the minister to wrong-foot his flock. Three-stage, plain Gothic tower and north aisle added, 1836, J B Papworth, giving the T-plan; aisle repeats the round-arched windows of the original. Elaborate stone bellcote, 1680, brought from Kirkmaiden Church. Remains of **stables** for the horses of worshippers.

521 **Physgill House**, late 17th century; extended *c*.1790; remodelled 1958, A C Wolffe
The 17th-century, three-storey, five-bay, harled and piend-roofed range now looks more

Top Ravenstone Castle. *Above* Interior, Mochrum Parish Church.

Georgian than the four-storey, four-bay, *c*.1790 rubble range. Present south front based on conjecture by the architect.

522 **Ravenstone Castle**, 16th century and later Complex structure with four main build periods, initially for the Kennedys of Blairquhan. South front has 16th-century, L-plan tower-house, re-entrant filled 17th century creating present twin-gabled front. Roll-moulded windows and one wide-mouth gunloop original, though elegant fish-tail stair and pedimented entrance, early 19th century. To the rear, early 19th-century addition, with bows to east and west, later sandwiched by Victorian baronial wing to balance the south front. Unroofed, 1948, shell now partly consolidated. Nearby, remains of 19th-century horse-powered water-pumping equipment.

ELRIG
Small village of 18th- and 19th-century origin up narrow valley running from Luce Bay.
Mochrum, pleasant little village curving
523 round T-plan **parish church** and **churchyard**, 1794, aisle lengthened, 1878, reseated about the same time, 1794 pulpit retained. Former manse, now **Greenmantle Hotel**, 1781, Anthony Park, with additions, 1822 and 1900-1, two-storey, two-bay symmetrical, with Roman-Doric doorcase. To the east well-preserved **Druchtag Motte**, earth mound that supported a 17th-century Scoto-Norman wooden castle.
Historic Scotland; open to the public

MONREITH
Small village, mainly 19th-century vernacular cottages, set on Luce Bay. On promontory to
524 south medieval **Kirkmaiden churchyard**; walls of medieval rubble nave reasonably complete, but chancel rebuilt late 19th century as mausoleum for the Maxwells of Monreith. **Monreith Cross**, ninth century, (see p.195) probably from this graveyard. Above the churchyard, **monument** to Gavin Maxwell, naturalist and author, born at House of Elrig, bronze otter on a rock, 1978, Penny Wheatley.

525 **Old Place of Mochrum**, 15th & 16th centuries Two towers, the west thick-walled, 15th-century tower house; the east tower 16th-century, generous on plan with spiral stair in

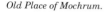

Old Place of Mochrum.

separate jamb. Both ruinous by 1780 and apparently never linked to allow direct access. Rebuilding of upper works and construction of linking block began 1873 under Richard Park of Newton Stewart for 3rd Marquess of Bute. Robert Weir Schultz took over for the 4th Marquess, 1903-8, kitting out interior with timber panelling, chunky furniture, iron-light fittings. **Walled garden** with **sundial** and well-head (Ernest Gimson) creates a protected idyll amid the blasted heath.

Monreith House.

526 **Monreith House**, 1791, Alexander Stevens Classical country house; two-storey, five-bay front. Ascetic Doric porch added, 1821, Sir Robert Smirke; lower west wing added, 1878. Full-height, bowed-bay to garden elevation. Rich interior mainly from 19th century; gilded friezes and plasterwork; tapestries and 18th-century floral appliqué work hung in the hall: handiwork of Lady Magdalene Maxwell and said to have originated as carpeting for Myreton Castle (ruinous, in grounds). Gavin Maxwell recalled Monreith as dismal, dank and *fusty* as a boy visiting his grandfather, the formidable Sir Herbert Maxwell.

Corsemalzie House Hotel, mid-19th century Two-storey-and-attic plain Tudor house, with single-storey canted bays, hood-moulded windows and triangular ball-finialed dormers. Rubble construction gives an informality unusual in a house of this character.

Left *Corsemalzie House Hotel.*
Below *House of Elrig.*

House of Elrig, 1912, Stewart & Paterson Birthplace of **Gavin Maxwell**, author of *Ring of Bright Water*. Successful essay in Lorimerian 17th-century Scots revival, two-storey and attic, with swept dormers, crowstepped rolled skewputs and older features of the style.

Above Craigeach. *Right* Port William.

Craigeach, 1890, Wigtown County Council
Built as a residential agricultural school, its
long two-storey frontage punctuated by three
crowstepped chimney gables. Dark rubble
hardly relieved by sandstone dressings.
Myrton Castle sits on 12th-century motte,
with overgrown and partly collapsed remains of
tower house, *c.*1500, with open roundels at the
corners. Rest of castle may be early 17th
century, converted to **doocot**, *c.*1870.

At **Drumtroddan**, east of Port William, a
group of **cup-and-ring markings** on rock face
of Bronze Age date and, close to **Drumtroddan
Farm**, an alignment of three **standing stones**,
two upright and one now fallen.
Historic Scotland; open to the public

PORT WILLIAM
Essentially a harbour village, serving the western
Machars, its plan dictated largely by topography.
Site in the valley of the Killantrae Burn where it
intersects the raised beach above Luce Bay;
certainly the irregular layout of the centre streets
suggests an early origin. As with most Galloway
villages, however, becoming planned settlement in
early 19th century, with **Main Street** running
north and **South Street** doing what it says.

527 The Square
Straight-edged on two sides, curved on the third
and bounded by **Mill Hill** to the east. Typical
vernacular buildings, most notable being
Monreith Arms Hotel, large **corn mill** (now
disused), **Bank of Scotland** and **primary
school**, both High Street, and small **Church of
Scotland**, off Main Street, now a house.

Harbour
The quayed mouth of Killantrae Burn with pier
extending into deeper water. Tipped-stone

north breakwater built recently, and south pier extended. Inner harbour, with its prominent gatepiers, retains its character. Built for trading vessels, harbour now used by small fishing craft and pleasure boats.

KIRKCOWAN
528 Single-street village running down to bridge over the River Bladnoch from present T-plan **parish church**, 1843, in pinnacled Perpendicular almost *de rigueur* in Galloway. **Old parish church**, 1732; only east gable remains with some fine carved 18th-century tombstones round about. **School**, *c.*1900, mildly Arts & Crafts. Mostly plain one- and two-storey houses, but **Tarff Hotel** and a few others have some distinction.

529 **Craichlaw House**, from 16th century Victorian baronial mansion incorporating remains of 16th-century tower, mostly taken down to first-floor level, rebuilt and *corrected*, 1864, Wardrop & Brown,with gabled asymmetric additions and by C S S Johnston at the turn of the century. Elaborate interior, Jacobean for the tower, Italianate elsewhere, almost all 1864. In 1954 Ian G Lindsay demolished the 1860s range, and returned the tower, approximately, to its 16th-century condition.

530 **Shennanton**, 1908, H E Clifford
Rare Galloway specimen of the English country house: red-roofed, Tudor-vernacular, writ large. L-plan layout; asymmetrical front with buttressed embattled porch at the angle, boldly handled roofline with gables and tall chimneys employed to great effect. Distinctive crazy paving rubble-work walls, mullioned and transomed windows. Internally, much Edwardian detail survives notably billiard room with timber panelling and ingle-nook fireplace.

Top *Kirkcowan.* Above *Craichlaw House.*

Shennanton.

New Luce Parish Church.

Boreland farmhouse

Earlier mid-19th-century symmetrical two-storey, three-bay differing from its peers in having shallow bays flanking the doorway, and low-pitched piended roof. Central chimneystack with 10 flues.

531 **Tarff Woollen Mills**

Previously two woollen mills here, two-storey and attic, a waulk mill, 1821, for finishing woollen cloth, and a larger, later mill, now ruined, but with tall octagonal brick chimney surviving.

532 **NEW LUCE**

Single street of 18th- and 19th-century houses, many much altered. **Parish church**, 1821, vestry added, 1957, interior refurnished 1975.

DUNRAGIT

In two sections: one a late 20th-century housing estate, the other a scattered 19th-century village, with castellated bow-ended **lodge** to Dunragit House, now harled, and

533 much-altered former **Dunragit Creamery**, one-time major employer. **Dunragit Station**, now closed, with two-storey station house and signal-box controlling passing loop-and-level crossing. **Station House**, probably 1877, when Dunragit became a junction between Girvan & Portpatrick Railway and Portpatrick & Wigtownshire Joint Railway.

Below Dunragit Creamery.
Bottom Glenluce Abbey.

534 **Dunragit House**, from late 18th century

Three-storey, four-bay symmetrical main range, with two centre bays advanced and pedimented, with chimney on apex. T-plan box porch, flat-roofed and railed to form balcony for the principal floor. Extensions, 19th century, to the rear.

535 **Glenluce Abbey**, 13th–15th centuries

Founded, 1190, by Roland, Earl of Galloway, as Cistercian daughter-house of Dundrennan, layout and decoration according with this pedigree. *Footprints* of nave and aisles discernible with fragments of south transept, only 15th-century chapter house reasonably complete. Lit by fine traceried windows, groin-vaulted ribbed roof springs from central column with richly carved capital. Portions of original tile floor survive, together with earthenware pipes carrying the water supply.
Historic Scotland; open to the public

Fragmentary remains survive of **Carscreugh Castle**, 1680, a long symmetrical palace-block flanked by twin towers with round stair towers nestling behind in re-entrant giving shallow U-plan; an arrangement similar to Castle Kennedy. Abandoned some 15 years after its completion. Revd Symson, in 1684, calls it *a stately house ... which Dalrymple of Stair has lately built de novo, according to the moderne architecture* and offers as explanation for its early demise *it might have been more pleasant if it had been in a more pleasant place*.

536 **GLENLUCE**

Hillside village, with varied cottages clambering up winding street, now bypassed and quiet, from the patched stone viaduct. Window and door replacement has taken a sad toll. **Village hall** with barometer, a distinctive touch, and subdued **parish church**, 1814, rather brutally altered, 1967, when it lost two forestairs, was *chancellised* internally and drearily drydashed.

Aerial view, Glenluce.

537 **Castle of Park**, 1590

Formerly Park Hay; lofty L-plan harled and crowstepped tower house inscribed *This verk vas begun in 1590 be Thomas Hay and Janet MacDoual*. Plan a less sophisticated version of Sorbie Tower: jamb entirely occupied by wide spiral stair, only relieved at third floor by small corbelled stair turret accessing garrets. Sadly, 18th-century piend-roofed flanking wings (more elaborate version of Carsluith), demolished *c*.1970. Tower consolidated by Historic Scotland, 1970-80, now converted for holiday letting by the Landmark Trust (colour page 191).

After the Reformation the properties of Glenluce Abbey were administered by a lay Commendator, whose house, Castle of Park, overlooks the Luce valley.

Castle of Park, c.1930s.

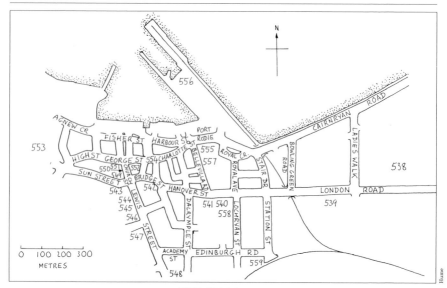

STRANRAER

Biggest and most prosperous town in former Wigtownshire, with administrative and educational responsibility for large, if sparsely populated, area. Situated on the neck of land that joins the Rhins of Galloway, the furthest south-west part of the area, to the rest of Galloway, at the head of **Loch Ryan**, a natural harbour, it was created a burgh of barony, 1595, and a royal burgh by James II, 1617. Market-town function recognised by burgh status continues. Since mid-19th century, also important ferry port, British terminus of the short sea crossing to Northern Ireland – one of the keys to its continuing prosperity. Two main roads converge here, A77 from Glasgow, and A75 *Euro Route* from Carlisle, which reaches the town at the brick abutment of a railway bridge built to carry the wartime line to Cairnryan (see p.208).

London Road

538 **Stranraer Academy** and **Rephad Primary School**, 1958-65, R M Clive, Wigtownshire County Architect
Academy originally two schools, senior and junior secondary, with shared physical education facilities; amalgamated as comprehensive school, 1967. Low two-storey buildings, typical 1960s, spiced-up by large post-modern addition, 1995, Dumfries and Galloway Regional Council.

Rephad House, *c.*1850, and **Viewfield**,

1876, High-Victorian villa, next to **Stair Park**, 1905, its most striking feature cast-iron
539 Saracen Foundry **bandstand** marking coronation of King George V in 1911.

Hanover Street
Lined by two-storey, late 18th- and 19th-century buildings, leading to the historic core.
540 **St Andrew's Church of Scotland**, 1896-8, John B Wilson, built as United Presbyterian church, in the compact style favoured at that period, with rich interior. Beyond, **L'Aperitif**
541 restaurant, formerly **Ivy House**, late 18th century, with ball-finialed pediment and Venetian windows in the *piano nobile*. Curious very tall French mansard roof over shop and house block in **Hanover Place**. Italianate former **Royal**
542 **Bank of Scotland**, Bridge Street, 1874, David Rhind, built as Commercial Bank, is the town's most commanding commercial building. Former **Relief Church**, 1821, now church hall, its three-bay frontage thoroughly domestic. Gothic
543 **Masonic Hall**, Sun Street, 1843, built as Original Secession Church. Beyond, low red sandstone **Council Offices**.

Lewis Street
Long, straight, early 19th century, with rendered-brick terrace with pleasing details.
544 Opposite, extraordinary Gothic **St Ninian's Church of Scotland**, 1883-4, Alexander Pettigrew, built for United Presbyterian congregation, with trade-mark rose window. Interior has stencilled ceiling and organ pipes.
545 Tudor **Sheriff Court**, 1871-4, Brown & Wardrop, red sandstone with cream sandstone dressings, and **War Memorial**, 1920, with bronze statue of a soldier on granite plinth.
546 **Lewis Street Gospel Hall**, 1843-4, built as Free Church, remodelled, 1845-6, John Boyd; triple-glazed Lewis Street frontage with central
547 bellcote. Unusually architectural **Fire Station**,

Top *Ivy House*. Above *St Ninian's Church of Scotland*.

Fire Station.

1960, M Purdon Smith & Partners, with curved concrete-framed awnings. Opposite, simple, well-proportioned post-war low-rise local authority 548 housing. **St Joseph's RC Church**, 1852-3; tower added, 1924, Charles J Menart, lacking coherence despite Menart's involvement.

Church Street

549 Remarkably rich architecturally: **Dunbar House**, 1823, three-storey villa with central shaped chimney gable. **No 12**, early 19th-century house with robust Doric-columned porch. Simple perpendicular **Old Parish** 550 **Church**, 1838-41, Hugh McDowall & Andrew McCrear, masons, and James Adair and Co, joiners. Ornate lamp-standards are former Provost's lamps of the burgh, set here, 1978. Opposite, two early 19th-century buildings – **Arkhouse Inn**, *c.*1800, with unusual doorpiece, and **No 71-75**, with Roman-Doric doorpiece.

George Street

Old market street of the burgh, its architectural 551 highlight the **old town hall**, 1777, with octagonal belfry and spire, extended to the rear, 1854-5, now town museum (colour page 192). 552 **George Hotel**, former coaching inn, probably remodelled, 1876, from earlier building, with Jacobean detailing and mansard roof. Late Victorian public house, the **Golden Cross**, 553 Queen Street. **Leswalt High Road**, dominated by the **High Kirk**, a dark building of whin, with sandstone dressings, with battlemented tower, 1841, chancel refurnished in Scots Catholic manner, 1912, Peter MacGregor Chalmers.

554 **Castle of St John**, *c.*1500, is the oldest building in the burgh. A large, four-storey-and-attic tower house, built for Ninian Adair of Kinhilt, remodelled, *c.*1600, and converted to prison, 1821-2; converted to **visitor centre**, 1988-90. Cast-iron **fountain**, probably Walter Macfarlane & Co, for Queen Victoria's Diamond Jubilee in 1897, relocated here from further west in George Street.

Top *Dunbar House*. Middle *Old town hall*. Above *Burgh arms, old town hall*.

Charlotte Street leads to the waterfront, past **No 32**, 1841, pleasing mildly Tudor villa. In 555 Port Rodie is **police station**, 1955-8, M Purdon Smith, and **North-West Castle Hotel**, incorporating large bow-fronted villa of *c.*1820, much extended in recent years.

556 Opposite, **East Pier**, 1861, James Leslie,

substantially extended, 1893-6, Dundas &
Melville, with railway station, 1898, with patent-
glazed awning, servicing railway-owned steamers
to Larne; demolished, 1978, replaced by much
smaller structure. New pier added, 1978-9, to
accommodate larger ferries. At the shore end of
the **West Pier**, little 1930s art deco **harbour
office**. **Harbour Street**, and its western
extension, **Market Street** and **Agnew Crescent**,
have been much altered, but Agnew Crescent still
presents a good vernacular front to the sea.

557 **Anne House**, Bellevilla Road, late Georgian
villa with Roman-Doric doorpiece. **Reformed
558 Presbyterian Church**, Dalrymple Street,
1824-5, with piended roof and high-set
windows in the end wall, and **hall**, 1898.
Garrick Hospital, Edinburgh Road, 1897-8,
Richard Park, thoroughly domestic in
character, brick railway terraces continue up
Victoria Street. Single-storey, former
Stranraer Town Station, Edinburgh Road,
very plain, next door smart *moderne* **fertiliser**
559 **store** for Scottish Agricultural Industries.
Station Street has former railway cottages
and the roofless locomotive shed.
    Near Castle Kennedy, very plain **Inch**
560 **Parish Church**, 1858-61, J Maitland Wardrop;
rebuilt after fire, 1895-6, Hamilton More-
Nisbet. East transept houses the Stair Pew, a
good example of a landowner's pew.

Top *Castle of St John.* Above *SAI
fertiliser store.*

561 **Castle Kennedy**, 1607
Palatial residence of the Kennedy Earls of
Cassilis, originally sited on an island; waters
parted, 19th century, to form **Black Loch** and
White Loch. Symmetrically planned with five-
storey square towers flanking rectangular
main block, paired stair towers tucked in rear
re-entrants, akin to Drumlanrig. Destroyed by

The Kennedy family had a strong
base in Wigtownshire, firstly at
Castle Kennedy and thereafter at
Culhorn, a rare example of an 18th-
century brick-built country house,
now demolished. Their influence is
attested in the 1684 rhyme:
*Twixt Wigton and the Town of Ayr
Portpatrick and the Cruives of Cree
No man need think for to bide their
Unless he court with Kennedie*

Castle Kennedy, from The
Antiquities of Scotland *by Francis
Grose, 1789.*

Top *Lochinch Castle*. Middle *Craigcaffie Castle*. Above *Lochryan House*.

On the shores of Loch Ryan are traces of the yards where concrete sections of the wartime **Mulberry harbours** (*below*) were fabricated to be used in the Normandy landings, June 1944. The harbours (code-named Mulberry) were designed to be floated out in sections and sunk on the Normandy Coast to land supplies for the invasion forces.

fire, 1716, and never restored becoming focal point in landscaped grounds first laid out by William Adam and William Boutcher, *c.*1722, for 2nd Earl Stair, subject to restorative overhaul, 1841, J C Loudon.

562 Lochinch Castle, 1864-7, Wardrop & Brown Wardrop's first large-scale solo commission, for 10th Earl of Stair. Frenchified baronial pile bristling with requisite pepper-pot turrets, crowsteps and battlements. Grounds include brick-arched balustraded bridge over canal; scattering of picturesque gabled lodges. *Gardens open to the public; guidebook available*

563 Craigcaffie Castle, 1570 Built for John Neilson and his wife, Margaret Strang; recently restored (colour page 192). Plain rectangular plan with commodious spiral-stair, vaulted ground floor with well and trapdoor to hall; an early form of dumb-waiter. Twin bartizans grace gable walls with *murder hole* over front door for dropping missiles on unwelcome guests. Elaborate moulded window surrounds comparable to MacLellan's Castle, Kirkcudbright.

CAIRNRYAN

One-sided village, whose rural tranquillity has been disturbed by the main road, and more obviously if less persistently, by creation of Second World War emergency port (now disused), long concrete jetty and by active modern ferry terminal. **Loch Ryan**

564 Lighthouse, 1847, Alan Stevenson.

565 Lochryan House, 1701 Very unusual and charming building, central block built for Colonel Andrew Agnew of Croach, originally as two-storey attic and basement. Middle three bays had a storey added, 1820-4, with crenellated top. Advanced wings have lean-to roofs giving the building its distinctive character. Behind, single-storey and basement wings and, to either side, single-storey service wings. In the grounds, circular **doocot**, 1846, William Ross, and 18th-century **garden**. Entrance from main road through high wall, with cannon flanking the gateway.

KIRKCOLM

Focus of parish, at north end of Rhins of **566** Galloway, is **Kirkcolm**, established, 1613, as a burgh of barony and then named Stewarton.

Re-established, 1780s, as planned village, on hillside sloping down to Loch Ryan. **Main Street** composed mainly of 19th-century vernacular buildings. Mid/late 20th-century housing in **Church Street** and notable T-plan **Ervie & Kirkcolm Parish Church**, 1824; birdcage belfry a 20th-century replacement, plain, much-altered interior. In the churchyard, **Kilmore Cross**, *c*.9th-10th century, with carvings on both faces, one in Celtic, the other in rose-style.

Balsarroch House, late 17th century
Only ruins remain of the house claimed as the missing link between tower-houses and the 18th-century classically inspired houses of the middle-ranking gentry. Here the hall moves down to ground level though it retains its traditional features of a great fireplace and aumbries. It was thatched and crowstepped with small regularly spaced first-floor windows.

Balsarroch House.

567 **Corsewall Lighthouse**, 1815, Robert Stevenson
An 86ft-high round tower, with two-storey keepers' houses, built of whin rubble and plagued by wind-borne damp for its first 20 years; a coating of raw linseed oil dashed with warm sand proved the cure. Copper-dome light-room, oil-burning lamp with 12 reflectors so powerful that daytime covers were provided to prevent spontaneous combustion. Now automated, and keepers' houses sensitively converted to **hotel** (colour page 192).

Corsewall Lighthouse.

568 **Corsewall Castle**, probably 15th century
Much-ruined but still-substantial remains of rectangular-plan tower house, for the Campbells of Corsewall. **Corsewall Farmhouse**, early 19th century, one-storey and attic, three-bay, with large diamond-pane

glazing. **Corsewall House** has, at its heart, late-Georgian mansion with spine-wall chimneystacks, much altered mid-19th century and 1905.

Mains of Cairnbrock, late 19th century Typical Galloway two-storey whitewashed rubble farmhouse and steading. Well-preserved two-storey rectangular cheese-loft, four window elevations with slatted vents below glazed upper sashes. Galloway was for long beef-cattle-rearing country. Better communications and eventually the railway sparked the change to large-scale dairying.

Top Marian Tower. Above Cheese loft, Mains of Cairnbrock.

569 **Marian Tower**, 1802
Hilltop rubble tower, in the centre of the parish, memorial erected by Arctic explorer Sir John Ross, to his wife.

LESWALT
Mostly modern public housing, with T-plan
570 **parish church**, 1827-8, with external gallery stair on the aisle and belfry. North gallery appears to be original, rest of interior recast, 1953. Tudor **primary school** and **schoolhouse**, 1875, S H Taylor. Ruined remains of earlier **parish church**, probably medieval in origin; north-east aisle, now obscured by ivy, housed **burial vault** and **loft** of the Agnews of Lochnaw.

571 **Lochnaw Castle**, 16th century
Early 16th-century simple rectangular tower-house with crenellated parapet, seat of the powerful Agnew family. Adjoining regular six-bay, two-storey range of 1663 with steeply pitched roofs, probably indicating original thatch. Gargantuan, 1822, Tudor addition, Archibald Elliot; demolished, 1953, remains laid out as garden. **Boat-house**, *c*.1900, barge-boarded and lattice-windowed. Various **lodges** in pinned whin rubble, gables, rustic porches and leaded windows.

Lochnaw Castle.

572 **Agnew Monument**, 1850
Atop the Tor of Craigoch in memory of Sir Andrew Agnew, square-plan buttressed four-storey tower finished with corbelled parapet.

573 **Galdenoch Castle**, 16th century
West of Lochnaw, shell of L-plan Agnew tower, stumps of angle turrets and corbels.

Crowstep detail peculiar to Wigtownshire formed by small rubble pinnings under stone slab.

574 **House of Knock**, 1908
Large, rambling two-storey house, on cliffs in south-west corner of the parish, baronialised by corner conical-roofed drum tower and projecting bay corbelled out from semi-octagonal to square at first floor.

PORTPATRICK
Furthest west settlement in Galloway, sited in an inlet in very rocky coast, convenient for trade with Ireland and the Isle of Man, and as fishing station, but exposed to prevailing westerly winds. Constituted a burgh of barony in 1620. Road

Portpatrick Harbour Lighthouse.

Portpatrick derives its name from the great Apostle of Ireland, who once, according to legend, here crossed the channel at a single stride, and left a deep footprint on a rock that was removed in the formation of the harbour. On another occasion, the savages of Glenapp had cut off his head; but picking it up, the Saint quietly walked to Portpatrick, plunged into the sea, and, *holding his head in his teeth*, swam safely to the opposite shore.
Groome's Ordnance Gazetteer

Left *Aerial view, Portpatrick.*
Below *Detail, Commercial Inn.*

improvement in second half of 18th century gave added importance, and pier built, 1774, John Smeaton. Packet service to Ireland started, 1790, proving so useful that, in 1818, John Rennie recommended that the crossing to Donaghadee be the prime Scottish/Irish route. Rennie's works, constructed, 1821-36, of Welsh limestone, damaged in 1839 storm, and never completed. Mail route moved to Stranraer, but the railway reached Portpatrick in 1862, and new basin constructed, 1859-66 (colour page 192).

The decline in the significance of Portpatrick as a packet station was, however, complemented by its rise as a holiday resort, a function it still retains; also a fishing station. Very attractive seaside town, but as with many settlements in south-west Scotland its character is being eroded by inappropriate window replacements.

211

Top Portpatrick Old Parish Church.
Middle Killantringan Lighthouse.
Above Portpatrick Hotel.

High Street
The town's form is constricted by the narrow valley through which it is approached. Towered 575 Gothic **Parish Church**, 1840-2, William Burn, and minute, harled **St Ninian's Episcopal Church**, 1937; early 19th-century **Commercial Inn**, with Roman-Doric doorcase and round-ended single-storey wing, facing the similarly round-ended **Ivy Cottage**.

Simple Gothic former **Free Church** (now a hall) on the corner with School Brae. Massive **Downshire Arms Hotel**, now four storeys, built as two-storey, early 19th century, its name marking the connection with Donaghadee, County Down. Early 19th-century villas, one 576 now **Harbour House Hotel**, their scale and underlying elegance reflecting the prosperity of the town at that time.

South Crescent, mainly 19th century, leads past small **limekiln**, tucked into a cliff, to **south pier** and its **lighthouse** of 1896, with keepers' houses of earlier Rennie light now used as **craft pottery**. **House o' Hill**, 1974-5, Ian Ballantine, tall villa with monopitch roof.

North Crescent, more mixed in character, some buildings appear to pre-date Rennie's harbour improvements, being set below present road level. **Basin**, 1859-66, with former lifeboat shed and steel-framed hand-operated derrick crane. Above, reached by footpath, is the dominant 577 **Portpatrick Hotel**, 1905, James Hunter, extended 1906-7, J M Dick Peddie, mainly baronial, affords fine views over the town and along the coast. Two other buildings to note: cruciform **Old Parish Church** (St Andrew's), St Patrick Street, 1628-9, now roofless, with earlier, perhaps 16th-century, four-storey **tower**, with conical slated roof and cupola of 1791. Tower, certainly a day mark for navigators, may have 578 displayed a light. **Primary School**, 1979,

Portpatrick Primary School.

Dumfries and Galloway Regional Council, highly original, brick-built, with radial buttresses, apparently growing out of the hillside setting.

579 **Killantringan Lighthouse**, *c*.1900, D A Stevenson
Tapering circular tower with diamond-paned lantern. Externally unaltered one- and two-storey keepers' houses now **guest-house**.

580 **Dunskey House**, 1901-4, James Hunter
Large house in simplified baronial fashionable at the time, with lavish interiors, replacing 1706 house.

581 **Dunskey Castle**, from early 16th century
Substantial remains of L-plan block, with tower-house on south-east angle, seat of the Adairs of Kinhilt. Extended to north-west, probably 1620s. Almost impossibly romantic setting on west-facing cliff.

582 **STONEYKIRK**
Small 19th-century village dominated by disused **parish church**, 1827, typical of Galloway, with south tower and pointed windows with Y-tracery. Interior recast, 1901-2, John B Wilson. Pleasing vernacular buildings round **churchyard**.

583 **SANDHEAD**
Mostly modern village on the shores of Luce Bay. The best building is **Sandhead Church of Scotland**, Main Street, 1962-3, I W A Macdonald, a wooden hall with stone porch and tapering bell tower.

ARDWELL
Unspoiled estate village for Ardwell House, consisting of a few whitewashed cottages, including unaltered, single-storey, mid-19th-century row. Dignified, steepled **Ardwell**
584 **Church**, 1900-2, Peter MacGregor Chalmers, in a simple Early English style, looks 20 years older. Interior is a good example of Chalmers' ecclesiological layout, arranged in the medieval manner with the communion table in place of the altar.

585 **Ardwell**, *c*.1720; remodelled 1956, H Anthony Wheeler
Another recovered laird's house like Logan (see pp.214-5) and Physgill (see pp.197-8); this one

South of Stoneykirk in trees to the left of the A716, small rubble tower of a **windmill**, late 18th/early 19th century. By analogy with comparable buildings in Ulster, probably scutching mill, preparing flax for spinning.

Below *Dunskey Castle*. Middle *Ardwell Church*. Bottom *Ardwell*.

Kirkmadrine Church, with Early Christian stones in porch.

The oldest of the Kirkmadrine stones are known as pillar stones. When discovered in the 19th century, two were being used as gateposts and the third as part of a stile in the churchyard wall. The oldest is inscribed, in Latin, *Here lie the holy and chief priests Ides, Uiventius and Mavorius.*

emerged, following demolition of Brown & Wardrop baronial additions. Reconstituted east front harled, crowstepped two-storey and basement, three-bay, with steps to central arched doorway. Curious window spacing likely to be Wheeler rather than 1720. Double-pile rear wing. Simple 18th-century curved staircase survives, but remaining interiors mostly 1956, reusing salvaged fragments.
Gardens open to the public

KIRKMADRINE
586 Site of one of the earliest Christian communities in Scotland. Present **church**, late 19th century, built as mortuary chapel for Lady McTaggart Stewart of Ardwell, in Romanesque, based on Cruggleton Church (see p.188). West porch adapted to contain inscribed and sculptured Early Christian stones recovered from graveyard, earliest of which dates from fifth century.
Historic Scotland; open to the public

Clachanmore School, 1831
En route to Kirkmadrine from Ardwell, U-plan, single-storey parish school, whinstone with sandstone dressings, crowsteps, pointed-arch windows and central boldly advanced stack rising from ground.

587 **Auchness**
Idiosyncratic amalgam with three-storey tower (too castellated to be true) linked to perfectly sane 19th-century, two-storey house. Dotty single-storey wing with central oculused pediment flanked by bulging bay windows.

588 **Chapel Rossan**, early 19th century
Charming, two-storey, L-plan, Gothick house, with Y-traceried windows. Semi-octagonal jamb facing the road.

589 **Logan House**, 1702
Early classical house, for Colonel Andrew McDouall, swallowed whole in 1874 by David Bryce's massively baronial reworking. McDouall's house born again for R Olaf Hambro, banker, after 1952 demolition of additions, and reconstitution to something of its original appearance, on the advice of David Style, interior decorator. East front three-storey, three-bay with pedimented entrance bay; window disposition slightly altered during resurrection. Somewhat solitary now, lacking the curved

Auchness.

quadrants and pavilions of the original. Bryce's work evidenced only in the rear service wing, stable block and quantities of red sandstone forming garden terraces.

590 **Logan Botanic Garden**
Created out of the designed landscape of Logan House, it has an amazing collection of sub-tropical plants; now outstation of Royal Botanic Garden, Edinburgh.
Open to the public

591 **Logan Windmill**, *c*.1680
Stump of windmill tower with stone barrel-vaulted basement, built by Patrick McDouall of Logan. The Revd Symson reported in 1684 that in summer the country *is very defective of mills, by reason that the little bournes are then dried up; the laird has lately built an excellent windmill very useful to his own lands and the whole country hereabouts.*

Left *Logan House.* Top *Logan Windmill.* Above *Balgowan Farmhouse.*

Logan Sawmill, probably early 19th century
Two-storey-and-basement rubble building, with all-iron overshot waterwheel; sawbench removed.

592 **Balgowan Farmhouse**, late 18th/
early 19th century
Delightfully idiosyncratic, two-storey, three-bay symmetrical house, with semicircular central bay entrance, with tripartite window at first floor. Flanking ground-floor windows are canted bays, probably 20th-century alteration.

Port Logan lighthouse.

PORT LOGAN
Established early 19th century as improved port by Colonel McDouall of Logan. Proposals for new harbour made, 1813, by John Rennie but harbour as built in 1818-22, John Young, differed from Rennie's design. Part of the pier reduced to rubble, but seaward end survives,
593 with circular granite **lighthouse** of 1830s. Village itself consists of row of houses along the shore. **School**, *c*.1860, to the north.

Logan Fish Pond.

594 **Logan Fish Pond**, 1788-1800
Most striking feature of the village, almost-
circular pond complex fringed with crenellated
rubble walls; entry through arch in castellated
cottage guarded by arrow slits. Rock-cut steps
zigzag down to 50ft-diameter pond linked to
sea by natural rock cleft with iron grille
allowing change of water at high tide while
preventing fish egress. Originally stocked with
carp for McDouall's bouillabaise, today's more
sanguine inmates await tourist titbits.
Open to the public

Below Killumpha. *Middle* Terally
Tile Works. Bottom *Kirkmaiden
Parish Church.*

595 **Killumpha**, *c.*1600
Small tower, remodelled 1823, probably with
dummy bartizans, and later extended by
irregular 1½-storey farmhouse, itself more
recently dressed up to echo the 1823 work.

596 **Terally Tile Works**, *c.*1840
Remains of drainage-tile works consist of small
rectangular brick building and substantial
remains of updraught tile kiln, the last
survivor of many which worked in Scotland.

KIRKMAIDEN
597 Tiny kirkton round T-plan **parish church**, dating
in essence from 1638 and later, altered 1885, one
of the oldest in Galloway. **North aisle** has, under
the gallery, burial vault of the McDoualls of Logan.
Carved wooden panel of 1534 on north wall.
Graveyard contains fine monuments, most
unusual being small stone model of a lighthouse,
monument to a son of a keeper of the Mull of
Galloway lighthouse, who died in 1852.

598 **DRUMMORE**
Small port on the east side of the Mull of
Galloway, with harbour protected by a north pier,
*c.*1845, 1889, and breakwater. Beside the harbour
is **Low Drummore**, a steading group; to the

north **Shore Street**, with terraced 19th-century, two-storey vernacular buildings including the **Ship Inn**, *c*.1860.

Mill Street

Principal street on a hill with fairly elaborate Victorian buildings, including **Queen's Hotel**. Note also large corrugated-asbestos-clad **shed**, probably Second World War, and, opposite, **grain mill**, *c*.1865, with small, late all-iron waterwheel.

Pleasant, slightly Arts & Crafts Gothic **St 599 Medan's Church of Scotland**, Stair Street, built 1903, as Kirkmaiden United Free Church, and **primary school**, Shaw Lane, 1974-5, John G Sowerby, Wigtown County Architect.

600 **Mull of Galloway Lighthouse**, 1828, Robert Stevenson

A 60ft-tall rubble tower, still functioning though without human input. Low ranges of keepers' cottages, flat-roofed behind a blocking course, each originally with byre, ash-pit and privy. **Foghorn**, 1894, on semicircular battery at water's edge. Supplies for the light landed at **East Tarbert**; the quay rubble-built on bedrock with granite rubble cottage/store set within neat garden walls.

Top *Grain mill.* Middle *Admiralty boatshed, Kirkmaiden Harbour.* Above *St Medan's Church of Scotland.* Left *Mull of Galloway Lighthouse.*

References

The following publications have proved particularly useful in the preparation of this guide: **The Making of Urban Scotland**, Ian Adams; **A Biographical Dictionary of British Architects, 1660-1840**, Howard Colvin; **The Scottish Castle**, Cruden; **A Dictionary of Scottish History**, Gordon Donaldson & Robert S Morpeth; **The Industrial Archaeology of Galloway**, Ian L Donnachie; **The Architecture of Scotland**, John Dunbar; **The Buildings of Scotland: Dumfries & Galloway**, John Gifford; **A History of Scottish Architecture**, Miles Glendinning, Ranald MacInnes & Aonghus MacKechnie; **Scottish Country Houses**, Gow & Rowan (eds); **The Ordnance Gazetteer of Scotland**, Groome; **Scottish Watercolours, 1740-1940**, Julian Halsby; **The Architecture of Scottish Post-Reformation Churches, 1560-1843**, George Hay; **The Industrial Archaeology of Scotland, Vol 1, The Lowlands and Borders**, John R Hume; **The Classical Country House in Scotland, 1660-1800**, James Macaulay; **The Castellated and Domestic Architecture of Scotland**, David MacGibbon & Thomas Ross; **Discovering Galloway**, Innes McLeod; **The Making of Scotch Whisky**, Michael S Moss & John R Hume; **Scotland's Art**, Ian O'Riordan & David Patterson; **Exploring Scotland's Heritage: Dumfries & Galloway**, Geoffrey Stell; **A Large Description of Galloway, 1684**, in **Macfarlane's Geographical Collections, Vol 2**, Edinburgh, 1907, Revd A Symson; **Regional History of the Railways of Britain, Vol 6, The Lowlands and the Borders**, John Thomas; **The Statistical Account** and **The New Statistical Account**. Finally, and crucially, the statutory **Lists of Buildings of Special Architectural and Historic Interest** compiled by Historic Scotland and its predecessors on behalf of the Secretary of State for Scotland have, as with other volumes in this series, been an invaluable resource.

Acknowledgements

The author would like to acknowledge the help of many individuals and bodies in the preparation of this guide, especially: Judith Anderson, who started out with me in this enterprise, and who contributed largely to its preparation; Graham Douglas; Anthony Wolffe; Sam Small; and the staffs of: the Royal Commission on Ancient and Historical Monuments of Scotland; the National Trust for Scotland; the Map Library of the National Libraries of Scotland; the Ewart Library, Dumfries; Stranraer Library; Historic Scotland, in particular Frank Lawrie, Chris Tabraham, Richard Fawcett, Deborah Mays, Pam Craig, Laura Mackay, Margaret Donaldson and the listing section, and Dumfries & Galloway Council and its predecessors, particularly Eric Wilson, Volkmar Nix and Gordon Mann.

Special thanks are due to Helen Leng and Susan Skinner of the Rutland Press and Dorothy Lena Smith of the RIAS, who have done more to make this book than many publishers; to Adrian Hallam, the Almond Consultancy, and Dorothy Steedman, Design Energy Associates for designing the book; and to Charles McKean and David Walker for their constructive comments.

Finally, grateful thanks to my wife and family, who have provided moral and practical support throughout the long gestation of this project.

INDEX

GLOSSARY

1. Architrave (projecting ornamental frame)
2. Astragal (glazing bar)
3. Barge (gable board)
4. Basement, raised
5. Bullseye, keyblocked (circular window with projecting blocks punctuating frame)
6. Buttress (supporting projection)
7. Caphouse (top chamber)
8. Cartouche (decorative tablet)
9. Cherrycocking (masonry joints filled with small stones)
10. Channelled ashlar (recessed horizontal joints in smooth masonry)
11. Chimneycope, corniced
12. Chimneycope, moulded
13. Close (alley)
14. Cobbles
15. Console (scroll bracket)
16. Corbel (projection support)
17. Crowsteps
18. Cutwater (wedge-shaped end of bridge pier)
19. Doocot, lectern
20. Dormer, canted & piended
21. Dormer, pedimented (qv) wallhead
22. Dormer, piended (see under 'roof')
23. Dormer, swept wallhead
24. Fanlight (glazed panel above door)
25. Finial (crowning ornament)
26. Fly-over stair
27. Forestair, pillared
28. Gable, wallhead
29. Gable, wallhead chimney
30. Gable, Dutch (curved)
31. Gibbs doorway (framed with projecting stonework)
32. Harling
33. Hoist, fishing net
34. Hoodmoulding (projection over opening to divert rainwater)
35. Jettied (overhanging)
36. Lucarne (small dormer on spire)
37. Margin, stone
38. Mercat Cross
39. Marriage Lintel
40. Mullion (vertical division of window)
41. Nave (main body of church)
42. Pavilion (building attached by wing to main building)
43. Pediment (triangular ornamental feature above windows etc)
44. Portico
45. Quoins, rusticated (corner stones with recessed joints)
46. Refuge (recess in bridge parapet)
47. Ridge, crested
48. Roof, flared pyramidal
49. Roof, leanto
50. Roof, ogival (with S-curve pitch generally rising from square plan and meeting at point)
51. Roof, pantiled
52. Roof, piended (formed by intersecting roof slopes)
53. Roof, slated
54. Skew (gable coping)
55. Skewputt, moulded (lowest stone of skew, qv)
56. Skewputt, scroll
57. Stair jamb (projection containing stairway)
58. Stringcourse (horizontal projecting wall moulding)
59. Transept (transverse wing of cruciform church)
60. Transom (horizontal division of window)
61. Voussoir (wedge-shaped stone forming archway)
62. Tympanum (area within pediment qv)
63. Window, bay (projecting full-height from ground level)
64. Window, oriel (corbelled bay qv)
65. Window, sash & case (sliding sashes within case)